Survival

GLOBAL POLITICS AND STRATEGY

Volume 67 Number 4 | August–September 2025

'Unlike Trump and his predecessors, whose red line was "no nuclear weapons" for Iran, Israel's red line has been "no nuclear-weapons capability". The latter is a vague criterion. Capabilities lie along a continuum.'

Mark Fitzpatrick, Attacking Iran and Tempting Fate, p. 11.

'Human oversight and control of AI-based systems demand substantial cognitive effort, and they have well-documented limits. Both can fray under stress, falter under excessive workload and fail altogether in moments of peak complexity, precisely when human judgement matters most.'

Anna M. Gielas, The Loop Is Broken: Why Autonomous-warfare Policy Must Reckon with Human Performance, p. 58.

'China's grand strategy is still a work in progress. Having resolved the question of the physical scope of China's strategic space a decade ago, there is still much for Chinese policymakers to discuss regarding how its "intangible" spaces – the ideological realm and China's sphere of influence as identified four decades ago by Colonel Xu – should be shaped.'

Nadège Rolland, Thinker, Lawyer, Soldier, Spy: The Makers of Xi Jinping's Grand Strategy, p. 88.

Survival
GLOBAL POLITICS AND STRATEGY
Volume 67 Number 4 | August–September 2025

Contents

War with Iran

7 **Attacking Iran and Tempting Fate** *Mark Fitzpatrick*
Although Israel and the United States did considerable damage to Iran's nuclear facilities, Iran may be able to produce the fissile material required for about ten nuclear weapons within half a year.

Commentary

25 **Israel's Perilous Revisionism** *Hasan T. Alhasan and Wolf-Christian Paes*
Regime collapse in Iran, which Israel endorses, could produce a more radical successor, imperil central-state control over Iran's missiles and other military capabilities, and spark a colossal refugee crisis.

33 **Iran's Shattered Missile Strategy** *Fabian Hinz*
The very fact that Israel undertook its 12-day air war against Iran reflects the failure of Iran's long-standing missile-based strategy, a key aim of which was to deter attacks on Iran proper.

43 **The Pentagon's Economic Blind Spot** *Philip M. Breedlove and Peter Devine*
While the United States' great-power rivals use their economies to build military power, the US military plans as if economic dynamism and military capability are independent – which they are not.

54 **Noteworthy: The Shangri-La Dialogue**

Technological Impediments

57 **The Loop Is Broken: Why Autonomous-warfare Policy Must Reckon with Human Performance** *Anna M. Gielas*
Effectively designing artificial-intelligence-based systems means treating the human operator not as a backup mechanism but as a dynamic actor whose cognitive readiness must be continuously supported and sustained.

67 **Offensive Cyber Attacks and Conventional Warfare** *Matthew F. Calabria*
When state-led cyber attacks have succeeded, it has been due to poor cyber security rather than good offensives.

Asian Currents

81 **Thinker, Lawyer, Soldier, Spy: The Makers of Xi Jinping's Grand Strategy** *Nadège Rolland*
Chinese President Xi Jinping – unlike Mao Zedong and Deng Xiaoping – values expert knowledge and has urged Chinese intellectuals to participate in policymaking.

On the cover
Smoke rises from Tehran after airstrikes by Israel on 15 June 2025.

On the web
Visit www.iiss.org/publications/survival for brief notices on new books on Russia and Eurasia; Cyber Security and Emerging Technologies; and Asia-Pacific.

Survival **editors' blog**
For ideas and commentary from *Survival* editors and contributors, visit https://www.iiss.org/online-analysis/survival-online.

95 **South Korea's Resilient Democracy** *Ramon Pacheco Pardo*
The strong institutional response to Yoon Suk-yeol's martial-law declaration indicates that South Korean democracy has matured to the point that no single individual can threaten it.

113 **Supply Chains and Southeast Asia: The Sino-American Shadow** *Amos Yeo*
While escalating tariff wars and deglobalisation will hit Southeast Asian economies especially hard, the US will be wary of alienating Southeast Asian states and pushing them closer to Beijing.

American Confusions

127 **America's 'Ungoverning' in Global Context** *Jodi Vittori*
The Trump administration's across-the-board dismantling of government institutions is unprecedented in mature democracies such as the United States, but it is not so rare elsewhere.

147 **A 'Reverse Kissinger'? Why Trump's Anti-China Rapprochement with Russia Is Likely to Fail** *Geraint Hughes and Zeno Leoni*
Whatever private tensions may have emerged between Vladimir Putin and Xi Jinping, their countries' bilateral relations are a long way from the border fighting of 1969 that conditioned the US rapprochement with China in 1972.

Review Essay

161 **Angela Merkel: A Status Quo Leader in a Revisionist Era** *Hanns W. Maull*
As her memoirs reflect, Angela Merkel's politics of compromise were insufficient for dealing with the return of Russian imperialism, the rise of American populism and China's arrival as an industrial juggernaut.

Book Reviews

169 **Russia and Eurasia** *Angela Stent*
176 **Cyber Security and Emerging Technologies** *Melissa K. Griffith*
180 **Asia-Pacific** *Lanxin Xiang*

Closing Argument

187 **Predicates and Consequences of the Attack on Iran** *Dana H. Allin and Jonathan Stevenson*
Israel's attack on Iran turned on Israel's vast strategic superiority – which could erode – and Donald Trump's disinclination to stop Israeli action.

Survival
GLOBAL POLITICS AND STRATEGY

The International Institute for Strategic Studies
2121 K Street, NW | Suite 600 | Washington DC 20037 | USA
Tel +1 202 659 1490   Fax +1 202 659 1499   E-mail survival@iiss.org   Web www.iiss.org

Arundel House | 6 Temple Place | London | WC2R 2PG | UK
Tel +44 (0)20 7379 7676   Fax +44 (0)20 7836 3108   E-mail iiss@iiss.org

14th Floor, GFH Tower | Bahrain Financial Harbour | Manama | Kingdom of Bahrain
Tel +973 1718 1155   Fax +973 1710 0155   E-mail iiss-middleeast@iiss.org

9 Raffles Place | #49-01 Republic Plaza | Singapore 048619
Tel +65 6499 0055   Fax +65 6499 0059   E-mail iiss-asia@iiss.org

Pariser Platz 6A | 10117 Berlin | Germany
Tel +49 30 311 99 300   E-mail iiss-europe@iiss.org

Survival Online www.tandfonline.com/survival and www.iiss.org/publications/survival

Aims and Scope *Survival* is one of the world's leading forums for analysis and debate of international and strategic affairs. Shaped by its editors to be both timely and forward thinking, the journal encourages writers to challenge conventional wisdom and bring fresh, often controversial, perspectives to bear on the strategic issues of the moment. With a diverse range of authors, *Survival* aims to be scholarly in depth while vivid, well written and policy-relevant in approach. Through commentary, analytical articles, case studies, forums, review essays, reviews and letters to the editor, the journal promotes lively, critical debate on issues of international politics and strategy.

Editor **Dana Allin**
Managing Editor **Jonathan Stevenson**
Associate Editor **Carolyn West**
Editorial Assistant **Anna Gallagher**
Production and Cartography **Alessandra Beluffi, Ravi Gopar, James Lemon, Jade Panganiban, James Parker, Kelly Verity-Cailes**

Contributing Editors

Chester A. Crocker	Melissa K. Griffith	Irene Mia	Karen Smith
Bill Emmott	Emile Hokayem	Meia Nouwens	Angela Stent
Franz-Stefan Gady	Nigel Inkster	Benjamin Rhode	Robert Ward
Bastian Giegerich	Jeffrey Mazo	Ben Schreer	Marcus Willett
Nigel Gould-Davies	Fenella McGerty	Maria Shagina	Lanxin Xiang

Published for the IISS by
Routledge Journals, an imprint of Taylor & Francis, an Informa business.

Copyright © 2025 The International Institute for Strategic Studies. All rights reserved. No part of this publication may be reproduced, stored, transmitted or disseminated, in any form, or by any means, without prior written permission from Taylor & Francis, to whom all requests to reproduce copyright material should be directed, in writing.

Inclusion of a territory, country or state – or terminology or boundaries used in graphics or mapping – in this publication does not imply legal recognition or indicate support for any government or administration

ISBN 978-1-041-07814-2 paperback / 978-1-003-64230-5 ebook

ISSN 0039-6338 print / 1468-2699 online

About the IISS The IISS, a registered charity with offices in Washington, London, Manama, Singapore and Berlin, is the world's leading authority on political–military conflict. It is the primary independent source of accurate, objective information on international strategic issues. Publications include *The Military Balance*, an annual reference work on each nation's defence capabilities; *Survival*, a bimonthly journal on international affairs; *Strategic Comments*, an online analysis of topical issues in international affairs; and the *Adelphi* series of books on issues of international security.

Director-General and Chief Executive
Bastian Giegerich

Executive Chairman
John Chipman

Chair of the Trustees
Bill Emmott

Chair of the Council
Chung Min Lee

Trustees
Caroline Atkinson
Neha Aviral
Hakeem Belo-Osagie
John O. Brennan
Florence Parly
Kasper Rørsted
Mark Sedwill
Grace R. Skaugen
Matt Symonds
Matthew Symonds

IISS Advisory Council
Caroline Atkinson
Linden P. Blue
Garvin Brown
Mark Carleton-Smith
Jong-moon Choi
Alejandro Santo Domingo
Thomas Enders
Yoichi Funabashi
Alia Hatoug-Bouran
Eyal Hulata

Badr Jafar
Bilahari Kausikan
Peter Maurer
Florence Parly
Charles Powell
Mark Sedwill
Debra Soon
Heizo Takenaka
Akiba Takeo
Marcus Wallenberg

SUBMISSIONS

To submit an article, authors are advised to follow these guidelines:

- Articles must be their authors' original work and not have been generated by any form of artificial intelligence.
- *Survival* articles are around 4,000–10,000 words long including endnotes. A word count should be included with a draft. Length is a consideration in the review process and shorter articles have an advantage.
- All text, including endnotes, should be double-spaced with wide margins.
- Any tables or artwork should be supplied in separate files, ideally not embedded in the document or linked to text around it.
- All *Survival* articles are expected to include endnote references. These should be complete and include first and last names of authors, titles of articles (even from newspapers), place of publication, publisher, exact publication dates, volume and issue number (if from a journal) and page numbers. Web sources should include complete URLs and DOIs if available.
- A summary of up to 150 words should be included with the article. The summary should state the main argument clearly and concisely, not simply say what the article is about.
- A short author's biography of one or two lines should also be included. This information will appear at the foot of the first page of the article.

Please note that *Survival* has a strict policy of listing multiple authors in alphabetical order.

Submissions should be made by email, in Microsoft Word format, to survival@iiss.org. Note that macro-enabled files will not be accepted. Alternatively, hard copies may be sent to *Survival*, IISS–US, 2121 K Street NW, Suite 801, Washington, DC 20037, USA.

The editorial review process can take up to three months. *Survival*'s acceptance rate for unsolicited manuscripts is less than 20%. *Survival* does not normally provide referees' comments in the event of rejection. Authors are permitted to submit simultaneously elsewhere so long as this is consistent with the policy of the other publication and the Editors of *Survival* are informed of the dual submission.

Readers are encouraged to comment on articles from the previous issue. Letters should be concise, no longer than 750 words and relate directly to the argument or points made in the original article.

Survival: Global Politics and Strategy (Print ISSN 0039-6338, Online ISSN 1468-2699) is published bimonthly for a total of 6 issues per year by Taylor & Francis Group, 4 Park Square, Milton Park, Abingdon, Oxon, OX14 4RN, UK. Periodicals postage paid (Permit no. 13095) at Brooklyn, NY 11256.

Airfreight and mailing in the USA by agent named World Container Inc., c/o BBT 150-15, 183rd Street, Jamaica, NY 11413, USA.

US Postmaster: Send address changes to Survival, World Container Inc., c/o BBT 150-15, 183rd Street, Jamaica, NY 11413, USA.

Subscription records are maintained at Taylor & Francis Group, 4 Park Square, Milton Park, Abingdon, OX14 4RN, UK.

Subscription information: For more information and subscription rates, please see tandfonline.com/pricing/journal/TSUR. Taylor & Francis journals are available in a range of different packages, designed to suit every library's needs and budget. This journal is available for institutional subscriptions with online-only or print & online options. This journal may also be available as part of our libraries, subject collections or archives. For more information on our sales packages, please visit librarianresources.taylorandfrancis.com.

For support with any institutional subscription, please visit help.tandfonline.com or email our dedicated team at subscriptions@tandf.co.uk.

Subscriptions purchased at the personal rate are strictly for personal, non-commercial use only. The reselling of personal subscriptions is prohibited. Personal subscriptions must be purchased with a personal cheque, credit card or BAC/wire transfer. Proof of personal status may be requested.

Back issues: Please visit https://taylorandfrancis.com/journals/customer-services/ for more information on how to purchase back issues.

Ordering information: To subscribe to the journal, please contact T&F Customer Services, Informa UK Ltd, Sheepen Place, Colchester, Essex, CO3 3LP, UK. Tel: +44 (0) 20 8052 2030; email subscriptions@tandf.co.uk.

Taylor & Francis journals are priced in USD, GBP and EUR (as well as AUD and CAD for a limited number of journals). All subscriptions are charged depending on where the end customer is based. If you are unsure which rate applies to you, please contact Customer Services. All subscriptions are payable in advance and all rates include postage. We are required to charge applicable VAT/GST on all print and online combination subscriptions, in addition to our online-only journals. Subscriptions are entered on an annual basis, i.e., January to December. Payment may be made by sterling cheque, dollar cheque, euro cheque, international money order, National Giro or credit cards (Amex, Visa and Mastercard).

Disclaimer: The International Institute for Strategic Studies (IISS) and our publisher Informa UK Limited, trading as Taylor & Francis Group ('T&F'), make every effort to ensure the accuracy of all the information (the 'Content') contained in our publications. However, IISS and our publisher T&F, our agents and our licensors make no representations or warranties whatsoever as to the accuracy, completeness or suitability for any purpose of the Content. Any opinions and views expressed in this publication are the opinions and views of the authors, and are not the views of or endorsed by IISS or our publisher T&F. The accuracy of the Content should not be relied upon and should be independently verified with primary sources of information, and any reliance on the Content is at your own risk. IISS and our publisher T&F make no representations, warranties or guarantees, whether express or implied, that the Content is accurate, complete or up to date. IISS and our publisher T&F shall not be liable for any losses, actions, claims, proceedings, demands, costs, expenses, damages and other liabilities whatsoever or howsoever caused arising directly or indirectly in connection with, in relation to or arising out of the use of the Content. Full Terms & Conditions of access and use can be found at http://www.tandfonline.com/page/terms-and-conditions.

Informa UK Limited, trading as Taylor & Francis Group, grants authorisation for individuals to photocopy copyright material for private research use, on the sole basis that requests for such use are referred directly to the requestor's local Reproduction Rights Organization (RRO). The copyright fee is exclusive of any charge or fee levied. In order to contact your local RRO, please contact International Federation of Reproduction Rights Organizations (IFRRO), rue du Prince Royal, 87, B-1050 Brussels, Belgium; email ifrro@skynet.be; Copyright Clearance Center Inc., 222 Rosewood Drive, Danvers, MA 01923, USA; email info@copyright.com; or Copyright Licensing Agency, 90 Tottenham Court Road, London, W1P 0LP, UK; email cla@cla.co.uk. This authorisation does not extend to any other kind of copying, by any means, in any form, for any purpose other than private research use.

Submission information: See https://www.tandfonline.com/journals/tsur20

Advertising: See https://taylorandfrancis.com/contact/advertising/

Permissions: See help.tandfonline.com/Librarian/s/article/Permissions

All Taylor & Francis Group journals are printed on paper from renewable sources by accredited partners.

August–September 2025

MILITARY BALANCE+
THE ONLINE DATABASE

DATA AND ANALYSIS TOOLS

MILITARY BALANCE+, the online database from the IISS Defence and Military Analysis team, provides indispensable information for the private sector, governments, armed forces, academia, the media and more.

- **Perform your analysis on Military Balance+**
  Utilising seven search engines and three data tools, you can ask complex questions of the data.

- **Save time and money**
  The Military Balance+ can do in seconds what would otherwise take hours of your researchers' time.

- **Data you can have confidence in**
  All data has gone through a rigorous verification process, meaning you can use it in your work without concern over its validity.

- **Original IISS insight**
  Military Balance+ contains a searchable library of original IISS analysis, charts and graphics.

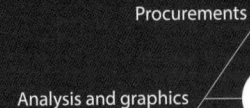

Deployments
Exercises
Forces
Equipment
Economics
Procurements
Analysis and graphics

A WORLD OF DEFENCE DATA TO DRIVE YOUR STRATEGY

173 countries and territories

Data tools

GSA Contract Holder
Contract # 47QTCA22D000H

www.iiss.org/militarybalanceplus

CONTACT

For an online demonstration, trial and subscription information:

Robert Hopgood
Sales Manager for Military Balance+

Direct: +44 (0)20 7395 9911
Mobile: +44 (0)7548 217 063
Email: robert.hopgood@iiss.org

Attacking Iran and Tempting Fate

Mark Fitzpatrick

The world's most deadly weapons in the hands of a determined adversary would be bad enough for the United States and its partners. The worst case would be an avoidable war waged over the issue, with an even more resentful Islamic Republic of Iran then acquiring nuclear weapons anyway.[1] The first part of this scenario played out when Israel from 13–24 June 2025 attacked Iran's nuclear infrastructure and other elements of its national power, with the US then joining in on 22 June to bomb three sites critical to uranium enrichment. Although these attacks badly damaged Iran's enrichment programme, they did not destroy it. The second part of the tragedy may materialise when Tehran, fuelled by nationalist fury and a sense of defensive necessity, moves secretly to use its still significant nuclear capabilities to produce at least a handful of weapons. Israel and the US may face the spectre of a new nuclear-armed enemy sooner than once feared.

Israeli Prime Minister Benjamin Netanyahu and US President Donald Trump are betting on a different outcome: that their strikes so severely set back Iran's nuclear capability as to make reconstitution impossible for years, and that, realising this, Iran's leadership will agree to give up the weapons quest. The evidence suggests this rosy scenario is wrong. Yet European partners seem to have bought into the optimism. At the G7 summit in Canada,

Mark Fitzpatrick is IISS Associate Fellow for Strategy, Technology and Arms Control, former Executive Director of IISS–Americas, and former head of the institute's work on non-proliferation. From 1979–2005, he served as a US Foreign Service Officer, with postings in Seoul, Tokyo, Wellington, Vienna and Washington DC, including as acting Deputy Assistant Secretary of State for Non-Proliferation.

the leaders issued a joint statement that Israel had a right to defend itself and that Iran should never be allowed to build nuclear weapons.[2] German Chancellor Friedrich Merz offered praise for 'the dirty work Israel is doing for all of us'.[3] NATO Secretary General Mark Rutte in text messages on 24 June called the US strikes 'truly extraordinary' and something 'no one else dared to do'.[4] Left unspoken by Western leaders was that the attacks were preventive rather than pre-emptive, because Iran was not about to hit first nor even threatening to do so.[5] French President Emmanuel Macron acknowledged that the attacks violated international law, while also saying there is 'a legitimacy in neutralizing Iran's nuclear structures'.[6]

Motivated by religious fervour and hatred of Israel, Iran's regime has been a major supporter of international terrorism, a would-be usurper of the regional order and a serial violator of human rights. It is hard to argue against Israeli perceptions that nuclear arms in the hands of the funder, supplier and trainer of the Hamas fighters who terrorised Israel on 7 October 2023 would pose an existential threat. The shameful irony of the June attacks, though, is that diplomacy had already practically checked Iran's nuclear ambitions before Trump, for no good reason, in 2018 withdrew from the 2015 nuclear deal negotiated by his predecessor Barack Obama and five leading powers, along with the European Union.

Called the Joint Comprehensive Plan of Action (JCPOA), the accord reduced Iran's enriched-uranium stockpile by 98%, sharply restricted development of dual-use nuclear technology for 15 years and allowed in perpetuity the most intrusive inspections ever agreed among sovereign states. When Trump pulled out of the deal, Iran had been honouring every aspect of it, and continued to do so for another year, before it began to ignore the restrictions in summer 2019. The deal was not perfect, but if allowed to run its course, it would have set back Iran's nuclear capabilities far longer than the June bombing is likely to do. While the JCPOA limits would be expiring by 2030, there would have been time for further diplomatic efforts to keep the nuclear capabilities in check, building on the trust gained through mutual adherence. Accordingly, the mantra that Iran should not be allowed nuclear weapons – intoned by every Western leader, including US presidents from both parties, for decades – is no justification for the Israeli and American attacks.

Unexhausted diplomacy

Diplomacy might again have succeeded in buying crucial time had Trump continued his initial effort to reach a peaceful outcome. His chief negotiator, fellow real-estate magnate and diplomatic rookie Steve Witkoff, had no business facing off against Iranian diplomats who had negotiated with the US for years. Witkoff had the advantage, however, of not wearing ideological blinders. When negotiations began in April 2025, he seemed to understand that a new deal could not be achieved unless, as in the JCPOA, Iran were allowed to maintain some level of uranium enrichment. But when he told Fox News on 14 April that Iran would have to reduce its enrichment level to 3.67% – the JCPOA standard – American Iran hawks reacted furiously.[7] The next day Witkoff back-pedalled and called for the complete dismantling of the uranium-enrichment programme.[8]

Reconciling the zero-enrichment demand with Iran's implacable insistence on a hard-earned right to nuclear technology darkened prospects for diplomatic success. Yet negotiators doggedly sought middle ground and had planned to meet for a sixth round in Oman on 15 June. The Iranians were expected to respond substantively to a Witkoff proposal for a framework to resolve the stand-off over enrichment.[9] Driven by a need to reduce the economic pain of America's chokehold on their commerce and the likelihood of more to come in the form of snapback United Nations sanctions, they were reportedly willing to consider creative alternatives, such as a multinational consortium for uranium enrichment, and wanted to explore further diplomatic and economic engagement with Washington.[10] They were even ready to allow US inspectors to join monitoring teams from the International Atomic Energy Agency (IAEA). Two Western researchers who visited Iran in late May and spoke with officials there stated that they saw no evidence that Iran was deliberately stalling. To the contrary, they said, the Iranian government was eager for a deal.[11]

On the day Israel launched its surprise attack, however, Trump said he had given Tehran 60 days to reach a new deal and that 13 June was the 61st day.[12] But Trump's first mention of a 60-day deadline was in a letter he sent to Supreme Leader Ayatollah Sayyid Ali Khamenei on 7 March, which would have made the 61st day 7 May. If the beginning of talks on 12

April started the clock, the 61st day would have been 11 June. In almost any negotiation, however, artificial deadlines are suspended as long as talks are proceeding in good faith.

Trump broke the faith with his negotiating partner when, on 9 June, he spoke with Netanyahu and reportedly did not repeat the 'hard no' he had previously given in response to the Israeli prime minister's desire to attack.[13] Former US diplomat Dennis Ross called Trump's response a 'plausible-denial green light'. While not accusing the US of deception, Ross said, 'there is no question that the Witkoff mission was a major contributor to the surprise. The Iranians would have assumed that Israel would not attack while the talks were under way and a meeting was about to take place.'[14]

Iranian Foreign Minister Abbas Araghchi suggested that talks with Witkoff had been an elaborate shadow play, cover for Israeli war preparations. 'So they had perhaps this plan in their mind, and they just needed negotiations perhaps to cover it up', he told NBC. 'We don't know how we can trust them anymore. What they did was in fact a betrayal to diplomacy.'[15] Trump's boast that he 'knew everything' about the 13 June attack in advance intensified the perception of bad faith.[16] Some Iranians have gone farther and claimed the attacks that started on 13 June were a joint Israeli–US operation, and that the US is thus responsible for hundreds of Iranian deaths. Iranian professor Foad Izadi in an Al Sharq News programme on 29 June insisted that US refuelling aircraft helped Israeli fighters return home after their attacks.[17] The distrust and suspicion toward the US is palpable.

Israel's attacks, code-named *Operation Rising Lion*, hit Iran's air-defence systems, command-and-control networks, communications nodes, nuclear facilities and missile sites. They also targeted energy infrastructure, Iran's broadcasting headquarters and several other government buildings, including the library of the Ministry of Foreign Affairs. Israel claimed it killed 11 nuclear scientists and engineers and over 30 military leaders and other security officials.[18] In announcing the operation, Netanyahu cited 'a clear and present danger to Israel's survival' from Iran's nuclear programme, claiming that Iran had 'recently taken unprecedented steps to weaponise' its uranium stockpile.[19] Public evidence does not support either of these claims. On 25 March, US Director of National Intelligence Tulsi Gabbard, reflecting the consensus of the intelligence community, testified that 'Iran is not building a nuclear weapon' and that Khamenei 'has not authorized the nuclear weapons program he suspended in 2003'.[20] There has been no indication that this assessment changed in the months that followed.[21]

In counterpoint to the mainstream media's scepticism about Israel's intelligence claims, *The Economist* reported on 18 June that it had gained insights from an authoritative source about the evidence. One data point was that an Iranian scientific team had squirrelled away a quantity of nuclear material not reported to the IAEA. Another was that the scientists had accelerated their work and were about to meet missile-corps commanders, apparently to prepare for the future mating of a nuclear warhead with a missile. Nevertheless, American intelligence agencies were reportedly sceptical.[22] To further justify the attacks, Israeli officials pointed to a 12 June IAEA board resolution finding that Iran was not in compliance with its safeguards obligations while stating that the agency was unable to verify that there had been no diversion of nuclear material.[23] This conclusion was no *casus belli*, however. It stemmed from Iran's failure to explain traces of anthropogenic uranium that IAEA inspectors in 2019 and 2020 had found at three sites where Iran had not reported any nuclear activity. The non-compliance finding had nothing to do with Iran's enriched-uranium stockpile.

A plausible explanation for Netanyahu's decision to attack is that Iran's prospective ability to produce nuclear weapons had simply gotten too close for comfort. Israel could not take the chance that the Islamic Republic would proceed with the last step of building a weapon before it could be discovered. Unlike Trump and his predecessors, whose red line was 'no nuclear weapons' for Iran, Israel's red line has been 'no nuclear-weapons capability'. The latter is a vague criterion. Capabilities lie along a continuum. Iran arguably has had such a capability since it first started producing highly enriched uranium (HEU, defined as over 20% U-235

> *American intelligence agencies were reportedly sceptical*

content) in 2010. An IAEA report dated 31 May 2025 indicating that Iran had produced more than 400 kilogrammes of 60% HEU was shocking. If further enriched to the 90%+ weapons-grade level, it would be enough for up to ten nuclear weapons.

There were undoubtedly several other contributing factors. The window of Iran's vulnerability due to Israel's decimation of Hizbullah and Hamas, the fall of its ally Bashar al-Assad in Syria, and Israel's elimination of Iran's air defences last autumn would close as Hizbullah and Hamas regrouped and Iran's air defences were replaced. Furthermore, Israel's covert pre-positioning of attack drones in Iran and pinpointing of the location of assassination targets might not have lasted long.[24] Netanyahu also may have wanted to derail any possibility of a US–Iran agreement that he would deem unacceptable. Although US hardliners had countermanded Witkoff's suggestion that Iran could be allowed a limited degree of indigenous uranium enrichment, forcing a retreat to zero, Netanyahu could not be certain that the unpredictable Trump would hold this line given his stated keenness to strike a deal.

Israeli domestic politics also played a role. Before the attack, Netanyahu's coalition was wobbly and his leadership under fire for failing to prevent the 7 October massacre. He was, moreover, facing criminal charges for corruption that prosecutors would pursue with greater dispatch upon his leaving office. Taking down the country deemed ultimately responsible for the atrocity would firm up his standing.[25] Netanyahu's place in history would be all the more enhanced if he could foster regime change in Iran. This objective was hardly disguised. Defence Minister Israel Katz on 20 June said he had instructed the Israel Defense Forces (IDF) to 'intensify strikes on regime targets in Tehran' to 'destabilize' the Iranian regime.[26] Similarly, Netanyahu described the Israeli operation as 'clearing the path' for the overthrow of the regime, and he called upon the Iranian people to liberate themselves.[27]

If regime change was the goal, it was fanciful. It has never been achieved through airpower alone, and few knowledgeable Iran watchers believe that its citizens would take to the streets.[28] If destroying diplomacy was Israel's aim, though, the operation was a success.

Operation Midnight Hammer

More focused deceit on Trump's part came a week later. While bruiting an onslaught of US bunker-busters to finish off Israel's attacks on the deeply buried enrichment plants, Trump as late as 19 June said Iran would have up to two more weeks to negotiate. By then, however, he had already made up his mind to join the attack. It was a feint meant to keep the Iranians off guard, several US officials told the *Atlantic*.[29] On the evening of 22 June, in what was code-named *Operation Midnight Hammer*, seven B-2 stealth bombers dropped 14 13,600-kg GBU-57/B 'massive ordnance penetrators' on the Natanz and Fordow enrichment sites.

Via Oman, the US wisely gave Iran advance warning so it could evacuate personnel. Unlike Israel's 12 days of strikes, which according to Iranian authorities killed 935 people, the US bombing caused no casualties.[30] Iran likewise provided warning of its symbolic missile attack against the Al Udeid Air Base in Qatar, America's largest military facility in the Middle East. All but one of the 14 short- and medium-range ballistic missiles were intercepted; the other one caused only minor damage. By contrast, Iran's barrage of 532 missiles targeting Israel killed 28 people and wounded 300.

Trump later mused about assassinating Khamenei, writing on social media that the US knew where the supreme leader was but was 'not going to take him out (kill!), at least not for now'.[31] Whether Trump wrote this to try to prod Iran into accepting his demand for 'unconditional surrender', to support Netanyahu's regime-change goal or for some other reason, the notion was ethically repugnant and tactically ignorant. It undermined trust in diplomacy and risked unnecessarily provoking Iran. In addition, US law since 1976 has prohibited political assassinations.[32]

Trump's deceit about *Operation Midnight Hammer* continued for days. In an address to the nation shortly after the 22 June strikes, he called them 'a spectacular military success', saying that 'Iran's key nuclear enrichment facilities have been completely and totally obliterated'.[33] Quickly contradicting this claim, a leaked initial battle-damage assessment by the US Defense Intelligence Agency judged that the strikes sealed off the entrances to two of the facilities, but did not collapse their underground buildings. With low confidence and subject to additional information, the report estimated that the strikes had delayed Iran's enrichment programme by less than six months.[34] Trump nevertheless continued to insist that the sites had been destroyed and required other US officials to say the same. A month earlier, Gabbard had fired two top National Intelligence Council officials for contradicting Trump's rationale for invoking the Alien Enemies Act and deporting alleged Venezuelan gang members without due process.[35] Now, by charging the media with disloyalty and dishonesty, and ordering the discontinuation of preliminary intelligence reports, he further increased pressure on intelligence analysts to tailor assessments to the administration's political needs.[36]

Trump's decision to stop giving diplomacy a chance appeared to be based on a whim. There was no inter-agency policy coordination, no declaration of war, no congressional authorisation for the use of force and no meaningful engagement with Congress, top Republicans having received only a brief heads-up. Some accounts suggested that Trump was goaded by Fox News, which was airing wall-to-wall praise of Israel's attacks and featuring guests urging Trump to pile on.[37] Wanting to share credit, Trump took to using the first-person plural to describe Israel's operations. 'We control the skies over Tehran. We are striking with tremendous force at the regime of the ayatollahs. We are hitting the nuclear sites, the missiles, the headquarters, the symbols of the regime', he said two days before the US airstrikes.[38] These pronouncements raised concerns at the Pentagon that Trump was giving Iran too much tactical warning about an impending strike.[39]

Iran's residual nuclear capability

Overall, it is unlikely that Iran will be able to reconstitute its nuclear-weapons capability at the industrial scale at which Natanz, Fordow and Esfahan were operating. Although the bunker-busters dropped on Fordow apparently did not reach the centrifuge hall itself, vibrations from the bombings and the loss of electricity would have made the centrifuges crash. The Natanz plant, being less deeply buried, suffered more damage. By contrast, some of the facilities at Esfahan are located so far underground that the US did not even try to drop bunker-busters on them, instead using submarine-launched *Tomahawk* cruise missiles to take out the most vulnerable targets there. It is probably safe to conclude that at Esfahan there will be no more production of uranium-hexafluoride gas and no conversion of HEU gas to metal for use in a weapon.

To produce a small arsenal of bombs, however, Iran does not need any more uranium hexafluoride. It already has over 400 kg of 60% enriched uranium, as well as other amounts of 40%, 20% and 3.5% enriched uranium, all of which was stored in scuba-tank-sized cylinders that Iran was able to hide before the attacks.[40] That is why no radiation leaks were reported after the bombing. The 60% HEU alone is enough for up to ten weapons if further enriched. Satellite imagery showed an unusual number of trucks moving in and out of the Fordow site hours before the US attack. Some observers assessed that Trump's boasts had indeed alerted Iran, enabling it to remove stockpiles and protect equipment.[41]

Iran also has an unknown number of centrifuges in storage or in production that it would be able to use, along with any centrifuges scavenged from Natanz and Fordow before or after the attacks. With these, it could further enrich the HEU stockpile to the 90% level considered to be weapons grade at a new enrichment plant where Iran recently told the IAEA it was ready to start installing centrifuges.[42] According to arms-control expert Jeffrey Lewis, Iran can install about 1.5 centrifuge cascades a week, so in six weeks, it could have nine cascades, each with 164–174 centrifuges. It would take Iran another two months to enrich the 60% HEU to weapons grade. From start to finish, the process would span about five months in total.[43]

In sum, Iran may be able to produce the fissile material required for about ten nuclear weapons within half a year. How long it would take Iran to fashion it into a weapon is unknown. The loss of the 11 nuclear scientists and engineers by assassination has undoubtedly lengthened the timeline. But Iran has more talent in the pipeline, as well as blueprint-based knowledge. Much of its weapons-development work had already been completed two decades ago, as detailed in the copious documents Mossad acquired in its January 2018 raid of a warehouse in suburban Tehran.[44] The most time-consuming bottleneck to overcome may be replacing the former capability at Esfahan to convert uranium gas to metal.[45] Iran's ability to reconstitute the nuclear capability will also be dependent on its ability to keep it protected from further Israeli attacks.

Another option if Iran cannot easily rebuild key facilities, such as a plant to convert HEU gas to metal, would be to seek North Korean help. There is ample precedent for such cooperation. The two regimes closely coordinated on missile development beginning in 1987, and Pyongyang provided Syria with a plutonium-production reactor in the early 2000s.[46] This was all before North Korea had a robust nuclear-weapons arsenal with which to protect itself if the transfer were discovered. Iran's oil would be a welcome commodity in exchange for weapons-related equipment or even possibly the nuclear warheads themselves.

It is mortifyingly ironic that Israel's attack has ensured that Iran will keep the stockpile of near-weapons-grade HEU hidden and increased the likelihood that it will use it as soon as possible to produce nuclear weapons. On 26 June, Iran's Guardian Council overwhelmingly approved a parliamentary bill ordering the suspension of cooperation with the IAEA until the security of nuclear sites and scientists were guaranteed and Iran's right to enrichment recognised.[47] President Masoud Pezeshkian officially signed the bill into law on 2 July. Commenting on it, Parliamentary Speaker Mohammad Bagher Ghalibaf claimed that the IAEA had shared information on its nuclear sites with Israel.[48]

Looking ahead

As of mid-July, Iran had not taken the next logical step and declared withdrawal from the Nuclear Non-Proliferation Treaty (NPT), a move it has several times threatened to make in response to affronts far less serious than Israel's and the United States' June attacks.[49] It has to be particularly galling to Iranians that one of the attackers was a non-NPT party and the other a former negotiating partner that has now twice upended the bargaining table. Leaving the treaty would trigger the snapback of UN sanctions that were lifted in 2015 in connection with the JCPOA. But the actual economic cost would be marginal, given that Iran is already subject to so many US secondary sanctions, and China and Russia would not implement UN measures. In any case, the snapback mechanism expires in October, so Iran need not wait long to evade the political as well as economic costs of UN sanctions. Meanwhile, Iran might keep the NPT-withdrawal card as a bargaining chip for future negotiations.

There might not be any negotiations, however. In a blistering commentary, former EU foreign-policy chief Enrique Mora, who was closely involved in nuclear negotiations with Iran, warned that the US strikes could finally induce Iran to decide it needs nuclear weapons to protect itself. 'June 21, 2025 may go down in history', he wrote, 'as the day a nuclear Iran was irreversibly born'.[50] Before the US bombing, senior US intelligence officials reportedly expected Iranian leaders to shift toward producing a bomb if the American military attacked Iranian uranium-enrichment sites.[51] Post-attack opinion polling in Iran – not available at this writing – is likely to show heightened support for the nuclear option. This is the natural human response to an unprovoked attack; unconditional surrender is not.

Iran's government steadfastly holds that its nuclear programme is entirely peaceful and that a fatwa issued by the supreme leader in 2009 prohibits nuclear-weapons production. Officials note, however, that the religious prohibition can be changed if circumstances warrant. Khamenei himself hinted at this last autumn.[52] Israel and the US, as well as their global partners, have been lucky that Iran's initial response to the attacks was so muted. In addition to refraining from withdrawing from the NPT and from ending the fatwa, Iran did not seek to close the Strait of Hormuz, bomb oil installations in the Middle East, rain cyber attacks against Western interests, or unleash terrorist attacks against Israeli or American companies or citizens by the Islamic Revolutionary Guard Corps or Iran's militia partners.[53] Such responses could still come at a time of Iran's choosing, as Iranian civilian and military leaders lick their wounds and consider how to restore deterrence against further Israeli attacks. In unleashing any retaliation to accomplish this, Iran would have to weigh the downsides of inciting further Israeli bombing, but Israel may not always enjoy the level of strategic superiority and freedom of action that it has established over Iran in the past two years.

Even if Tehran itself continues its forbearance to some degree, the attacks could well produce a grave second-order result: the breakdown of the non-proliferation regime and the global nuclear order. Iran has joined the list of beleaguered states without nuclear arms that have been attacked by states that have them – a list that includes Iraq, Libya and Ukraine. Some states that until now have adhered to the NPT may reconsider their pledges. North Korea is the only country to have pulled out of the NPT, having done so in

2003, three and a half years before testing its first, crude nuclear bomb. It has now assembled a formidable arsenal estimated at 50 nuclear weapons.[54] Even before the June attacks, Iranian parliamentarians and other citizens had been increasingly inclined to follow North Korea's path. The North Korean case is *sui generis*. The main factor precluding a South Korean attack on North Korea is geography rather than North Korea's possession of nuclear weapons: Seoul's proximity to the border allows conventional North Korean artillery to hold South Korea's population hostage.[55] Be that as it may, however, a natural inference for a country attacked for nearing nuclear-weapons capability is that the capability itself would produce a stronger deterrent.

What, then, is Trump's strategy for dealing with the first- and second-order consequences? The spur-of-the-moment nature of the US attack order suggests he is not capable of anticipatory planning. As law professor and former Pentagon official Rosa Brooks put it in a recent podcast, rather than three- or four-dimensional chess, Trump is playing one-dimensional checkers.[56] His triumphalist accounting of *Operation Midnight Hammer* showed his concept of war as being 'one shot and done', whereby a cowering adversary is supposed to roll over in abject and permanent fear. Modern history paints a different pattern of war that lingers.

It is hardly reassuring to watch the unimpressive and unqualified cabinet members with whom Trump has surrounded himself. In no normally competent administration would a Fox News co-host serve as secretary of defense, a former senator hold the positions of both secretary of state and national security advisor, a national guardsman with no career military service be chairman of the Joint Chiefs of Staff, and appointees with no direct experience in intelligence work be heads of the two main intelligence services. The sycophantic and defensive responses of Trump's key aides to any perceived criticism of the president suggest that none of them will be ready to give him unwelcome advice.[57]

The voice that has proven most persuasive to him, however, has been that of Netanyahu, to the point where Trump has tied America's destiny to Israel's. The fact that Netanyahu has so often been wrong does not factor into the president's thinking. Netanyahu encouraged him to abandon the JCPOA, which was operating flawlessly and had 12 more years to run before the limits on enrichment would be lifted. Netanyahu and other JCPOA opponents considered this too short. Yet the military course of action they goaded Trump to take will buy far less time – two years perhaps – than the agreement originally did. It makes little sense to hold diplomacy to much higher standards than military action. Granted, the comparison between the 15 years bought by the JCPOA's limits compared to the two years perhaps bought by bombing is apples and oranges due to the different times and circumstances of the starting points. But the Iran hawks who claimed 15 years was too short cannot possibly know that bombing has done a better job.

The question now is whether diplomacy might again play a role. A return to agreed limits verified by close monitoring is still the best solution to the Iran nuclear crisis. But both sides have expressed ambivalence about reconvening. On 25 June, Trump suggested there was no further need for an agreement with Iran since bombing, in his view, had destroyed the enrichment programme.[58] Yet on 27 June, reports emerged that his administration had been exploring economic incentives, including the idea of a $30 billion investment by Arab Gulf states in Iran's civilian nuclear infrastructure in return for an end to uranium enrichment, floated to Iran the day before Israel launched its attacks.[59]

*   *   *

Bloodied or bribed, Iran continues to insist it will not give up enrichment. National pride in the scientific achievements of its nuclear programme is embedded in the Iranian psyche. The nuclear-hedging motivation behind the programme is immutable. All the same, it may not be impossible to find a way to overcome the impasse. For example, a time-limited 'voluntary' halt to enrichment would make practical sense, given that Natanz and Fordow are now out of operation anyway. Iran's HEU stockpile would have to be shipped abroad or down-blended. The only way Iran might agree to this, however, is if the US accepted the principle that Iran could resume enrichment. For Trump – and Netanyahu – such a compromise might sound too akin to the JCPOA that both judged to be unacceptable.

It was a strategic tragedy that Trump abrogated an agreement that was working in 2018, thereby ensuring that Iran would increase enrichment levels and install thousands of more efficient centrifuges. The 12 months ensured by the JCPOA before Iran could break out and produce the fissile material for a weapon was reduced to about a week. Israel's military action compounded the tragedy by pre-empting any new deal in progress. The tragedy will be repeated if, or more likely when, Israel learns about Iran's reconstitution progress and conducts further strikes. This cycle could be repeated more than once. Eventually, however, Iran is likely to emerge nuclear armed and objectively paranoid – the worst of all outcomes.

Notes

1   See Mark Fitzpatrick, *The Iranian Nuclear Crisis: Avoiding Worst-case Outcomes*, Adelphi 398 (Abingdon: Routledge for the IISS, 2008).
2   See G7, 'G7 Leaders' Statement on Recent Developments Between Israel and Iran', 16 June 2025, https://g7.canada.ca/en/news-and-media/news/g7-leaders-statement-on-recent-developments-between-israel-and-iran/.
3   Quoted in, for example, Natan Odenheimer et al., 'Israel Says It Assassinated Iran's Most Senior Military Commander', *New York Times*, 17 June 2025, https://www.nytimes.com/2025/06/17/world/middleeast/israel-iran-assassination-general.html.
4   Quoted in, for example, John Paul Tasker, 'NATO Chief Praises Trump's "Truly Extraordinary" Actions Against Iran in Text Messages', CBC News, 24 June 2025, https://www.cbc.ca/news/politics/nato-chief-praises-trump-iran-1.7569579.
5   See Tom Nichols, 'Israel's Bold, Risky Attack', *Atlantic*, 12 June 2025, https://www.theatlantic.com/ideas/archive/2025/06/israel-iran-war/683160/.
6   Clea Caulcutt, 'Macron: US Strikes on Iran Aren't Legal', *Politico*, 23 June 2025, https://www.politico.eu/article/emmanuel-macron-iran-israel-us-legal-war-mena/. The UN Charter prohibits the use of force between member states, except in cases of self-defence or when authorised by the Security Council.
7   See Marc Rod, 'Witkoff Sends Mixed Messages on Iranian Nuclear Enrichment', *Jewish Insider*, 16 April 2025, https://jewishinsider.com/2025/04/steve-witkoff-iran-nuclear-talks-oman/.
8   See 'United States and Iran Begin Nuclear Talks', *Arms Control Today*, May 2025, https://www.armscontrol.org/2025-05/united-states-and-iran-begin-nuclear-talks.
9   See Michael R. Gordon, 'In Twist, U.S. Diplomacy Served as Cover for Israeli Surprise Attack', *Wall Street Journal*, 13 June 2025, https://www.wsj.com/world/middle-east/in-twist-u-s-diplomacy-served-as-cover-for-israeli-surprise-attack-c79b2206?.
10 See Ned Price, 'Israel Should Have Let Diplomacy Run Its Course', *Foreign Policy*, 16 June 2024, https://foreignpolicy.com/2025/06/16/israel-iran-strikes-diplomacy-trump-nuclear-negotiations/.
11 See Eli Clifton and Eldar Mamedov, 'America Is Sleepwalking into

Another Unnecessary War', *Guardian*, 18 June 2025, https://www.theguardian.com/commentisfree/2025/jun/18/iran-us-nuclear-negotiaons-israel-war.

12   See 'Trump Says He Gave Iran a 60-day Ultimatum: "Today Is Day 61 … Now They Have, Perhaps, a Second Chance!"', *Times of Israel*, 13 June 2025, https://www.timesofisrael.com/liveblog_entry/trump-says-he-gave-iran-a-60-day-ultimatum-today-is-day-61-now-they-have-perhaps-a-second-chance/.

13   One analyst judged that Trump's previous 'red light shifted to a yellow light'. Ryan Costello, 'Will Trump Take on George W. Bush's Foreign Policy Legacy?', *American Conservative*, 19 June 2025, https://www.theamericanconservative.com/Will-Trump-Take-On-George-W-Bushs-Foreign-Policy-Legacy/.

14   Gordon, 'In Twist, U.S. Diplomacy Served as Cover for Israeli Surprise Attack'.

15   Dan De Luce and Andrea Mitchell, 'Iran Not Sure It Can Trust America After Israeli Attack, Iran's Foreign Minister Tells NBC News', NBC News, 20 June 2025, https://www.nbcnews.com/world/iran/iran-not-sure-can-trust-america-israeli-attack-irans-foreign-minister-rcna214139.

16   Steve Holland, '"We Knew Everything", Trump Tells Reuters About Israel's Strikes on Iran', Reuters, 13 June 2025, https://www.reuters.com/world/middle-east/trump-tells-reuters-its-unclear-if-iran-still-has-nuclear-program-2025-06-13/.

17   I was his interlocutor on the programme.

18   Howard Goller and Jonathan Landay, 'Israeli Official Says Iran Strikes Killed Over 30 Security Chiefs, 11 Nuclear Scientists', *Times of Israel*, 28 June 2025, https://www.timesofisrael.com/israeli-official-says-iran-strikes-killed-over-30-security-chiefs-11-nuclear-scientists/. Earlier, Israel's ambassador to France, Joshua Zarka, claimed 14 nuclear scientists and engineers had been killed.

19   Quoted in, for example, Julian Borger, Peter Beaumont and Deepa Parent, 'Israeli Strikes Hit More than 100 Targets in Iran Including Nuclear Facilities', *Guardian*, 13 June 2025, https://www.theguardian.com/world/2025/jun/13/israel-strikes-iran-nuclear-program-netanyahu.

20   Office of the Director of National Intelligence, 'DNI Gabbard Opening Statement for the SSCI as Prepared on the 2025 Annual Threat Assessment of the U.S. Intelligence Community', 25 March 2025, https://www.dni.gov/index.php/newsroom/congressional-testimonies/congressional-testimonies-2025/4059-ata-opening-statement-as-prepared.

21   See, for instance, Julian E. Barnes, 'U.S. Spy Agencies Assess Iran Remains Undecided on Building a Bomb', *New York Times*, 19 June 2025, https://www.nytimes.com/2025/06/19/us/politics/iran-nuclear-weapons-assessment.html.

22   See 'Inside the Spy Dossier that Led Israel to War', *The Economist*, 18 June 2025, https://www.economist.com/middle-east-and-africa/2025/06/18/inside-the-spy-dossier-that-led-israel-to-war.

23   International Atomic Energy Agency, 'NPT Safeguards Agreement with

the Islamic Republic of Iran', GOV/2025/38, 12 June 2025, https://www.iaea.org/sites/default/files/25/06/gov2025-38.pdf.

24 See Daniel Byman, 'Intelligence Window Might Have Been a Factor in Timing of Israeli Attack on Iran', *Foreign Policy*, 18 June 2025, https://foreignpolicy.com/2025/06/18/intelligence-window-israel-iran-attack-nuclear/.

25 See *ibid.*

26 Emanuel Fabian, 'Katz Says He Instructed IDF to "Destabilize" Iranian Regime with Intensified Strikes Against It', *Times of Israel*, 20 June 2025, https://www.timesofisrael.com/liveblog_entry/katz-says-he-instructed-idf-to-destabilize-iranian-regime-with-intensified-strikes-against-it/.

27 Prime Minister of Israel, 'Prime Minister Benjamin Netanyahu Addresses the Iranian People', YouTube.com, 13 June 2025, https://www.youtube.com/embed/fO8WlACdCB8?list=PLt-RWNOCtivaWKB8u1XwxnBqCxN6M9DQs.

28 See 'Israel's Dazzling, Daunting, Dangerous Victory', *The Economist*, 24 June 2025, https://www.economist.com/middle-east-and-africa/2025/06/24/israels-dazzling-daunting-dangerous-victory.

29 See Michael Scherer et al., 'Trump's Two-week Window for Diplomacy Was a Smoke Screen', *Atlantic*, 22 June 2025, https://www.theatlantic.com/politics/archive/2025/06/trump-israel-iran-bomb/683275/.

30 '935 People Killed in Israeli Strikes on Iran, Official Says', Reuters, 30 June 2025, https://www.reuters.com/world/middle-east/935-people-killed-israeli-strikes-iran-iran-judiciary-spokesperson-says-2025-06-30/.

31 Sarah D. Wire, 'Trump Says US Won't Kill Iran's Supreme Leader, "At Least Not for Now"', *USA Today*, 17 June 2025, https://www.usatoday.com/story/news/politics/2025/06/17/trump-iran-supreme-leader/84243930007/.

32 See Charles A. Ray, 'A Red Line Has Been Crossed: Navigating the Crossroads of Policy and Diplomacy', The Steady State, Substack, 26 June 2025, https://steadystate1.substack.com/p/a-red-line-has-been-crossed-navigating.

33 Elena Moore and Megan Pratz, 'U.S. Strikes 3 Nuclear Sites in Iran, in Major Regional Conflict Escalation', NPR, 22 June 2025, https://www.npr.org/2025/06/21/nx-s1-5441127/iran-us-strike-nuclear-trump.

34 Julian E. Barnes et al., 'Strike Set Back Iran's Nuclear Program by Only a Few Months, U.S. Report Says', *New York Times*, 24 June 2025, https://www.nytimes.com/2025/06/24/us/politics/iran-nuclear-sites.html. Israeli intelligence assessments concluded that the damage was more extensive. Two Israeli officials said that intelligence showed Iran's stockpile of enriched uranium was buried beneath rubble at Esfahan and Fordow. See Barak Ravid and Zachary Basu, 'Israeli Officials See "Significant" Damage to Iran's Nuclear Facilities', *Axios*, 25 June 2025, https://www.axios.com/2025/06/25/iran-nuclear-program-israel-damage-intelligence.

35 See Warren P. Strobel, 'Gabbard Fires Leaders of Intelligence Group

that Wrote Venezuela Assessment', *Washington Post*, 14 May 2025, https://www.washingtonpost.com/national-security/2025/05/14/gabbard-intelligence-venezuela-tren-de-aragua/.

36 See Stephen Collinson, 'Why Trump Needs the World to Believe Iran's Nuclear Program Is "Obliterated"', CNN, 26 June 2025, https://www.cnn.com/2025/06/26/politics/trump-iran-nuclear-program-damage.

37 See Mark Mazzetti and Jonathan Swan, 'Shifting Views and Misdirection: How Trump Decided to Strike Iran', *New York Times*, 22 June 2025, https://www.nytimes.com/2025/06/22/us/politics/trump-iran-decision-strikes.

38 See Graeme Baker and Helen Sullivan, 'Trump Approves Iran Attack Plan but Has Not Made Final Decision, Reports Say', BBC, 19 June 2025, https://www.bbc.com/news/articles/c4g8r8rj87vo.

39 See Mazzetti and Swan, 'Shifting Views and Misdirection'.

40 See David E. Sanger, 'Officials Concede They Don't Know the Fate of Iran's Uranium Stockpile', *New York Times*, 22 June 2025, https://www.nytimes.com/2025/06/22/us/politics/iran-uranium-stockpile-whereabouts.html.

41 See Cheryl Rofer, 'Mission Accomplished', Lawyers, Guns, Money blog, 23 June 2025, https://www.lawyersgunsmoneyblog.com/2025/06/mission-accomplished-8.

42 See Stephanie Liechtenstein, Jon Gambrell and Aamer Madhani, 'Iran Announces a New Nuclear Enrichment Site After UN Watchdog Censure', Associated Press, 12 June 2025, https://apnews.com/article/iran-nuclear-iaea-sanctions-728b811da537abe942682e13a82ff8bd.

43 See Jeffrey Lewis (@armscontrolwonk.bsky.social), post to Bluesky, 22 June 2025, https://bsky.app/profile/armscontrolwonk.bsky.social/post/3lsagielkcc2l.

44 See, for instance, David E. Sanger and Ronen Bergman, 'How Israel, in Dark of Night, Torched Its Way to Iran's Nuclear Secrets', *New York Times*, 15 July 2018, https://www.nytimes.com/2018/07/15/us/politics/iran-israel-mossad-nuclear.html.

45 See William J. Broad and Ronen Bergman, 'Israel and U.S. Smashed Iran Nuclear Site that Grew After Trump Quit 2015 Accord', *New York Times*, 28 June 2025, https://www.nytimes.com/2025/06/28/science/iran-nuclear-uranium-metal.html.

46 See Mark Fitzpatrick, 'Iran and North Korea: The Proliferation Nexus', *Survival*, vol. 48, no. 1, Spring 2006, pp. 61–80; and David E. Sanger and Mark Mazzetti, 'Israel Struck Syrian Nuclear Project, Analysts Say', *New York Times*, 14 October 2007, https://www.nytimes.com/2007/10/14/washington/14weapons.html.

47 See 'Iran Signals Cut in Ties with IAEA as Focus Shifts to Restoring Deterrence, Public Trust', Amwaj.media, 25 June 2025, https://amwaj.media/en/media-monitor/iran-signals-cut-in-ties-with-iaea-as-focus-shifts-to-restoring-deterrence-public.

48 See Alexandra Sharp, 'Khamenei Vows to "Never Surrender" to the U.S. in Defiant Speech', *Foreign Policy*, 26 June 2025, https://foreignpolicy.com/2025/06/26/khamenei-iran-

strikes-us-israel-nuclear-weapons-iaea/?tpcc=recirc_latest062921.
49 See Mark Goodman and Mark Fitzpatrick, 'What If Iran Withdraws from the NPT?', *Bulletin of the Atomic Scientists*, 25 June 2025, https://thebulletin.org/2025/06/what-if-iran-withdraws-from-the-npt.
50 Enrique Mora, 'El día que nació un Irán nuclear', *Política Exterior*, 26 June 2025, https://www.politicaexterior.com/el-dia-que-nacio-un-iran-nuclear/. An English translation can be found at https://amwaj.media/en/article/the-day-a-nuclear-iran-was-born.
51 See Barnes, 'U.S. Spy Agencies Assess Iran Remains Undecided on Building a Bomb'.
52 See Reuel Marc Gerecht and Ray Takeyh, 'Why Iran May Dash for the Bomb', *Wall Street Journal*, 10 November 2024, https://www.wsj.com/opinion/iran-may-dash-for-the-bomb-nuclear-weapon-escalation-a5c744ca; and International Institute for Strategic Studies, 'Iran's Weakened Position and the Status of Its Nuclear Option', *Strategic Comments*, vol. 30, no. 35, December 2025, https://www.iiss.org/publications/strategic-comments/2024/11/irans-weakened-position-and-the-status-of-its-nuclear-option/.
53 For a rundown of potential Iranian revenge responses, see Colin P. Clarke, 'How Iran Might Strike Back', *New York Times*, 22 June 2025, https://www.nytimes.com/2025/06/22/opinion/iran-nuclear-strike-israel-war.html.
54 Arms Control Association, 'Arms Control and Proliferation Profile: North Korea', June 2024, https://www.armscontrol.org/factsheets/arms-control-and-proliferation-profile-north-korea.
55 See, for example, Brad Lendon, 'North Korea Showcases Artillery that Poses a Deadly Threat to the South', CNN, 7 March 2024, https://www.cnn.com/2024/03/07/asia/north-korea-artillery-exercise-seoul-threat-intl-hnk-ml.
56 See 'Unconventional Wisdom About the Iran Crisis and the NATO Summit', The DSR Network, 25 June 2025, https://podcasts.apple.com/us/podcast/unconventional-wisdom-about-the-iran-crisis-and/id1245002955?i=1000714553144.
57 See Josh Marshall, 'Thoughts on Israel's Iran Campaign and Donald Trump', *Talking Points Memo*, 17 June 2025, https://talkingpointsmemo.com/edblog/thoughts-on-israels-iran-campaign-and-donald-trump.
58 See Danielle Cohen, 'Trump Announces Meeting with Iran but Says a Nuclear Agreement "Is Not Necessary"', *Jewish Insider*, 25 June 2025, https://jewishinsider.com/2025/06/trump-announces-meeting-with-iran-nuclear-agreement-not-necessary-nato-summit/.
59 See Abigail Williams and Dan De Luce, 'Trump Administration Exploring $30 Billion Civilian Nuclear Deal for Iran', NBC News, 27 June 2025, https://www.nbcnews.com/politics/national-security/trump-administration-exploring-30-billion-civilian-nuclear-deal-iran-rcna215679.

Commentary

Israel's Perilous Revisionism

Hasan T. Alhasan and Wolf-Christian Paes

Few in the Middle East are likely to concur with US Press Secretary Karoline Leavitt's assessment that Israel's June 2025 war with Iran, including the US strikes on Iran's nuclear facilities, are making the world 'a much safer place'.[1] It is still unclear how severe a setback Iran's nuclear programme has suffered.[2] Meanwhile, the war has exposed the deep rift separating Israel and its Western allies from key Middle Eastern states. Some in Europe and North America have applauded Israel for doing the 'dirty work' of stopping Iran from acquiring nuclear weapons.[3] But Israel's apparent plan to reshape the Middle East has produced growing unease in the region.

Israel has emerged from the regional sidelines, from which it had merely watched Iran, Qatar, Saudi Arabia, Turkiye and the United Arab Emirates (UAE) compete for influence across the Middle East during the Arab Spring and several years thereafter. Following the Hamas attack on 7 October 2023, however, Israel asserted itself in the region through sheer military force. Israeli Prime Minister Benjamin Netanyahu's ambition is to redraw the map of the Middle East, geopolitically if not literally.[4] Animated by a strategic doctrine of preventive warfare and buoyed by wide domestic support, Israel's government has waged war against Iran's network of armed non-state partners in Gaza (Hamas), Lebanon (Hizbullah) and Yemen (the Houthis), destroyed much of Syria's advanced

---

Hasan T. Alhasan is IISS Senior Fellow for Middle East Policy. **Wolf-Christian Paes** is IISS Senior Fellow for Armed Conflict.

military capabilities following the fall of Syrian dictator Bashar al-Assad and engaged in multiple rounds of direct hostilities with Iran itself.[5]

The latest round of attacks in June 2025 was different, however. Israel established complete air supremacy, decapitated much of the country's military leadership and seemed intent on eliminating Iran's supreme leader, possibly prompting the collapse of the regime, and in doing so clearly violated international law.[6] Despite pleas from Arab Gulf partners not to intervene and an ambivalent American public, the United States joined Israel, for the first time in its history launching direct strikes against Iran's nuclear facilities.

Changing regional dynamics

Iran is facing its largest strategic setback since the Iran–Iraq War in the 1980s. Israel has exposed the weakness of Tehran's military apparatus. Iran's air defences, centred on the domestically produced *Bavar*-373 surface-to-air missile system, were incapable of shooting down a single Israeli aircraft. Moreover, the regime's much-touted ballistic-missile programme failed to inflict significant military damage on Israel.[7] Meanwhile, since October 2023, Israel has significantly weakened Iran's 'axis of resistance' – the network of armed groups it supports – that for decades has been the cornerstone of Iran's deterrence strategy.

Some American and Israeli observers have inferred that Arab partners of the West – the Arab Gulf states, Egypt and Jordan – discreetly approve of the attacks on Iran.[8] This betrays a degree of naivety and wishful thinking. In fact, Arab threat perceptions have shifted. While much of the Arab world remains deeply wary of Tehran, Saudi Arabia and the UAE have learned sober lessons about the limits of military power in Yemen, where they were engaged in a bloody conflict with the Iran-supported Houthi rebels between 2015 and 2022. With China's assistance, they pursued a thaw in relations with Iran that led to a de-escalation of tensions in the Gulf. Washington's permissive attitude emboldened Israel, which has now disrupted relative regional stability.

Fearful of potential damage to their economic ambitions, the Arab Gulf states had sought to avert this confrontation. Addressing the World

Economic Forum at Davos, Saudi Foreign Minister Prince Faisal bin Farhan Al Saud stated that 'a war between Iran and Israel … is something we should try to avoid as much as possible'.[9] Oman has facilitated a ceasefire deal between the United States and the Houthis, and hosted multiple rounds of US–Iran nuclear talks. Once those talks began, Riyadh solemnly encouraged Tehran to conclude a deal with US President Donald Trump to deny Netanyahu a pretext for launching an attack on Iran.[10]

A weaker Iran is not necessarily a less dangerous Iran, especially to its Arab Gulf neighbours. They are within range of Iran's short-range missiles and uninhabited aerial vehicle (UAV) arsenals, which remain largely intact. A closure of the Strait of Hormuz could shut down their ability to export oil, the lifeblood of their economies. As hosts to US military facilities and forces, the Gulf states are at risk of Iranian retribution every time US–Iranian tensions rise, a point driven home by Iran's attack against Al Udeid Air Base in Qatar, which hosts US Central Command's forward headquarters, on 23 June 2025. Although the attack had been telegraphed by Iran and duly intercepted, the images of Iranian ballistic missiles lighting up Qatar's night sky suggested that Iran was not inclined towards abject capitulation.

The Arab Gulf states have balked at the prospect of regime change in Tehran, endorsed by Israel and somewhat more ambiguously by the United States.[11] A collapse of the regime in Iran, a country of over 90 million people, could pave the way for a more radical successor, imperil central state control over Iran's stock of missiles and other military capabilities, and spark a refugee crisis of colossal proportions.

Simmering tensions elsewhere

Israel's heavy-handed military campaign in Gaza has placed its relations with Egypt under immense strain. Israel has taken control of the Philadelphi Corridor, a demilitarised buffer zone along Gaza's border with Egypt, in a move Cairo has protested as a violation of the 1979 Egypt–Israel peace treaty and 2005 Philadelphi Accord.[12] Egypt also condemned, but ultimately acquiesced to, Israel's ground invasion of Rafah.[13] Suspecting Israeli designs to engineer an exodus of Palestinian refugees from Gaza into Egypt, Cairo has beefed up its military presence in the Sinai.[14]

In turn, some Israeli officials have become quietly leery of Egypt's military modernisation. Much of the build-up can be explained by the need to replace ageing Soviet-era platforms, and it does not constitute an imminent threat.[15] Nevertheless, last February, Lieutenant-General Herzi Halevi, then Israel's chief of defence staff, cautioned that Egypt's growing military capabilities were troubling, noting in reference to Egypt's short-lived Muslim Brotherhood government of 2012–13 that the 'situation can change in a moment' and propel a hostile leadership to power.[16]

Arguably, Jordan is in the most precarious position. The Hashemite Kingdom depends on Israel for its water and power-generation needs, and on the United States for foreign assistance, while facing immense pressure from its population to take a stronger position against Israeli excesses in the occupied Palestinian territories. Military exchanges between Israel and Iran have routinely embarrassed Amman, which weakly justified its interception of Iranian missiles and UAVs to a sceptical domestic audience as protecting Jordanian airspace rather than defending Israel. If Israel's low-intensity military campaign in the West Bank turns into full-blown ethnic cleansing at the behest of Netanyahu's extreme-right ethno-supremacist allies, the mass displacement of Palestinian refugees into Jordan would upset Jordan's demographic balance, jeopardising the Hashemites' hold on power.

Tensions between Israel and Turkiye have also increased. In Syria, the Turkish-backed Islamist group Hay'at Tahrir al-Sham toppled the Assad regime in December 2024, disquieting Israel. Turkiye's neo-Ottoman ambitions in the Middle East and Eastern Mediterranean, and its government's ideological ties to the Muslim Brotherhood, have placed it on a collision course with Israel. With Iran severely weakened, Turkiye is now the only regional power capable of posing a credible military challenge to Israel. Sensing danger, Turkish President Recep Tayyip Erdoğan has described Israel's aggression against Iran as 'state terrorism' and pledged to expand stockpiles of medium- and long-range missiles to deter threats.[17]

Eroding the norm-based order

Beyond the Middle East and the Gulf region, Moscow and Beijing were quick to condemn the attacks on Iran.[18] This is hardly surprising given their close ties to the Iranian regime and geopolitical competition with the United States. But some US allies and partners were also unhappy. Japan, for example, called for 'maximum restraint'.[19] Indian Prime Minister Narendra Modi, in a call with Iranian President Masoud Pezeshkian, endorsed immediate de-escalation.[20] With few exceptions, Asian, Latin American and African governments have been similarly critical of the attacks, exposing the depth of the rift between Israel and its Western allies on the one hand, and the rest of the world on the other.

At the heart of this fracture is the growing realisation in much of the Global South that the United States and many of Israel's European allies, for all their rhetoric to the contrary, are willing to accept grave violations of international law if the target is Iran's nuclear programme. The hypocrisy of this position will likely further erode the norm-based international order and allow Moscow and Beijing to find new allies among non-aligned states. Many of them sympathise with the Palestinians, whose plight resonates with their own anti-colonial struggles for liberation. Within multilateral institutions, chiefly the United Nations, Russia and China are likely to invoke the 12-day war of June 2025 the next time a Western country appeals to the international community to uphold international law in another conflict. More ominously, other states could elect to follow Israel's example and deal militarily with their adversaries under a presumptively acceptable doctrine of preventive warfare.

*   *   *

It remains to be seen whether Israel's campaign against Tehran will improve its security in the long run. Although the Iranian regime appeared shaky during the conflict, it seemed to regain its footing following the ceasefire. The United States' erratic trajectory, which lurched between military action and frantic pressure for a truce, kept both its allies and its enemies guessing, reflecting Washington's lack of a longer-term vision for the region. Tehran is now likely to be more distrustful of Washington, which effectively used diplomacy as cover for Israel's surprise attack. With Tehran poised to curtail its cooperation with the International Atomic Energy Agency, Iran will probably resume and possibly accelerate its pursuit of nuclear weapons.

Without a credible pathway towards de-escalation, the region remains on edge. The root causes of conflict between Israel and Iran are still in place. As Egypt and Turkiye scramble to close gaps in capabilities, border tensions and ideological differences with Israel risk spiralling out of control. Now cognisant of the United States' inability or unwillingness to rein in Israel, the Arab Gulf states are awakening to the fact that they have no credible partner for peace in Washington.

Notes

[1] Quoted in, for example, Tyler Pager, 'In NATO Visit, Trump Casts Himself as a Global Peacemaker', New York Times, 26 June 2025, https://www.nytimes.com/2025/06/26/us/politics/trump-nato-visit-nobel-prize.html.

[2] See, for example, 'Natasha Bertrand, Katie Bo Lillis and Zachary Cohen, 'Exclusive: Early US Intel Assessment Suggests Strikes on Iran Did Not Destroy Nuclear Sites, Sources Say', CNN, 24 June 2025, https://edition.cnn.com/2025/06/24/politics/intel-assessment-us-strikes-iran-nuclear-sites.

[3] German Chancellor Friedrich Merz quoted in, for instance, Roger Cohen, 'An Islamic Republic with Its Back Against the Wall', New York Times, 19 June 2025 (updated 20 June 2025), https://www.nytimes.com/2025/06/19/world/middleeast/iran-islamic-republic-regime.html.

[4] See Lazar Berman and Sam Sokol, 'Netanyahu Heads to Washington to Meet Trump, Hoping to "Redraw" Middle East', Times of Israel, 2 February 2025, https://www.timesofisrael.com/netanyahu-heads-to-washington-to-meet-trump-hoping-to-redraw-middle-east/.

[5] On domestic support, see 'Public Support for Iran Strikes High Among Jewish Israelis, Deeply Divided from Arab Israelis', Jerusalem Post, 17 June 2025, https://www.jpost.com/israel-news/article-858069.

[6] See United Nations, 'UN Experts Condemn Israeli Attack on Iran and Urge End to Hostilities', 20 June 2025, https://www.ohchr.org/en/press-releases/2025/06/un-experts-condemn-israeli-attack-iran-and-urge-end-hostilities.

[7] See Fabian Hinz, 'Israel's Attack and the Limits of Iran's Missile Strategy', IISS Online Analysis, 18 June

2025, https://www.iiss.org/online-analysis/online-analysis/2025/06/israels-attack-and-the-limits-of-irans-missile-strategy/.

8   See 'Gulf Nations Quietly Applauding Israel, but Fear Iran Strikes Could Destabilize Region', *Times of Israel*, 13 June 2025, https://www.timesofisrael.com/gulf-nations-quietly-applauding-israel-but-fear-iran-strikes-could-destabilize-region/.

9   Quoted in Joanie Margulies, 'War Between Israel and Iran Should Be Avoided, Saudi FM Says', *Jerusalem Post*, 21 January 2025, https://www.jpost.com/breaking-news/article-838602.

10 See 'Exclusive: Saudi Warned Iran to Reach Nuclear Deal with Trump or Risk Israeli Strike', Reuters, 30 May 2025, https://www.reuters.com/world/middle-east/saudi-warned-iran-reach-nuclear-deal-with-trump-or-risk-israeli-strike-2025-05-30/.

11 See, for example, 'Gulf States Want No Winner in the Conflict Between Israel and Iran', *Conversation*, 23 June 2025, https://theconversation.com/gulf-states-want-no-winner-in-the-conflict-between-israel-and-iran-259471.

12 See State Information Service (Egypt), 'Egypt Warns Israeli Retaking of Philadelphi Corridor Would Violate Peace Treaty', 16 January 2024, https://www.sis.gov.eg/Story/191152/Egypt-warns-Israeli-retaking-of-Philadelphi-Corridor-would-violate-peace-treaty.

13 See Beatrice Farhat, 'Egypt Outraged Over Israeli Takeover of Rafah Crossing but Shows Restraint', *Al-Monitor*, 7 May 2024, https://www.al-monitor.com/originals/2024/05/egypt-outraged-over-israeli-takeover-rafah-crossing-shows-restraint.

14 See Aya Batrawy, 'Trump Wants Palestinians Out of Gaza. Here Are Egypt's Plans to Keep Them There', NPR, 3 March 2025, https://www.npr.org/2025/03/03/g-s1-51326/gaza-reconstruction-cairo-egypt; and Ariel Kahana, 'Israel Confronts Egypt Over "Major" Peace Treaty Violation', *Israel Hayom*, 31 March 2025, https://www.israelhayom.com/2025/03/31/israel-confronts-egypt-over-major-peace-treaty-violation/.

15 See IISS, *The Military Balance 2025* (Abingdon: Routledge for the IISS, 2025), p. 333.

16 Quoted in 'Israeli Military Chief "Very Concerned" About Egyptian Security Threat', *Middle East Eye*, 17 February 2025, https://www.middleeasteye.net/news/israeli-military-chief-very-concerned-about-threat-egypt.

17 See Suzan Fraser, 'Erdogan Vows to Boost Turkey's Missile Production as Israel–Iran War Escalates', Associated Press, 20 June 2025, https://apnews.com/article/turkey-israel-iran-war-missile-production-41c6471f2b5c958c7e08a956f64e4972.

18 See 'US Attacks on Iran Risk Global Conflict, Russia and China Warn', Al-Jazeera, 23 June 2025, https://www.aljazeera.com/news/2025/6/23/us-attacks-on-iran-risk-global-conflict-russia-and-china-warn.

19 Quoted in Hiroshi Asahina and Kana Baba, 'Japan Distances Itself from G7 Statement on Israel–Iran Conflict', Nikkei Asia, 20 July 2025, https://asia.

nikkei.com/Politics/Middle-East-crisis/
Japan-distances-itself-from-G7-
statement-on-Israel-Iran-conflict.

20 See Kallol Bhattacherjee, 'PM Calls
for "Immediate De-escalation"
After U.S. Bombs Nuclear Sites in
Iran', *Hindu*, 23 June 2025, https://
www.thehindu.com/news/national/
pm-modi-calls-for-immediate-de-
escalation-after-the-us-bombs-fordow-
natanz-esfahan-nuclear-sites-in-iran/
article69724310.ece.

Commentary

Iran's Shattered Missile Strategy

Fabian Hinz

In June 2025, after months of rising tension and a series of limited reciprocal strikes, Israel launched a large-scale operation targeting Iran's nuclear infrastructure and conventional military assets. Called *Operation Rising Lion*, it evolved into a 12-day war that negated Tehran's assumptions about deterrence and left the Iranian leadership facing difficult choices about how to recalibrate its broader military strategy.

Operation Rising Lion

Israel initiated its campaign on 13 June with a massive air assault reportedly involving more than 200 aircraft. Although some nuclear facilities were struck during this opening phase, the initial focus appears to have been on time-sensitive targets, including human ones – not only the air-defence systems and the ballistic-missile bases expected to support Iran's anticipated retaliation, but also nuclear scientists and senior military figures.[1] Israel employed small uninhabited aerial vehicles (UAVs) and long-range anti-tank guided missiles, smuggled into Iran by Israeli intelligence services, to target some of Iran's mobile air-defence systems and ballistic-missile launchers.[2]

Iran's air-defence network was rapidly degraded, affording the Israeli Air Force operational freedom over Iranian territory, including Tehran. Israel was thus able to deploy relatively vulnerable intelligence,

---

Fabian Hinz is IISS Research Fellow for Missile Technologies and UAVs.

surveillance and reconnaissance, and strike platforms, including fourth-generation fighter aircraft, without using stand-off munitions. The ability to exploit these assets at scale sustained the tempo and intensity of the air campaign, during which Israel reportedly conducted more than 1,500 sorties and destroyed up to half of Iran's estimated 400 medium-range ballistic-missile (MRBM) launchers.[3] Over time, Israel broadened its target set to include less time-sensitive sites, among them additional nuclear facilities and locations linked to regime security and domestic repression. Israel conducted more comprehensive strikes against Iran's large missile bases in the west of the country and extended operations to missile bases farther inland, as far east as Yazd.[4]

Subsequently, the Israeli Air Force extended strikes to elements of Iran's missile-production infrastructure. In its limited October 2024 attack, Israel had already targeted key production choke points at three of Iran's four known solid-propellant-motor manufacturing sites. In *Operation Rising Lion*, the Israeli strikes eventually encompassed all four sites, as well as facilities involved in the production of liquid-propellant missiles and mobile launchers. The campaign proceeded farther down the supply chain, with strikes on sites linked to the production of missile-guidance systems, carbon fibre, liquid propellants and missile-related precursor chemicals. Even so, Israel appears to have maintained its strategy – likely shaped by sortie availability and possibly munitions constraints – of selectively targeting critical choke points at production sites rather than seeking the wholesale destruction of entire facilities.

Operation True Promise 3

The night after Israel's attack, Iran began its retaliatory campaign, *Operation True Promise* 3, following the pattern of its predecessor operations on 13 April and 1 October 2024. The first day's counterstrikes reportedly involved around 150 ballistic missiles, notably fewer than the 200 launched during *Operation True Promise* 2 in October.[5] That a broader assault on Iranian territory triggered a weaker response suggests that the earlier strikes had significantly disrupted Iran's missile operations.[6]

Iran continued daily missile barrages until the final day of the conflict, although the volume of fire declined. By the later stages, daily launches consisted of several dozen missiles, occasionally falling to single-digit counts. While precise figures remained unconfirmed as of mid-July, statements by the Israel Defense Forces suggest that Iran launched approximately 530 MRBMs over the course of the war.[7] Although Iran introduced a few new features, such as submunitions, the majority of systems employed were the same as those used in 2024.[8]

The main shift in Iran's strategy appeared to consist not in the number or quality of missiles, but in the selection of targets. Whereas *True Promise* 1 and 2 focused heavily on remote military facilities such as Ramon and Nevatim air bases, *True Promise* 3 appears to have placed a greater emphasis on urban areas. The result was a higher human toll: 28 fatalities and over 3,000 hospitalisations.[9] Open-source data on Iran's targeting of more remote military facilities during *Operation True Promise* 3 remained limited as of mid-July, but available low-resolution imagery showed no evidence of significant damage to any of Israel's main air bases, though Iran claimed to have targeted them.

Israeli forces and later supporting US forces made full use of both endo-atmospheric and exo-atmospheric missile-defence systems such as *Arrow* 2, *Arrow* 3, Terminal High Altitude Area Defense (THAAD) and Standard Missile-3 during the conflict. The Israeli military claimed an interception rate of 86%, and open sources recorded 33 missile impacts in non-military areas. Some press reports suggested that, towards the end of the conflict, Israel began to run low on *Arrow* interceptors.[10] To what extent and whether interceptor availability influenced Israel's political calculus remain unclear. Israel also used shorter-range interceptors not originally designed to counter MRBMs.[11] It is uncertain whether this was intended to conserve higher-end interceptors or simply to increase engagement opportunities.

On 23 June, in response to US airstrikes on key nuclear facilities at Natanz, Fordow and Esfahan, Iran launched 19 missiles at US forces stationed at Al Udeid Air Base in Qatar.[12] All but one were reportedly intercepted. Iran gave advance warning and appeared to follow a highly scripted pattern, much as it had done in response to the United States' targeted killing of Qasem Soleimani in 2020.

Iran accompanied its missile campaign against Israel with the large-scale use of one-way attack UAVs, launching approximately 1,000. The effort appears to have largely failed, with only a single impact recorded in open sources and the vast majority of UAVs reportedly intercepted and neutralised through electronic-warfare measures.[13] Notably, while the Houthis continued sporadic missile launches on Israel during the period of *True Promise* 3, there were no indications of significant action by other elements of Iran's so-called axis of resistance, such as Iraqi Shia militias and Lebanese Hizbullah.

A failed strategy

Iran managed to impose costs on Israel until the final day of the conflict and publicly celebrated its operations as a victory. But the very fact that *Operation Rising Lion* occurred at all reflects the failure of Iran's long-standing strategy against Israel, a key aim of which was to deter attacks on Iran proper.

Starting with the Iran–Iraq War, Iran has invested heavily in ballistic missiles as a means of offsetting an adversary's strategic depth and imposing costs in the absence of a capable air force. Reinforcing the ballistic missiles were the rocket and missile arsenals of Iran's non-state allies, positioned to encircle Israel under what Israeli officials often described as Iran's 'ring of fire' concept. With an eye to leveraging their geographical proximity to Israel, Hizbullah and various Palestinian groups amassed large numbers of simple rocket systems. The idea was to constrain Israel's regional freedom of action, entangle it in peripheral conflicts and gradually build a deterrent capable of dissuading direct attacks on Iranian territory. Although Iran had in recent years undertaken major efforts to improve its air defences, its strategy remained rooted in deterrence by punishment.

In decimating Hizbullah's rocket and missile arsenal in 2024 during the Gaza war, Israel removed a key pillar of that strategy. The limited effectiveness of Iran's own missile barrages in April and October 2024, which failed to inflict significant damage or casualties, further eroded its deterrent. Israeli counterstrikes in late October 2024 also disabled

Iran's Russian-supplied S-300 system, its most advanced air-defence capability, diminishing its already limited capacity for deterrence by denial.[14] These developments helped clear the path for Israel's large-scale campaign in June 2025.

Iran also relied on its ability to accurately gauge the risk tolerance and pain thresholds of its adversaries and assumed that the costs that its missiles and its proxies' rockets could visit on Israel would be sufficient to deter aggression. The relevant parameters shifted rapidly after Hamas's 7 October 2023 attacks, as Israel began to perceive the regional conflict in existential terms, adapted to a prolonged state of war and markedly increased its risk tolerance. The change in Israeli calculations was most evident with respect to Hizbullah, whose deterrent vis-à-vis Israel all but collapsed in 2024 despite the absence of major changes to either side's strategic arsenal prior to Israel's assault. The effect ultimately extended to Iran itself, as the threat of Iranian MRBMs to Tel Aviv proved insufficient to prevent Israel from launching massive attacks on Iranian territory.

Iran's constricted strategic choices

Prospects for restoring Iran's network of non-state allies, and their missile and UAV arsenals, to a central role in its regional-security strategy appear increasingly bleak. Those groups may still be useful to Iran for shaping local political dynamics, confronting weaker regional states and conducting limited, deniable attacks. But their value as a strategic deterrent against Israel is likely to remain limited for the foreseeable future.

Hizbullah, long regarded as the most capable and loyal of Tehran's militia partners, was effectively neutralised by Israel's 2024 campaign. The fall of the Bashar al-Assad regime in Syria, which had served as a critical logistics node for Hizbullah, and growing domestic pressure on the group within Lebanon will hinder its rearmament. In Gaza, both Hamas and Palestinian Islamic Jihad have been severely degraded, their rocket arsenals largely destroyed. While the Houthis in Yemen remain operationally resilient and capable of projecting power into the Red Sea and the Gulf of Aden, their direct military utility against Israel is limited by distance, which restricts their ability to amass stockpiles comparable to those once held by Hizbullah.

Iran will probably continue to prioritise its national ballistic-missile programme and may even increase its investment in it. Although its missiles failed to deter Israeli action and did not significantly degrade Israeli military capabilities, they still imposed tangible costs on Israel. For Tehran, this outcome alone could justify their continued production, development and deployment in the absence of viable alternatives. One contributing factor is the powerful symbolic imagery of missile impacts in Israeli cities, which carries special weight in authoritarian and ideologically driven regimes. Another is sunk costs. Decades of investment have produced extensive production infrastructure and entrenched bureaucratic interests with a strong stake in the missile programme's perpetuation. Statements by Israeli officials suggesting that Iran was close to producing missiles in numbers capable of overwhelming Israeli defences and posing an existential threat will only reinforce perceptions that the strategy was sound but had not reached its full potential.[15]

Rebuilding the missile arsenal and restoring the industrial base to pre-war capacity will, of course, require considerable time and resources. Solid-propellant-missile production is likely paralysed for the time being, unable to resume without specialised equipment, particularly planetary mixers. Nevertheless, Iran demonstrated after the October 2024 strikes that it could reconstitute production relatively quickly. If it succeeds in repairing damaged facilities and returns to its previous output of approximately 50 missiles per month, it would take about a year to replace the missiles expended during the conflict.[16] Iran will also need to replace the large number of launchers destroyed during the war.

*   *   *

Should Iran decide to restore the missile programme, it will still face critical decisions regarding its strategic direction. One key issue is whether to maintain its long-standing emphasis on precision, reportedly mandated by Supreme Leader Sayyid Ali Khamenei himself, with the aim of eventually fielding missiles capable of effective counterforce strikes. Alternatively, Iran could opt for a more explicit counter-value posture, prioritising larger-scale production of simpler, less accurate systems designed to target civilian areas, thus imposing higher costs. Another unanswered question is whether Iran will cease concentrating its missile arsenal in underground bases. While such facilities offer significant protection, they also risk rendering missiles unuseable when entrances are targeted before the missiles are launched.

It also remains to be seen whether Iran will move beyond its self-imposed range limit of 2,000 kilometres. Thus far, Tehran has pursued a hedging strategy in long-range-missile development, acquiring relevant technologies under the cover of its space-launch-vehicle programme led by the Islamic Revolutionary Guard Corps.[17] The United States' unprecedented direct military intervention could prompt a shift in this approach and lead to the open development of intercontinental-range systems.

Finally, the war has glaringly exposed the critical weakness of Iran's air defences, which are central to both deterrence by denial and – insofar as they protect offensive capabilities – deterrence by punishment. Strengthening this capability rapidly will be both difficult and urgent. Russia could offer technologies to support Iran's domestic air-defence development, but is unlikely to supply complete systems in meaningful numbers due to its own wartime requirements. China is a more viable source, with a broad portfolio of ground-based air-defence systems and the industrial capacity to deliver them at scale. It could also play a key role if Iran elects to revitalise its long-neglected air force – an option that could gain traction following Pakistan's successful employment of Chinese fighter aircraft and long-range air-to-air missiles against India. Of course, it is difficult to know whether China would be willing to incur the political costs associated with large-scale arms transfers to Iran. The potential activation of snapback sanctions by the E3 (France, Germany and the United Kingdom), which would reinstate the United Nations arms embargo on Iran, would further complicate any such arrangement for Beijing. From Tehran's point of view, however, firming up air defences appears to be the paramount step among several strategically mandatory ones for restoring a comprehensively diminished regional deterrent.

Notes

1. See Emanuel Fabian, 'IDF: 200 Aircraft Involved in Opening Strikes on Iran, with Several Top Officials Killed', *Times of Israel*, 13 June 2025, https://www.timesofisrael.com/liveblog_entry/idf-200-aircraft-involved-in-opening-strikes-on-iran-with-several-top-officials-killed/.
2. See Dov Lieber and Andrew Dowell, 'How Israel's Mossad Smuggled Drone Parts to Attack Iran from Within', *Wall Street Journal*, 15 June 2025, https://www.wsj.com/world/middle-east/how-israels-mossad-smuggled-drone-parts-to-attack-iran-from-within-633516a9.
3. See Emanuel Fabian, 'The Stars Aligned: Why Israel Set Out for a War Against Iran, and What It Achieved', *Times of Israel*, 27 June 2025, http://timesofisrael.com/the-stars-aligned-why-israel-set-out-for-a-war-against-iran-and-what-it-achieved/; and Felice Friedson, 'Israeli Military Official Says Iran's Missiles Can Hit Europe, Aiming to Reach East Coast of US', *Jerusalem Post*, 4 July 2025, https://www.jpost.com/international/article-860021.
4. See Emanuel Fabian, 'IDF Publishes Footage of Strikes on Iranian Ballistic Missile Facility 2,200 km Away', *Times of Israel*, 22 June 2025, https://www.timesofisrael.com/liveblog_entry/idf-publishes-footage-of-strikes-on-iranian-ballistic-missile-facility-2200-km-away/.
5. See Emanuel Fabian, 'IDF Estimates that Iran Has Fired 150 Missiles at Israel in Two Barrages', *Times of Israel*, 13 June 2025, https://www.timesofisrael.com/liveblog_entry/idf-estimates-that-iran-has-fired-150-missiles-at-israel-in-two-barrages/.
6. See Famaz Fassihi, 'A Miscalculation by Iran Led to Israeli Strikes' Extensive Toll, Officials Say', *New York Times*, 13 June 2025, https://www.nytimes.com/2025/06/13/world/middleeast/iran-israel-strikes-nuclear-talks.html.
7. See 'Iran Strikes Israel: Updated Tracker of Every Iranian Ballistic Missile Fired at Israel', *Haaretz*, 25 June 2025, https://www.haaretz.com/israel-news/security-aviation/2025-06-23/ty-article-magazine/.premium/iran-strikes-israel-updated-tracker-of-every-iranian-ballistic-missile-fired-at-israel/00000197-97f8-d5ef-a9bf-b7fedfc30000.
8. See Fabian Hinz, 'Israel's Attack and the Limits of Iran's Missile Strategy', IISS Online Analysis, 18 June 2025, https://www.iiss.org/online-analysis/online-analysis/2025/06/israels-attack-and-the-limits-of-irans-missile-strategy/.
9. See Emanuel Fabian, 'Medical Officials Say 28 People Were Killed, Over 3,000 Wounded by Iranian Missiles During Conflict', *Times of Israel*, 24 June 2025, https://www.timesofisrael.com/liveblog_entry/medical-officials-say-28-people-were-killed-over-3000-wounded-by-iranian-missiles-during-conflict/.
10. See Shelby Holliday, 'Israel Is Running Low on Defensive Interceptors, Official Says', *Wall Street Journal*, 18 June 2025, https://www.wsj.com/world/middle-east/

israel-is-running-low-on-defensive-interceptors-official-says-fd64163d.
11   See Sebastien Roblin, 'How Did Israel's Air Defenses Fare Against Iran's Ballistic Missiles?', *Forbes*, 30 June 2025 (updated 4 July 2025), https://www.forbes.com/sites/sebastienroblin/2025/06/30/how-did-israels-air-defenses-fair-against-irans-ballistic-missiles/.
12   See 'Iran Attacks US Air Base in Qatar: What We Know So Far', Al-Jazeera, 23 June 2025, https://www.aljazeera.com/news/2025/6/23/iran-attacks-us-air-base-in-qatar-what-we-know-so-far.
13   See Emanuel Fabian, 'IDF Says It Has Been Intercepting Dozens of Iranian Drones Using Electronic Warfare Means', *Times of Israel*, 23 June 2025, https://www.timesofisrael.com/liveblog_entry/idf-says-it-has-been-intercepting-dozens-of-iranian-drones-using-electronic-warfare-means/.
14   See Louis Casiano and Jennifer Griffin, 'Israel's Strike on Iran Took Out Missile Defense Systems, Islamic Republic "Is Essentially Naked"', Fox News, 29 October 2024, https://www.foxnews.com/world/israels-strike-iran-took-missile-defense-systems-islamic-republic-is-essentially-naked.
15   See Lazar Berman, 'Netanyahu Claims "Historic Victory," Says "We Sent Iran's Nuclear Program Down the Drain"', *Times of Israel*, 25 June 2025, https://www.timesofisrael.com/netanyahu-claims-historic-victory-says-we-sent-irans-nuclear-program-down-the-drain/.
16   See Barak Ravid, 'Exclusive: U.S. Fears Iran's Response to Israeli Strike Would Be Mass Casualty Event', *Axios*, 12 June 2025, https://www.axios.com/2025/06/12/israel-strike-iran-response-witkoff.
17   See Fabian Hinz, 'The IRGC's Space Programme and a Move Towards Longer-range Missiles', IISS Online Analysis, 13 December 2023, https://www.iiss.org/online-analysis/online-analysis/2023/12/the-irgcs-space-programme-and-a-move-towards-longer-range-missiles/.

Commentary

The Pentagon's Economic Blind Spot

Philip M. Breedlove and Peter Devine

For years, the White House has hosted a monthly meeting of chief economists from federal agencies to discuss the most challenging economic issues. Yet the Department of Defense (DoD), despite being the largest agency by far, has never sent a representative, because it does not have a chief economist or a unified economic strategy.

The failure is more than a bureaucratic oversight – it is a strategic blind spot that weakens national security. While China treats economic policy as warfare and Russia appointed an economist as defence minister, the Pentagon continues to view economic strategy as separate from military planning. The DoD has offices that perform some of the functions of economic strategy, but none will stand up and say it is their responsibility, so they lack the specialised personnel and authority to manage conflicting priorities within the Pentagon and to coordinate with outside agencies. The fact that the department has only balkanised and undervalued economic shops means it tends to underappreciate the long-term trade-offs it is making for short-term goals. The result is a procurement system that allows costs to balloon far beyond a programme's relative value; technology policies that stifle US innovation while failing to block adversaries' progress; and an alliance strategy that ignores the economic foundations of military power.

Gen. (Retd) Philip M. Breedlove, United States Air Force, is the former Commander, Supreme Allied Command, Europe (2013–16) and a Distinguished Professor of the Practice at Georgia Tech, Sam Nunn School of International Affairs. **Peter Devine** was a fellow at the White House National Economic Council (2023–24) and is Assistant Professor of the Practice at Boston College Department of Economics.

The consequences of this neglect are tangible and pervasive. In defence procurement, a lack of economic foresight has led to monopolistic pricing and production bottlenecks that threaten both submarine deterrence and the United States' Pacific strategy. In technology policy, ill-conceived export controls on semiconductors are eroding US competitiveness instead of slowing China. In Ukraine, NATO has a military strategy but no economic strategy, undermining its viability. These are not isolated problems; they are symptoms of a broad failure to integrate economic strategy into defence planning.

Great-power competitions are won economically. Whoever innovates faster will outpace rivals, advancing technological capabilities so significantly that they overcome other relative weaknesses. While we think of this 'offset strategy' as a purely military strategy, it is an economic strategy, maximising economic advantages to achieve defence objectives by optimising capabilities per dollar and accelerating the rate of innovation. The DoD's lack of an economic strategy means the effects of its disparate policies and the efforts of its byzantine web of innovation organisations are uncoordinated and occasionally misguided.

To address this, the DoD should institutionalise economic expertise by directing the deputy secretary of defense to establish a clear economic strategy and to install qualified economists, well versed in defence priorities, as liaisons to coordinate with US economic agencies. Without this, the Pentagon will continue making decisions that trade long-term strength for short-term fixes, leaving the US vulnerable in the next great-power conflict.

The defence-industrial base

Economists rarely interact with the DoD and often assume that the defence industry isn't really a market because the weapons systems are often sourced from a single producer, purchased by a single buyer, and provide a necessary but only occasionally useful capability to society. But how the government incentivises defence firms matters a great deal. Without a centralised economic strategy, the DoD's procurement decisions are driven by short-term pressures rather than long-term capability growth. Bringing in economists and familiarising them with the DoD's unique challenges will help the deputy secretary avoid simply reacting to cost overruns and use an economic strategy to ensure that procurement maximises readiness.

Nowhere is this more pressing than in the submarine fleet, where the cost overruns per boat are so large they threaten to swamp every other DoD priority. Last November, the White House was forced to ask for an extra $7.3 billion to cover cost overruns on three *Virginia*-class attack submarines and one *Columbia*-class ballistic-missile submarine. Both are well off the construction timelines needed to meet national-security requirements. Poor budgeting, inconsistent demand and a diminished manufacturing base have all played a part in this. The dominant factor, however, is how the DoD has incentivised the firms. Since 1997, all new contract bids for submarines have been from a single government-sponsored monopoly composed of General Dynamics Electric Boat (EB) and Huntington Ingalls Industries (HII).[1] This DoD policy was designed to preserve US production capacity if the department's demand increased in the future.

Since that decision, America's demand for submarines has increased nearly 500%, and the AUKUS agreement – a trilateral agreement between Australia, the United Kingdom and the US to improve defence capabilities in the Indo-Pacific that in part involves the construction of additional nuclear submarines in the US to be sold to Australia – will add even more. However, the EB and HII monopoly has raised prices and delayed deliveries with cost overruns and sliding timelines.[2] The team is also a monopsony buyer to its suppliers, lowering the prices the industrial base receives and further degrading future capacity. Neither EB nor HII will dissolve the monopoly and compete, nor can the DoD force them apart without further damaging production in the critical 2027–35 window. Today, the US can't produce submarines at a cost and scale sufficient for national security, and won't be able to any time soon. Meanwhile, the cost overruns are threatening Australia's ability to remain in the AUKUS agreement, and are forcing the DoD to redirect funds from more promising future-capability programmes.[3]

How the DoD rebuilds its undersea capabilities matters. While the department and US Navy cannot introduce new competitors into the crewed-submarine market overnight, they can increase competition for capabilities across programmes and improve submarine production by:

- directly contracting with suppliers and supplying equipment to the prime contractors
- expanding public maintenance yards, clearing space at EB and HII for new construction
- assisting intellectual-property transfers between EB and HII as a credible procedure to *eventually* break their teaming arrangement
- requiring contractors to use open architecture and modular subsystems with standardised interfaces to open competition for each component
- creating reference-implementation digital test beds, or virtual environments where designs can be cheaply tested and refined, dedicated to collaboration, competition and innovation across agencies and firms.

Fortunately, there are many small and innovative firms in the autonomous underwater vehicle (AUV) industry. The DoD should continue to encourage them and look to substitute crewed-system capabilities with uncrewed systems, preventing EB and HII from horizontally monopolising and helping the best innovators to compete in the underwater industry.

The DoD needs to understand the risks of a 'more subs at all costs' mindset. The navy is reallocating budgets from other programmes, including its collaborative combat aircraft (drones), to cover submarine-cost overruns. This could mean that promising technologies, which might one day prove decisive, are sacrificed. The DoD's lack of an economic strategy means it is failing to understand how its short-term optimal policy is damaging its long-term capabilities. Charging the deputy secretary to develop an economic strategy will allow the department to ask industry for a competitive capability rather than a specific system, channelling funds to the most promising technologies and preventing the next capability shortfall before it becomes a crisis.

The CHIPS programme and US geo-economic strategy

Senior defence-department officials confuse economics with procurement. That is a problem. Economics is not a section of the DoD's portfolio; it is a lens, a way of thinking about the entire portfolio. The Pentagon hasn't developed an economic strategy to inform its decision-making, but instead is haphazardly influencing and executing geo-economic policies without that road map to counter China's rising significance in US supply chains.

The CHIPS (Creating Helpful Incentives to Produce Semiconductors) programme is an example of where the Pentagon's lack of economic expertise is evident. Instead of a coordinated strategy that balances security with innovation, the DoD's autarkic stance risks weakening US technological leadership in an area critical to military readiness. The CHIPS programme aims to increase America's advantage over China in semiconductor technology. Whether an action increases or decreases that advantage is how a geo-economic strategy should be evaluated.

There are roughly four parts to the CHIPS programme: increasing American research-and-development (R&D) leadership; preventing advanced technology from going to China; onshoring manufacturing for supply-chain security; and segmenting technology specific for military use into a secure enclave. But these are in tension in a 'stock and flow' problem. There is a trade-off between forgoing revenue to prevent technology from going to China today, versus reinvesting that revenue in R&D and expanding our capabilities tomorrow.

Advancing US leadership in semiconductor R&D requires significant investment, but the potential gains are exponential. NVIDIA stated that its global sales revenue funded its unequalled pace of innovation, allowing the American firm to comfortably outpace Chinese competitors.[4] However, the sales of US technology that drive that revenue also supply technology to other states, including China. The DoD is concerned about US technology flowing into the militaries of its adversaries. This is a reasonable concern, but choosing the best course of action to mitigate that requires careful economic analysis. Blunt export controls on American technology may have prevented some technology going to China, but they also accelerated China's rotation towards self-sufficiency and deprived American chip designers of a few more years of R&D revenue. More importantly, the policy forced other countries to price in American supply risk. China is offering a guaranteed flow of Huawei technology to these third-party states while America applies complex restrictions that could starve their economies of vital inputs. These policies are transferring a revenue stream that directly financed American R&D to Huawei.

Before the DoD advocates for a completely domestic supply chain, it must understand that the policy will sacrifice innovation. It could be worth the cost – in some cases, it certainly is. If a rival has a realistic probability of denying access to a strategic input, then the price for resilience could be less than the cost of forgone innovation. But the DoD needs to understand the economic argument. Onshoring semiconductor manufacturing by subsidising domestic production saps revenue with higher construction and operating costs, diverting those resources from new innovations. The DoD must not overlook such trade-offs when evaluating whether a proposed strategy would restrict or aid China in closing a capability gap.

By institutionalising economic expertise, the Pentagon's role in geoeconomic policy can have a clearer and more coordinated economic effect. As in the case of submarine procurement, the CHIPS programme shows how policies developed in the absence of an explicit economic strategy within the Pentagon can undermine rather than enhance capabilities. A long-term, defence-integrated economic strategy would help ensure that technology policy protects national security without undermining US innovation. The CHIPS programme should allow American industry to iterate faster than China, especially in foundational technologies where sacrificing revenue reinvestment is exponentially costly.

The war in Europe
The war in Ukraine is not just an example in our analysis; it is a microcosm of our central hypothesis that economics and national security are inextricably linked. Ukraine's battlefield resilience has been aided by US military logistics, but its future security depends on economic growth. DoD strategists must incorporate long-term economic considerations into their planning to achieve lasting security objectives.

The scale of Ukraine's economic challenge is hard to overstate. Since 1990, its population has declined by more than 25%, and its GDP per capita, adjusted for purchasing power, has stagnated. While Ukraine faces external threats from Russia, its greatest internal threat is the resulting depopulation. Of about 38 million people, a net 6.5m refugees have left Ukraine and another 3.5m are internally displaced.[5] Ukraine's population was shrinking prior to the 2022 invasion, but now the numbers are stark.

This population loss is a serious threat to Ukraine's economy and its ability to fight Russian aggression over time. The refugees are not a random sample of the population; data from Ukrainian refugees in Poland shows they are significantly better educated, 40% are children, and 70% of the adults are female (with much higher tertiary-education rates).[6] Consequently, Ukraine's recovery depends on repatriating its population. If there isn't a repatriation strategy to restart Ukraine's economic growth in tandem with security support, Ukraine will be in perpetual need of military assistance.

The DoD cannot and should not be expected to design Ukraine's refugee and reconstruction policy. But as the largest agency responsible for Ukraine's security assistance, it should ensure that its military commitments align with a viable economic endgame. Practically, this means coordinating with the Treasury and State departments, and with international allies to prioritise economic-stabilisation efforts.

If the Pentagon fails to internalise this linkage, security assistance will be perpetually undermined by a hollowed-out economy and labour flight. Ultimately, lasting deterrence against Russian aggression requires economic strength. The DoD must integrate economic outcomes into its strategic assessments and alliance planning.

American policymakers once understood this. The Marshall Plan was neither written by nor originally named for General George Marshall. It was developed by committee and spearheaded by Robert Lovett, the former assistant secretary of war and future secretary of defense.[7] Lovett integrated military and economic considerations, collaborating closely with senator Arthur Vandenberg to secure congressional approval. The Marshall Plan was the necessary twin of NATO, recognising that economies and defence needs move in tandem. Additionally, president Harry Truman understood that the American public and Congress were reluctant to send more US tax dollars to Europe and needed to see European economic recovery as an essential security measure. President Truman explicitly used General Marshall's public stature as the five-star general, chief of staff of the army, who won the war, to uniquely argue that the economic initiative was a strategic military imperative. This effort successfully stabilised Europe and deterred Soviet aggression on the continent for generations.[8]

*   *   *

While the United States' great-power adversaries wield their economies to multiply military power, the US military continues to plan as if economic dynamism and military capability are independent. They are not. Without an integrated economic strategy, the Pentagon's procurement system will continue overpaying for underperformance, its technology policies will slow American innovation, and its alliance strategy will fail to build lasting collective security.

From submarine-cost overruns that threaten key alliances and future drone technologies, to the missteps in semiconductor-export controls that threaten US technological pacing, to its alliance strategy, the DoD's absence from the US government's economic dialogue represents a significant vulnerability. These failures are not separate issues; they are symptoms of a systemic blind spot that is eroding US military power.

In great-power competition, the side that most effectively compounds economic and military strength wins. The Pentagon should act accordingly. The deputy secretary of defense should establish and maintain a formal economic strategy that aligns procurement with long-term capability growth and integrates the DoD into US geo-economic planning. Without harnessing economics as a weapon of war, the Pentagon will continue trading future military strength for short-term expediency – an error China is counting on.

Notes

1 Congressional Research Service, 'Navy Virginia-class Submarine Program and AUKUS Submarine (Pillar 1) Project: Background and Issues for Congress', RL32418, 28 March 2025, p. 4, https://www.congress.gov/crs-product/RL32418.

2 See 'New US Subs Running $17 Billion over Budget, Lawmaker Says', Bloomberg, 19 September 2024, https://www.bloomberg.com/news/articles/2024-09-19/new-us-submarines-running-17-billion-over-budget-lawmaker-says.

3 AUKUS submarines were already projected to be the most expensive defence project in the United States' history. If costs balloon by anywhere close to 75% (as projected from 2024's overruns), then Australia may not be able to afford AUKUS's keystone programme, and it may be forced to focus on more affordable, less strategic military options. Daniel Hurst, 'US Congress Research Warns of Risk of Cost Blowouts for Australia in Aukus Submarine Program', 17 October 2024, https://www.theguardian.com/world/2024/oct/18/aukus-submarine-deal-us-australia-cost-blowouts.

4 See 'Donald Trump Is Right to Ditch Joe Biden's Chip-export Rules', *The Economist*, 8 May 2025, https://www.economist.com/leaders/2025/05/08/donald-trump-is-right-to-ditch-joe-bidens-chip-export-rules; Ben Thompson, 'An Interview with Nvidia CEO Jensen Huang About Chip Controls, AI Factories, and Enterprise Pragmatism', *Stratechery*, 19 May 2025, https://stratechery.com/2025/an-interview-with-nvidia-ceo-jensen-huang-about-chip-controls-ai-factories-and-enterprise-pragmatism/; Meaghan Tobin, 'Nvidia's Chief Says U.S. Chip Controls on China Have Backfired', *New York Times*, 21 May 2025, https://www.nytimes.com/2025/05/21/business/nvidia-china-washington-chip-controls-failure.html; and 'Nvidia Seeks Shanghai R&D Site After US Chip Curbs, Say Sources', 16 May 2025, https://www.reuters.com/world/china/nvidia-seeks-shanghai-rd-site-after-us-chip-curbs-say-sources-2025-05-16/. The authors also communicated with NVIDIA directly.

5 Council on Foreign Relations, 'Rebuilding Ukraine', February 2025, https://www.cfr.org/report/rebuilding-ukraine.

6 Katie Toth, 'After Two Years in Poland, Ukrainian Refugees Ask When – and If – They Will Go Home', *New Humanitarian*, 5 March 2024, https://www.thenewhumanitarian.org/news-feature/2024/03/05/poland-ukrainian-refugees-ask-when-they-will-go-home; and Nataliia Zaika and Volodymyr Vakhitov, 'A Way Home: Returning Intentions of Ukrainian Refugees and Migrants', American University Kyiv, May 2024, https://er.auk.edu.ua/server/api/core/bitstreams/a57365b4-29fa-45bf-a819-a99bb8e8f97c/content.

7 See Harry S. Truman Library and Museum, 'Oral History Interview

with Robert A. Lovett', 1971, https://www.trumanlibrary.gov/library/oral-histories/lovett.

8 See George C. Marshall Foundation, 'The Marshall Plan', https://www.marshallfoundation.org/the-marshall-plan/.

Copyright © 2025 The International Institute for Strategic Studies

Noteworthy

Shangri-La Dialogue 2025

'Let us be clear, we have several risks of double standards in our current environment. Double standards in Ukraine. For a lot of countries. In Latin America (LATAM), Africa, Asia, here. I hear the narrative and most of the time what is shared is a sort of equidistance between Ukraine and Russia and the fact that it is a European conflict and that we are clearly spending too much energy, too much time, and creating too much pain for the rest of the world with what is happening in Ukraine. Allow me to say this is a total mistake, because if we consider that Russia could be allowed to take a part of the territory of Ukraine without any restriction, without any constraint, without any reaction of the global order, how would you phrase what could happen in Taiwan? What would you do the day something happened in the Philippines? There [are] no several global order[s] by definition if we stick to our principles; this is true in Europe and this is true elsewhere. So, what is at stake in Ukraine is our common credibility, to be sure that we are still able to preserve territorial integrity and sovereignty of people. No double standard.

[…]

I believe our key challenge is how to preserve peace and stability and prosperity in this current environment. And in a moment when the competition between China and the United States for global leadership could create constraints and a side effect for each of us, without us willing or even able to imagine handing our interests over to one or the other, how to react? And I will be clear. France is a friend and an ally of the United States and is a friend – and we do cooperate, even if sometimes we disagree and compete – with China. And I do intend to remain so, loyally, with a demanding approach of our own interests. But France is no less attached to what is essential for herself: strategic autonomy, freedom of sovereignty. And we do defend this approach for Europe and for [the] Indo-Pacific.

[…]

We have a challenge of revisionist countries that want to impose, under the name of spheres of influence – in reality, spheres of coercion – countries that want to control areas from the fringe of Europe to the archipelagos in the South China Sea at the exclusion of regional partners, oblivious to international law; countries that want to appropriate resources, whether fishing or mineral, and crowd out others from their benefit; countries that want to impose on free countries their foreign-policy choices or prejudice their alliances. No way for these spheres of coercion.

[…]

We live in a time of a potential erosion of long-time alliances whose credibility and clout is under threat. Alliances, by the element of balance they brought, had been essential to maintain stability in Europe and Asia; and the sense that their promise might not be ironclad is ushering in a new instability. We see it every day. And the credibility of the alliances, which is to be confirmed, is a very important point for stability. [Moreover] we have now a big risk of nuclear proliferation. This is why the situation in Iran is so critical, and this is why we do consider that the work which is being done by the United States of America in Iran is so critical. And this is why especially the E3 [France, Germany and the United Kingdom] wants to be a reliable and consistent partner in order to avoid any type of nuclear proliferation in Iran, because it would trigger all sorts of justification to proliferate elsewhere with a domino effect. But let us be clear: the situation is very challenging as well in Europe. When Ukraine, the country that renounced nuclear weapons in 1991, is the one that Russia is repeatedly invading, how could there not be a second thought? When the Democratic People's Republic of Korea (DPRK) is developing a massive nuclear arsenal unconstrained by China and is now entering an alliance with Russia, a nuclear-weapons state, permanent member of the UN Security Council, supposed to act responsibly, how are regional countries threatened by the DPRK supposed to act? What can reasonably be on their mind when they owe their people before anything else their security? In Europe and in Asia, how can mid-sized countries faced with aggressive nations ensure that they won't have to surrender or live in fear?'

French President Emmanuel Macron delivers the keynote address at the 22nd IISS Shangri-La Dialogue in Singapore on 30 May 2025.[1]

'President Trump was elected to apply America First on the world stage. Getting a chance to watch him first-hand in the Oval Office and around the world, the world is incredibly fortunate to have an American president with the combination of being a peace seeker and a strong leader. President Trump has the unique ability to make possible things that seem impossible, moving the Overton window. He is the ultimate dealmaker. To that end, from day one, President Trump gave me a clear mission at the Defense Department: achieve peace through strength. To accomplish this mission, our overriding objectives have been equally clear: restore the warrior ethos, rebuild our military and re-establish deterrence.

[…]

Beyond our borders and beyond our neighbourhood, we are reorienting toward deterring aggression by communist China … Elsewhere and around the world, we are engaging with, enabling and empowering our allies, sometimes with tough love, but love nonetheless. We are pushing our allies in Europe to own more of their own security, to invest in their defence, things that are long overdue. We still believe the 'N' in NATO stands for North Atlantic and that our European allies should maximise their comparative advantage on the continent. Thanks to President Trump, they are stepping up.

[…]

We are not here to pressure other countries to embrace or adopt policies or ideologies. We are not here to preach to you about climate change or cultural issues. We are not here to impose our will on you.

[…]

President Trump and the American people have an immense respect for the Chinese people and their civilisation, but we will not be pushed out of this critical region. We will not let our allies and partners be subordinated and intimidated.

China seeks to become a hegemonic power in Asia, no doubt. It hopes to dominate and control too many parts of this vibrant and vital region. Through its massive military build-up and growing willingness to use military force to achieve its goals, including grey-zone tactics and hybrid warfare, China has demonstrated that it wants to fundamentally alter the region's status quo. We cannot look away and we cannot ignore it. China's behaviour toward its neighbours and the world is a wake-up call, and an urgent one.

> […]
> Any unilateral attempt to change the status quo in the South China Sea and the first island chain by force or coercion is unacceptable.
> […]
> Again, to be clear, any attempt by communist China to conquer Taiwan by force would result in devastating consequences for the Indo-Pacific and the world. There is no reason to sugarcoat it. The threat China poses is real, and it could be imminent. We hope not, but it certainly could be. Facing these threats, we know that many countries are tempted by the idea of seeking both economic cooperation with China and defence cooperation with the United States.
> Now, that is a geographic necessity for many. However, beware the leverage that the Chinese Communist Party (CCP) seeks with that entanglement. Economic dependence on China only deepens their malign influence and complicates our defence decision space during times of tension. Nobody knows what China will ultimately do, but they are preparing, and therefore we must be ready as well.'
>
> *US Defense Secretary Pete Hegseth speaks on 'The United States' New Ambitions for Indo-Pacific Security' at the Shangri-La Dialogue on 31 May.*[2]
>
> 'With respect, my question on cooperation is not so appropriate at the atmosphere of this Shangri-La Dialogue platform. It seems that labelling China, blaming China, verbally attacking China are political rights here. Still, no matter how China is misinterpreted, China will develop in its peaceful way.'
>
> *Senior Colonel Lu Yin, a professor at the National Security College, National Defense University, China, participates in the Q&A during the sixth plenary session of the Shangri-La Dialogue on 1 June.*[3]

Sources

[1] IISS, 'President of the French Republic Emmanuel Macron Delivers the Keynote Address', Shangri-La Dialogue, Singapore, 30 May 2025, https://www.iiss.org/events/shangri-la-dialogue/shangri-la-dialogue-2025/plenary-sessions/keynote-address/.

[2] IISS, 'United States' New Ambitions for Indo-Pacific Security', Shangri-La Dialogue, Singapore, 31 May 2025, https://www.iiss.org/events/shangri-la-dialogue/shangri-la-dialogue-2025/plenary-sessions/first-plenary/.

[3] IISS, 'Enhancing Security Cooperation for a Stable Asia-Pacific', Shangri-La Dialogue, Singapore, 1 June 2025, https://www.iiss.org/events/shangri-la-dialogue/shangri-la-dialogue-2025/plenary-sessions/sixth-plenary/.

Copyright © 2025 The International Institute for Strategic Studies

The Loop Is Broken: Why Autonomous-warfare Policy Must Reckon with Human Performance

Anna M. Gielas

In September 2024, the US Army became the first-ever American military service to integrate a generative artificial intelligence (AI) platform into its operations.[1] Developers are now reportedly able to code 35 times faster, acquisition experts to complete 50 tasks in the same time it previously took them to complete one, and other military personnel to analyse thousands of documents in minutes rather than days.[2] The US Department of Defense (DoD) has over 800 active AI projects, focusing on areas such as process efficiency, threat evaluation and battlefield decision-making.[3] None of this is likely to surprise scholars and policymakers.

Far less attention has been devoted to the interface technologies – ranging from wearable sensors to brain–computer machines – that operationalise human–machine interaction. These interfaces encompass not only physical devices but also software, prompting some to dismiss them as mere technical enablers. This perspective downplays their critical function as the primary mediators of human agency in AI-integrated systems, facilitating inter-operability between human operators and autonomous technologies. To overlook them is to take for granted the very mechanisms that translate policy requirements, such as 'human control', into practice. This neglect carries significant consequences – not only for the efficacy and safety of military operations, but also for ensuring compliance with core principles

---

Anna M. Gielas is an associate of the Centre for Global Knowledge Studies at the University of Cambridge. She holds a PhD in the history of science and is pursuing a second PhD in war studies focused on the integration of emerging neuro-technologies into the armed forces.

of international humanitarian law. Accountability, distinction and proportionality are increasingly mediated through interfaces that determine how information is perceived and define the scope of human decision-making in complex, time-sensitive environments.

The dangers of inadequate interface design are starkly illustrated by the Israeli military's reported use of the 'Lavender' system in Gaza. This AI-driven tool is said to have generated kill lists by identifying suspected militants based on behavioural patterns and data correlations, allegedly with minimal human oversight.[4] While AI-based identification and targeting raise profound ethical concerns, the pressing technical issue lies in the system's streamlined and opaque interface, which reportedly prompts the 'human on the loop' to review targets in less than 20 seconds.[5] Such interface design – by no means unique to the Israeli military – threatens humanitarian norms. As long as debates on automation and autonomy remain preoccupied with abstract concepts like 'human on the loop', security experts and policymakers forfeit an important opportunity to promote interface designs that bring AI and military personnel into a shared, better-informed and more accountable decision-making process that makes human control more tangible, operationally meaningful and ethically defensible.

Human limits

Human oversight and control of AI-based systems demand substantial cognitive effort, and they have well-documented limits. Both can fray under stress, falter under excessive workload and fail altogether in moments of peak complexity, precisely when human judgement matters most. These vulnerabilities are not theoretical. During the 2003 Iraq War, two friendly-fire incidents involving the US Army's *Patriot* missile-defence system illustrated how human–machine interaction failures can lead to fatal outcomes – even with highly trained crews operating sophisticated automated systems. In two separate events, the *Patriot* system misidentified friendly aircraft as incoming enemy missiles. In both cases, operators failed to override the system's automatic engagement sequence, resulting in the pilots' deaths. Post-incident analyses indicated that the system's interface design and automation logic encouraged human over-reliance on machine-generated recommendations. Operators trusted the automated identification and threat classification so heavily that it sidelined their own situational judgement. The episodes demonstrated that when human–machine integration fails to support critical oversight, and automation is too rigid or opaque, even expert personnel may place undue trust in system outputs, leading to fatal consequences.[6]

This example underscores two critical needs. The first is a scientifically grounded understanding of human cognitive strengths and limitations under operational conditions. The second is interface technologies that reliably connect high-performing – but inherently fallible – humans with AI-enabled systems in ways that accommodate both the variability of human performance and the rigidity of machine logic. Unless security experts and policymakers begin to address these two imperatives, governance frameworks for autonomy will remain dangerously disconnected from how these systems actually function in the field. In that context, vague commitments to keeping a 'human in the loop' risk becoming not safeguards but rather perilous illusions of control.

Adaptive automation

As states race to field ever-faster autonomous weapons and AI-enabled systems, the 'human in the loop' remains a curiously underspecified figure – a normative placeholder, always presumed to be equally competent, available and alert. This assumption lacks grounding in empirical reality. Research fields such as neuroscience and human factors offer increasingly substantial evidence-based toolkits for turning human control and oversight from rhetorical commitment into operational reality.[7] Decades of studies across domains such as aviation, air-traffic control, nuclear-power plants, intensive-care units and manufacturing industries have mapped the conditions under which human control and oversight succeed or fail.[8] These findings make one point abundantly clear: human control and oversight are not on–off switches. They are rooted in a complex, dynamic interplay of biological and social variables, including attention, cognitive load, situational awareness and trust in automation – all of which fluctuate under pressure, uncertainty and time constraints.[9]

One valuable research strand in the field of human factors is adaptive automation, which offers critical insights for shaping design and policy frameworks surrounding the deployment and regulation of autonomous systems. Instead of framing debates in terms of 'how to keep the human (meaningfully) in the loop', adaptive automation reframes the issue as 'how much autonomy is appropriate given human cognitive abilities and limits at different phases of military engagement'. Contemporary technologies already enable real-time monitoring of an operator's cognitive workload using physiological markers such as brain activity, eye movement and heart rate.[10] This data can be used to dynamically adjust a system's level of autonomy during an ongoing mission.[11] When an operator's workload crosses a pre-defined threshold, the AI system can temporarily assume specific tasks, returning control once the operator regains sufficient capacity.

Adaptive automation offers a genuinely human-centred approach to autonomy because it roots the design of autonomous systems in the realities of human capacity. Leveraging measurable neurophysiological signals to dynamically calibrate the appropriate degree of autonomous activity acknowledges that human control and oversight are not static attributes but contingent capabilities that must be actively supported. This perspective reframes human–machine interaction as ongoing, co-constructed teaming rather than a rigid division of tasks between human and machine.[12]

The accidents with the *Patriot* missile system and other incidents reveal that human operators – though nominally 'on the loop' – lacked the interface support necessary to maintain effective oversight in ambiguous threat environments. Adaptive automation could have meaningfully informed the interface design. For example, rather than presenting binary 'friend or foe' indications, the interface could have displayed confidence intervals to help operators better interpret target ambiguity. It might have provided decision rationales or prompted additional confirmation before authorising lethal engagement. During periods of high stress or cognitive overload, adaptive automation could have reconfigured the user interface by simplifying displays, reducing non-essential alerts and highlighting only the most critical data relevant to engagement decisions. In scenarios involving multiple fast-moving targets, the system might have temporarily managed lower-priority tracks, freeing the operator to focus on the most uncertain or threatening contacts. While not features of the current *Patriot* system, these adaptive techniques stem from decades of research and could inform future designs to make human oversight more resilient and dependable.

Human in the mesh

The traditional models of human involvement – human in the loop, on the loop and out of the loop – view the human actor as static and technologically determined. Contrary to popular belief, concerns regarding this static approach are not a recent issue. In 1983, Lisanne Bainbridge articulated what remains one of the sharpest warnings. She stated that the more reliable and autonomous the machine, the more likely it is that the humans' role will be reduced to rare, high-stakes interventions precisely when they are least prepared to act.[13] When human engagement becomes mainly passive – that is, relegated to mere oversight – attention fades, skills atrophy and the operator becomes most vulnerable exactly when vigilance and rapid decision-making are needed most.[14] In static automation architectures, waiting until a crisis to hand control back to an underprepared human is not a fallback plan; it is a failure mode. National-security decision-makers who take Bainbridge's insight to heart would pursue automation design for resilience, recovery and re-engagement.

Designing for resilience, recovery and re-engagement means treating the human operator not as a backup system, but as a dynamic actor whose cognitive readiness must be continuously supported and sustained. For instance, rather than sidelining the operator during routine autonomous operations, the system can periodically prompt low-stakes decisions, request confirmations or present simulated edge cases to maintain better situational awareness and cognitive sharpness. In high-stress scenarios, such systems can assist in human recovery by offering decision aids – say, contextual explanations and replay functions – enabling the operator to reconstruct what has occurred and why, even after a temporary lapse in attention. Re-engagement mechanisms might include phased control transfer, where the operator regains control in stages, rather than being overwhelmed with full responsibility all at once. Most importantly, a human-centred approach does not assume human perfection, as abstract frameworks like 'human in the loop' often do. Instead, it acknowledges the natural oscillation between peak performance – marked by focus and agility – and inevitable states of distraction, cognitive overload and fatigue.

Given the stakes involved, national-security discourse ought to incorporate empirically rooted insights into human–machine integration. Yet the effort remains sporadic. This absence of sustained attention has left critical conceptual gaps, particularly when it comes to rethinking outdated frameworks of human control. One promising alternative to the loop frameworks is the concept of 'human in the mesh' (HITM), drawn from human-factors research and related scientific fields.[15] Unlike the traditional static view of human control, HITM reconceives the human operator as deeply embedded in a dynamic network of autonomous processes. This model seeks to reflect the increasing operational complexity of command-and-control environments far more accurately.

A current research-and-development solicitation by US Special Operations Command offers a way to illustrate the evolving concept of HITM. Imagine a special-operations team moving through a heavily restricted urban area. Autonomous drones, outfitted with radio-frequency, acoustic and visual sensors, serve as the team's scouts, mapping both the physical and digital terrain in real time. These drones detect wireless hotspots, communication nodes and electronic devices that could indicate a variety of threats, including improvised explosive devices, surveillance tools or human adversaries. The drones transmit the collected data to a centralised system that fuses multiple sensor streams, performs threat assessments, flags anomalies and generates predictive insights into potential adversary behaviour.[16] Complementing these processes, countermeasure systems deploy jamming and decoy signals to mask the special-ops team's electromagnetic signature and complicate enemy efforts to locate and target the team.[17] Most of this activity unfolds with minimal human intervention, but an operator still confronts numerous outputs such as alerts. Additionally, an AI-based assistant informs the operator of options that require decisions, such as choices of routes or contingency plans in response to unforeseen threats.

In this HITM scenario, the human operator takes on an adaptive leadership role, shaping the behaviour of the autonomous network through a blend of active decision-making, passive monitoring and collaborative interaction. Rather than intervening at isolated moments, the operator remains continuously engaged by providing context-sensitive input throughout the mission. In a security discourse still preoccupied with locating the human in relation to autonomous systems, HITM gives rise to a different conversation that abandons rigid metaphors of control and oversight, and instead embeds the human within a distributed, adaptive network of autonomous agents. Crucially, HITM challenges us to move beyond abstract 'loop' frameworks and confront a defining reality of modern conflict: no single agent – human or machine – can perceive the full battlespace. Perception, and by extension oversight and control, are increasingly networked phenomena.

More broadly, an HITM-informed approach invites a rethinking of key assumptions in human–machine integration, raising a range of important questions. How can systems be designed to adapt dynamically to fluctuations in human cognitive capacity, ensuring that human control remains viable under operational conditions? Can fundamental principles – such as the norms of international humanitarian law – be embedded into interface designs that govern joint human–machine activity? And are there interface cues or system behaviours that can help guard the human against innate biases, particularly in time-sensitive, high-stakes scenarios? Such questions have yet to assume prominence in policy debates about 'meaningful human control'. This omission is all the more striking given that human control depends on human–machine interaction, which is shaped not only by doctrine or ethics, but also by biological and social realities.

*   *   *

Security experts, policymakers and the DoD should seek to influence AI policies in ways that reflect the operational realities of the US armed forces. Future policy could require that all autonomous systems undergo rigorous testing not only for technical performance, but also for cognitive compatibility with human operators. Trials should include stress testing, fatigue simulations and human–machine interaction studies that replicate the high-pressure conditions of real-world operations. Moreover, the DoD should further institutionalise collaboration with neuroscientists, cognitive engineers and human-factors experts during both the design and acquisition phases of AI and autonomous systems. If these voices are not heeded early on, policy and procurement may default to technically sophisticated but operationally flawed systems. In addition, rules of engagement and use-of-force protocols should be updated to account for situations in which human intervention is not feasible, reliable or safe, and define autonomous-system behaviour accordingly. In high-speed engagements or complex threat environments, assuming that a human can consistently evaluate relevant information, make an informed decision and approve the system's next steps is not merely tactically unrealistic; it may also be ethically indefensible.

US policy must move beyond viewing human control or oversight as static safeguards. Instead, policymakers should champion human-centred standards that acknowledge the dynamic, context-sensitive nature of human agency. In an era of increasingly autonomous systems, meaningful human control is not an abstract ideal or a mere legal formality. Rather, it must be actively sustained across all human–machine interaction, particularly within the interface that binds them. This interface fundamentally shapes human perception, the understanding of options and the scope of possible decisions. When it fails to account for human capabilities and limitations, control is not so much surrendered to AI and automation as never truly present to begin with. Autonomous-warfare policy must therefore treat interface design and human performance not as ancillary technical concerns, but as foundational pillars of operational effectiveness and ethical responsibility.

Notes

[1] See Evan Lynch, 'US Army Launches Generative AI Platform in Groundbreaking Move', AFCEA, 10 September 2024, https://www.afcea.org/signal-media/us-army-launches-generative-ai-platform-groundbreaking-move.

[2] See *ibid.*; and Tate Nurkin and Julia Siegel, 'Battlefield Applications for Human–Machine Teaming: Demonstrating Value, Experimenting with New Capabilities, and Accelerating Adoption', Atlantic Council, Scowcroft Center for

3 See Frank Bajak, 'Pentagon's AI Initiatives Accelerate Hard Decisions on Lethal Autonomous Weapons', Associated Press, 25 November 2023, https://apnews.com/article/us-military-ai-projects-0773b4937801e7a0573f44b57a9a5942; Kyle Hiebert, 'The United States Quietly Kick-starts the Autonomous Weapons Era', Centre for International Governance Innovation, 15 January 2024, https://www.cigionline.org/articles/the-united-states-quietly-kick-starts-the-autonomous-weapons-era/; and Adib Bin Rashid et al., 'Artificial Intelligence in the Military: An Overview of the Capabilities, Applications, and Challenges', *International Journal of Intelligent Systems*, November 2023, p. 16.
4 See Yuval Abraham, '"Lavender": The AI Machine Directing Israel's Bombing Spree in Gaza', *+972 Magazine*, 3 April 2024, https://www.972mag.com/lavender-ai-israeli-army-gaza/; and Callum Fraser, 'AI's Baptism by Fire in Ukraine and Gaza Offers Wider Lessons', IISS Military Balance Blog, 22 April 2024, https://www.iiss.org/online-analysis/military-balance/2024/04/analysis-ais-baptism-by-fire-in-ukraine-and-gaza-offer-wider-lessons/.
5 Abraham, '"Lavender"'.
6 See Raja Parasuraman, Thomas B. Sheridan and Christopher D. Wicken, 'A Model for Types and Levels of Human Interaction with Automation', *IEEE Transactions on Systems, Man, and Cybernetics – Part A: Systems and Humans*, vol. 30, no. 3, June 2000, pp. 286–97; and Jitu Patel et al., 'Give Us a Hand, Mate! A Holistic Review of Research on Human–Machine Teaming', *BMJ Military Health*, 2024, p. 2, https://militaryhealth.bmj.com/content/jramc/early/2024/12/24/military-2024-002737.full.pdf.
7 See Raja Parasuraman, 'Designing Automation for Human Use: Empirical Studies and Quantitative Models', *Ergonomics*, vol. 43, no. 7, July 2000, pp. 931–51.
8 See Margherita Bernabei and Francesco Costantino, 'Adaptive Automation: Status of Research and Future Challenges', *Robotics and Computer-integrated Manufacturing*, vol. 88, August 2024, article 102724.
9 See Frédéric Dehais et al., 'Dual Passive Reactive Brain–Computer Interface: A Novel Approach to Human–Machine Symbiosis', *Frontiers in Neuroergonomics*, vol. 3, April 2022, article 824780, p. 2, https://www.frontiersin.org/journals/neuroergonomics/articles/10.3389/fnrgo.2022.824780/full; Parasuraman, Sheridan and Wicken, 'A Model for Types and Levels of Human Interaction with Automation', pp. 290–1; and Emilie M. Roth et al., 'Function Allocation Considerations in the Era of Human Autonomy Teaming', *Journal of Cognitive Engineering and Decision Making*, vol. 13, no. 4, November 2019, pp. 199–220.
10 See Xinyue Ma et al., 'Determining Cognitive Workload Using Physiological Measurements: Pupillometry and Heart-rate Variability', *Sensors*, vol. 24, no. 6,

March 2024; Eydis H. Magnusdottir et al., 'Assessing Cognitive Workload Using Cardiovascular Measures and Voice', *Sensors*, vol. 22, no. 18, September 2022; and Jesse A. Mark et al., 'Mental Workload Assessment by Monitoring Brain, Heart, and Eye with Six Biomedical Modalities During Six Cognitive Tasks', *Frontiers in Neuroergonomics*, vol. 5, March 2024, https://www.frontiersin.org/journals/neuroergonomics/articles/10.3389/fnrgo.2024.1345507/full.

11 See Bernabei and Costantino, 'Adaptive Automation'; and Grace Teo et al., 'Adaptive Aiding with an Individualized Workload Model Based on Psychophysiological Measures', *Human–Intelligent Systems Integration*, vol. 2, no. 5, December 2020, pp. 1–15.

12 See Gianluca Di Flumeri et al., 'Brain–Computer Interface-based Adaptive Automation to Prevent Out-of-the-loop Phenomenon in Air Traffic Controllers Dealing with Highly Automated Systems', *Frontiers in Human Neuroscience*, vol. 13, September 2019, article 296, p. 3; Roth et al., 'Function Allocation Considerations in the Era of Human Autonomy Teaming', p. 206; and Paul Scharre, *Army of None: Autonomous Weapons and the Future of War* (New York: W. W. Norton & Co., 2018).

13 See Lisanne Bainbridge, 'Ironies of Automation', *Automatica*, vol. 19, no. 6, November 1983, pp. 775–9, https://ckrybus.com/static/papers/Bainbridge_1983_Automatica.pdf.

14 See Di Flumeri et al., 'Brain–Computer Interface-based Adaptive Automation to Prevent Out-of-the-loop Phenomenon in Air Traffic Controllers Dealing with Highly Automated Systems'; and Parasuraman, Sheridan and Wicken, 'A Model for Types and Levels of Human Interaction with Automation', p. 291.

15 See Bernabei and Costantino, 'Adaptive Automation'.

16 See US Special Operations Forces Acquisition, Technology, and Logistics Directorate of Science and Technology, 'Broad Agency Announcement USSOCOM-BAAST-2020, Amendment 5 for Technology Development and Advanced Technology Development', 16 November 2023, https://govtribe.com/file/government-file/ussocombaast2020-ussocom-baast-2020-amendment-5-final-dot-pdf.

17 See US Special Operations Forces Acquisition, Technology, and Logistics Directorate of Science and Technology, 'Broad Agency Announcement USSOCOM-BAAST-2020, Amendment 6 for Technology Development and Advanced Technology Development', 30 November 2024, https://www.highergov.com/document/ussocom-baast-2020-amendment-6-final-20240924-pdf-248d96/.

Offensive Cyber Attacks and Conventional Warfare

Matthew F. Calabria

When could offensive cyber attacks tip the balance in conventional warfare, reaching a point at which they could decide, or help decide, the outcome of war in an aggressor's favour?[1] Scholarship abounds on the use of cyber attacks in war but remains remarkably scant in confronting why such attacks have proven ineffective in resolving conflict favourably for the offence. This article looks to fill this gap by evaluating how cyber attacks can be useful in war and identifying the conditions under which they could become decisive in securing military victory.

The case against cyber weapons in conventional war

Cyber attacks in and of themselves have neither vanquished peer-level adversaries in a large-scale war nor degraded an opponent's armed forces to precipitate total defeat. For example, Russia has fought several wars since the end of the Cold War, introducing cyber attacks to the battlespace, but failed to win any of them. In 2008, it conducted a massive cyber offensive against neighbouring Georgia before invading with conventional forces.[2] Yet the cyber offensive was not a major, or even minor, determinant of the trajectory of that war. Seven years later, of course, Russia employed complex malware to shut down much of Ukraine's power grid – hinting at how offensive cyber power

---

Matthew F. Calabria is former Director for Cyber Operations and Incident Response in the Office of the National Cyber Director, Executive Office of the President, and an adjunct professor at George Washington University's Elliott School of International Affairs. The views expressed in this article are solely those of the author and do not necessarily reflect the views or position of the US government.

could set conditions for military victory. Yet despite Russia's stature as a major cyber power, the 'cyber blitzkrieg' Russia watchers expected in the opening salvo in Russia's invasion of Ukraine in February 2022 never transpired.[3]

The cyber attacks that Russia launched at the onset of the invasion were subdued, with unidentified hackers disrupting broadband satellite-internet access in Ukraine to support the invasion, but still failing to degrade Ukraine's readiness.[4] Russian forces also reportedly launched a separate missile strike at the TV Tower in Kyiv in coordination with widespread cyber attacks on Kyiv-based media in the early months of the war.[5] Although CrowdStrike, an information-security firm, assesses that cyber operations have since 'directly contributed' to the ongoing conflict, they have not culminated in any significant battlefield victories.[6] These and other cyber operations have rarely succeeded in carrying the initiative, even tactically, in a war that Russia is not clearly winning.[7] The battles in Ukraine have been decided by drones, artillery and concentrated conventional combat power.

China, for its part, would unleash a bruising combination of cyber and kinetic attacks during a Taiwan-invasion scenario, according to a Center for Strategic and International Studies report.[8] Last year, the US Cybersecurity and Infrastructure Security Agency (CISA) found that cyber actors sponsored by China were seeking to pre-position themselves on IT networks for disruptive or destructive cyber attacks against US critical infrastructure in the event of a major crisis or conflict with the United States.[9] Yet China's offensive cyber capability, while potent, remains unproven in a major war. A war over Taiwan would almost certainly involve a range of actors across East Asia, indicating a degree of complexity that would make the cyber effect on the war's outcome indeterminate and, in all likelihood, negligible with current technologies. China's People's Liberation Army would still need to prevail in massive, force-on-force battles along the coastline while landing troops and subduing major cities – operations only marginally affected by cyber – to enforce Beijing's rule. Unless war breaks out, whether Chinese cyber attacks could be decisive will remain unknowable.

Cyber–military integration is poor in most countries, as they have not adapted their armed forces to the digital age. In wartime, cyber attacks tend to be scattershot, unfocused and ineffective against hardened systems, including military command-and-control networks. Cyber attacks often require extensive preparation and precise execution, making them less appropriate for the fluid, substantially unpredictable conditions of battle. Weapons like bespoke malware can be used only once and, once deployed, are often easily neutralised. Their effectiveness diminishes as victims recognise the threat, patch vulnerabilities and shrink attack surfaces. The conflict in Ukraine has shown that strategic cyber attacks are also prone to high rates of failure and severe challenges owing to the difficulties of integrating them with conventional military operations.[10]

On account of the specialised, non-strategic nature of cyber attacks, they have not been primary sources of power for fighting forces. That said, gaining direct control over or destroying an opposing force's individual platforms, weapons systems or combat units through cyber intrusions or hacks is possible. Thirteen years ago, Iran, a middling cyber power, was able to find, target and hack a US-controlled RQ-170 *Sentinel* drone.[11] Modern warplanes are designed to operate independently and are therefore harder to disable than drones. Since crewed aircraft and other contemporary combat systems are increasingly hyperconnected, however, impeding their operability by cyber means is becoming more feasible. All US Air Force air operations rely on cyberspace as a matter of doctrine, and its combat systems depend on datalink technologies that connect to an expansive, albeit restrictive, networked architecture.[12] On balance, the hyperconnectivity of modern military platforms increases the risk of wider cyber compromise.

Perhaps the extreme difficulty of compromising an enemy military's network integrity is why belligerents have never perpetrated hacks in wartime that could induce significant casualties in opposing forces. If cyber attackers could 'find and fix' an entire enemy air squadron in one fell swoop, such effects would already be far more common in war – indeed, war itself would arguably be more common. Yet no major power has demonstrated this offensive capability against cutting-edge, military-grade hardware, which verges on the implausible at almost any level of the cyber kill chain. As cyber defences evolve in tandem with offensive capabilities, these capabilities, though important complementary tools, may remain unreliable stand-alone means of achieving victory.

Cyber attacks, as the war in Ukraine has shown, are also all but ineffectual during long, grinding campaigns of attrition. Since 2022, drones and First World War-style trench warfare – including heavy use of long-range artillery, steady access to shells and land grabs – have been the crucial factors. Russian strategy has relied on relatively cheap recruits, artillery and missile strikes to deplete Ukrainian forces in Ukraine's countryside, which is not well connected to grids or other infrastructure and therefore largely invulnerable to cyber-physical effects. Cutting off the internet in Kyiv or shutting down power in other major cities, even if it were possible, would afford the Kremlin negligible advantages in its bloody campaign on Ukraine's eastern plains against dug-in forces across the 1,000-kilometre front. Cyber attacks might be more suited to tipping the balance in a war in the Pacific, in which hyperconnected air and naval platforms reliant on Global Positioning Systems would be vulnerable to jamming and hacks.[13]

When state-led cyber attacks have succeeded, it has been due to poor cyber security rather than good offensives. As Rebecca Slayton has concluded, 'the current success of [cyber] offense results primarily from poor defensive management and the relatively simpler goals of offense; it can be very costly to exert precise physical effects using cyberweapons'.[14] Cyber security is also improving, which will make cyber attacks less effective as instruments of war. Defensive technologies have evolved globally into formidable obstacles for aggressors looking to win conventional wars via attacks originating from cyberspace, further discouraging cyber attacks to achieve decisive military objectives. As defensive technologies become more sophisticated, attackers face higher costs and thus diminishing returns on their efforts. Integrating zero-trust architectures – security models that assume no one inside or outside a network should be trusted by default – complicates aggressors' infiltration of critical systems. At the same time, international collaboration on cyber-security standards has strengthened global resilience against and resistance to cyber threats.[15] Shortly after the Russian invasion began, CISA and the State Service of Special Communications and Information Protection of Ukraine brokered a memorandum of cooperation to strengthen collaboration on shared cyber-security priorities.[16]

Meanwhile, Fortune Business Insights has forecast that the cyber-security market will balloon to $425 billion by 2030 – nearly 2.5 times greater than its valuation in 2023.[17] Cyber-security titans Palo Alto Networks, CrowdStrike and others will have the money, bespoke tools and leading-edge software programmes to confront major offensive cyber threats, and their reputations will be on the line. Virtual private networks and cloud technologies have kept pace with global cyber threats. Complex combinations of cloud architecture, artificial intelligence (AI), quantum computing and 5G network security, among other emerging technologies, could sustain the status quo in the defence's favour. AI will also generate better warning of potential security incidents by more discriminately analysing and extrapolating data and patterns. In addition, defensive technologies have become more decentralised, making network compromises that much harder.[18]

The persistent case for cyber weapons

The underperformance of cyber attacks does not necessarily translate into their terminal irrelevance in determining whether wars end favourably. Four years ago, Robert Jervis warned that 'cyber conflict and competition are intensifying, increasing the chances of escalation into a true global crisis'.[19] Cyber aggressors like Russia, despite limiting factors, still prosecute cyber war regularly, especially in combat zones like Ukraine. China, Iran and North Korea are all aggressively deploying advanced cyber capabilities for offensive purposes.[20] Marcus Willett, the first director of cyber at the United Kingdom's Government Communications Headquarters (GCHQ), sums up the present outlook authoritatively:

> Cyber operations have a proven strategic utility for both liberal-democratic and authoritarian states even if this utility mostly stems from 'softer', below-the-threshold activities rather than from 'hard' physically destructive attacks, and normally depends on cyber operations being synchronised with other levers of national power. Nevertheless, there is as much jeopardy in underestimating as overestimating the disruptive and destructive potential of cyber capabilities, with the risk that states will fail to imagine what is possible until it occurs.[21]

Modern state aggressors recognise that offensive cyber weapons offer numerous operational advantages. As Google's Threat Analysis Group concluded last year, 'cyber capabilities can be quickly deployed at minimal cost to regional rivals' and 'are a tool of first resort'.[22] Over a decade ago, analysts judged that the growth of cyber arsenals was 'outpacing the design of doctrines to limit their risks'.[23] The trend is not abating. Cyber attacks have become quite useful. They tend to be unattributable, surprising and, with the right toolsets and access, employable en masse. Recall that the NotPetya malware infected millions of systems worldwide in 2017. They also tend to be much cheaper than military operations and can be calibrated to the deployer's particular degree of aggression and inclination to escalate.

> *Offensive cyber weapons offer numerous advantages*

The onset of major conflict is the point at which offensive cyber operations would be most useful for preparing the battlespace in the aggressor's favour by weakening the adversary, which is essential to modern operational art. Deep political divisions in France in both 1914 and 1939, for example, invited Germany's aggression. During the Cold War, the KGB's active measures in Afghanistan cultivated an environment that the Soviet high command determined was ripe for invasion.[24] To an extent, contemporary aggressors have absorbed this lesson, routinely launching cyber attacks ahead of large-scale combat operations. The National Intelligence Council's (NIC) *Global Trends* stated that 'belligerents are increasingly likely to target their adversaries' computer networks, critical infrastructure, electromagnetic spectrum, financial systems, and assets in space, threatening communications and undermining warning functions'.[25] These cyber attacks could create divisions and stoke the victim population's distrust of their government, facilitating an invasion.[26] Even so, state aggressors with the most advanced cyber capabilities generally have not chosen to use them offensively at the beginning of hostilities.

To be sure, improved defensive technologies curtail the operational advantages of next-generation offensive cyber weaponry. But cyber attackers are refining their capabilities to target physical systems in ways that can shape conflict to their advantage. Well-timed, well-executed cyber operations can trigger cascading effects in physical environments. Thirteen years ago, Leon Panetta, then director of the CIA, warned of the possibility of a 'cyber-Pearl Harbor' that would include 'cyber-actors launching several attacks on our critical infrastructure at one time, in combination with a physical attack'.[27] Attacking the population of a country and hacking its water supply, for example, might bend the victim to the will of the aggressor without the attacker (or victim) firing a shot.

Offensive cyber capabilities are also constantly improving. As they do, physically damaging cyber attacks launched by states can increasingly complicate cyber defences, with considerable potential to shape and win future conflicts. 'The development of cyber weapons, doctrine, and procedures, in conjunction with other weapons, is likely to mature significantly during the next 20 years, increasing the consequences of cyber conflict', according to *Global Trends,* published in March 2021.[28] Signs that this prediction will come true are already emerging. For example, while Russia seems to improve its malware with each passing year, Ukraine has fought back with innovative offensive systems of its own to even the score, even employing malware-equipped drones to sabotage captured Russian systems.[29] Although improved cyber defence and cloud computing could also blunt the impact of the offence across increasingly target-rich environments, cyber weapons may outpace cyber defences in some areas.

Meanwhile, operational-technology (OT) systems that control physical devices and infrastructure, such as energy grids and transportation networks, are becoming vulnerable to cyber attacks despite integrating with cloud-security architecture and other defences.[30] The most capable states are using cyber intrusions into OT systems for pre-conflict hedging. Earlier this year, the Department of Homeland Security found that 'adversarial state cyber actors will continue to seek access to, or to pre-position themselves on, US critical infrastructure networks'.[31]

These OT vulnerabilities underscore how distinctions between cyber offence and defence are blurring. The Institute for the Future, a non-profit research service, estimates that an average of one million devices per square kilometre of coverage area worldwide will connect to the internet by 2040, compared with only tens of thousands today.[32] Approximately 85% of US critical infrastructure is currently held by the private sector. That translates into a lot of hardware and software for non-government actors to secure against an array of cyber threats of which these private defenders may be unaware.[33] The US Army War College concluded that cyber attacks on critical infrastructure are highly likely to impact global military mobilisations by 2035.[34] As the NIC assesses, 'greater connectivity almost certainly will increase the vulnerability of connected individuals, institutions, and governments, as the presence of hundreds of billions of connected devices vastly increases the cyber–physical attack surface'.[35]

Accordingly, adversaries should be expected to sharpen their tools and improve their capabilities continually, whether through augmenting technologies with AI and quantum computing or marrying offensive cyber components with conventional forces and the physical environment. AI could help cyber attackers analyse exploitation pathways to hard targets, present contingencies for commanders, and further integrate cyber weapons with conventional systems and programmes. According to the NIC, 'AI will enhance the performance of existing weapons, defenses, and security systems, both physical and cyber, while counter-AI techniques, designed to negate or confuse AI decision making, also are likely to emerge'.[36] Though it is worth noting that quantum-resistant and quantum-enabled encryption and communications are being developed, quantum-enabled cyber attacks could still eventually enable cyber aggressors to circumvent encryption in opposing military networks.

Conditions favouring cyber operations in conventional war

Given operational limitations, it is not an absolute certainty that offensive cyber attacks will provide war-fighting advantages to state aggressors. But favourable conditions could well materialise in at least three ways.

Firstly, tactical cyber effects in the battlespace could become capable of delivering operational or strategic results. Effects of cyber attacks vary, but most are non-strategic. Today, cyber attacks can affect individual systems, including hardened encrypted units, or – like *WannaCry* – even global networks, but only occasionally and inadvertently. Once cyber attacks can extend beyond low-scale hacks and subdue civil society or infrastructure, or sap an opponent's will to fight, they can help achieve military victory. Future aggressors might enhance cyber capabilities with new technologies, such as AI or quantum computing, and pair them with electronic warfare or saturation strikes in large-scale cyber attacks that can dismantle an entire opposing force. Had Russia invaded Ukraine in 2015 immediately after deploying malware that enabled it to cut Ukraine's power, it would have enjoyed far greater operational and strategic advantages than it did in the actual event.

Secondly, dedicated and operationally integrated offensive cyber units could optimise conventional operations in real time. Soldiers acting in the fog of war must make split-second decisions to carry the initiative. If timely offensive cyber attacks could slow the advance of a defensive force's response or reduce prospects for retaliation at crucial points early in a conflict, they could surprise and demoralise the defending force.

Thirdly, offensive technologies could simply outpace defensive ones, as the tank, ineffective and plodding in the First World War, did in the Second World War. Cyber war tends to favour defenders.[37] Amplifying a cyber attack like the one on Ukraine's power grid in 2015 could translate into a breakthrough capability, particularly if applied by way of surprise attack in the opening stages of war, before the enemy is dug in.

*   *   *

The US Department of Defense recognises that wars are won by dismantling infrastructure or affecting tangible assets, such as electric grids or water supplies, while integrating emerging technologies into war planning. The Joint Force is practising 'cyberspace operations that require the deployment of cyberspace forces within the physical domains', enhancing the prospect of winning conventional wars via cyber operations.[38] The United States Cyber Command's Cyber National Mission Force is also introducing into cyber operations AI that provides a 'roadmap' to victory in future war.[39] But next-generation defensive tools, including AI-driven anomaly detection and quantum-resistant encryption, could undermine cyber attacks' offensive impact. States may find that using an AI system to scan for threats in the battlespace and then eliminate them physically is more useful for ending conflict on their terms than launching precision cyber attacks.

Accordingly, policymakers should temper their expectations about the transformative potential of cyber weapons in warfare, incorporating cyber's limitations as well as its potential into simulations, training and war games. War plans should still turn on scale, speed and force concentration at decisive points against the enemy's centre of gravity while treating cyber weapons as niche assets best suited for pre-conflict operations and not as direct means to victory. But they should also account for the possibility that powerful offensive cyber capabilities could eventually overwhelm physical defences and recognise how this could change conventional war.

Notes

1   This narrow definition, for our purposes, does not include cyber espionage, influence operations or other activities in cyberspace that are neither damaging nor disruptive.
2   See John Markoff, 'Before the Gunfire, Cyberattacks', *New York Times*, 12 August 2008, https://www.nytimes.com/2008/08/13/technology/13cyber.html.
3   See Paul Rosenzweig, 'Where Is Russia's Cyber Blitzkrieg?', *Hill*, 16 March 2022, https://thehill.com/opinion/cybersecurity/597272-where-is-russias-cyber-blitzkrieg/; and Marcus Willett, 'The Cyber Dimension of the Russia–Ukraine War', *Survival*, vol. 64, no. 5, October–November 2022, pp. 7–26.
4   See Daryna Antoniuk, 'Ukraine Says Russia Is Coordinating Missile Strikes, Cyberattacks and Information Operations', *Record*, 18 January 2023, https://therecord.media/ukraine-says-russia-is-coordinating-missile-strikes-cyberattacks-and-information-operations; and James Pearson et al., 'Exclusive: US Spy Agency Probes Sabotage of Satellite Internet During Russian Invasion, Sources Say', Reuters, 11 March 2022, https://www.reuters.com/world/europe/exclusive-us-spy-agency-probes-sabotage-satellite-internet-during-russian-2022-03-11/.
5   See James Pearson and Christopher Bing, 'The Cyber War Between Ukraine and Russia: An Overview', Reuters, 10 March 2022, https://www.reuters.com/world/europe/factbox-the-cyber-war-between-ukraine-russia-2022-05-10/.
6   See CrowdStrike, '2024 Global Threat Report', https://go.crowdstrike.com/rs/281-OBQ-266/images/GlobalThreatReport2024.pdf.
7   See Michael Kimmage, 'Russia Has Started Losing the War in Ukraine', *Foreign Policy*, 19 May 2025, https://foreignpolicy.com/2025/05/19/russia-military-putin-war-ukraine-nato-europe/.

8   See James A. Lewis, 'Cyberattack on Civilian Critical Infrastructures in a Taiwan Scenario', Center for Strategic and International Studies, August 2023, https://csis-website-prod.s3.amazonaws.com/s3fs-public/2023-08/230811_Lewis_Cyberattack_Taiwan.pdf.

9   See Cybersecurity and Infrastructure Security Agency, 'CISA Cybersecurity Advisory AA24-038A', 7 February 2024, https://www.cisa.gov/news-events/cybersecurity-advisories/aa24-038a.

10 See Frederik A.H. Pedersen and Jeppe T. Jacobsen, 'Narrow Windows of Opportunity: The Limited Utility of Cyber Operations in War', *Journal of Cybersecurity*, vol. 10, no. 1, August 2024, https://doi.org/10.1093/cybsec/tyae014.

11 See 'Iran Shows "Hacked US Spy Drone" Video Footage', BBC News, 7 February 2013, https://www.bbc.com/news/world-middle-east-21373353.

12 See Patrick Tucker, 'Air Force, Industry Seek to Cyber-protect Weapons, Fighter Jets', *Defense One*, 25 January 2017, https://www.defenseone.com/defense-systems/2017/01/air-force-industry-seek-to-cyber-protect-weapons-fighter-jets/190331/; and US Air Force, 'Air Force Doctrine Publication 3-12: Cyberspace Operations', 1 February 2023, https://www.doctrine.af.mil/Portals/61/documents/AFDP_3-12/3-12-AFDP-CYBERSPACE-OPS.pdf.

13 See Anthony P. Carrillo, 'Surface Crews Need More Tools to Navigate Without GPS', *Proceedings*, July 2022, https://www.usni.org/magazines/proceedings/2022/july/surface-crews-need-more-tools-navigate-without-gps.

14 See Rebecca Slayton, 'What Is the Cyber Offense–Defense Balance? Conceptions, Causes, and Assessment', *International Security*, vol. 41, no. 3, Winter 2016/17, pp. 72–109.

15 See Anand Oswal, 'Zero Trust for Critical Infrastructure', Palo Alto Networks, 2023, https://www.paloaltonetworks.com/cybersecurity-perspectives/zero-trust-for-critical-infrastructure.

16 See US Cybersecurity and Infrastructure Security Agency, 'United States and Ukraine Expand Cooperation on Cybersecurity', 27 July 2022, https://www.cisa.gov/news-events/news/united-states-and-ukraine-expand-cooperation-cybersecurity.

17 Fortune Business Insights, 'Cyber Security Market Size, Share & Industry Analysis', 2023, https://www.fortunebusinessinsights.com/industry-reports/cyber-security-market-101165.

18 See SignalFire, 'The Rise of Decentralized Cybersecurity: Trends & Opportunities', 7 November 2022, https://www.signalfire.com/blog/rise-decentralized-cybersecurity-trends-opportunities; and Sharada Yeluri, 'The Evolution of Network Security', APNIC, 25 June 2024, https://blog.apnic.net/2024/06/25/the-evolution-of-network-security/.

19 Quoted in Trey Herr and Stewart Scott, 'How to Reverse Three Decades of Escalating Cyber Conflict', Atlantic Council, 11 July 2023, https://www.atlanticcouncil.org/blogs/

new-atlanticist/how-to-reverse-three-decades-of-escalating-cyber-conflict/.
20 See White House, 'National Cybersecurity Strategy', March 2023, https://bidenwhitehouse.archives.gov/wp-content/uploads/2023/03/National-Cybersecurity-Strategy-2023.pdf.
21 Marcus Willett, *Cyber Operations and Their Responsible Use*, Adelphi 511–513 (Abingdon: Routledge for the IISS, 2024), pp. 168–9.
22 Sandra Joyce and Shane Huntley, 'Tool of First Resort: Israel–Hamas War in Cyber', Google Blog, 14 February 2024, https://blog.google/technology/safety-security/tool-of-first-resort-israel-hamas-war-in-cyber/.
23 Lucas Kello, 'The Meaning of the Cyber Revolution: Perils to Theory and Statecraft', *International Security*, vol. 38, no. 2, Fall 2013, pp. 7–40.
24 See Vasili Mitrokhin, 'KGB Active Measures in Southwest Asia in 1980–82', Wilson Center, April 2004, https://digitalarchive.wilsoncenter.org/document/kgb-active-measures-southwest-asia-1980-82.
25 US National Intelligence Council, Office of the Director of National Intelligence, 'Global Trends 2040: A More Contested World', March 2021, p. 102, https://www.dni.gov/files/ODNI/documents/assessments/GlobalTrends_2040.pdf.
26 See Henry Durojaye and Oluwaukola Raji, 'Impact of State and State Sponsored Actors on the Cyber Environment and the Future of Critical Infrastructure', Cornell University, December 2022, https://arxiv.org/pdf/2212.08036.
27 Quoted in Elisabeth Bumiller and Thom Shanker, 'Panetta Warns of Dire Threat of Cyberattack', *New York Times*, 11 October 2012, https://www.nytimes.com/2012/10/12/world/panetta-warns-of-dire-threat-of-cyberattack.html.
28 US National Intelligence Council, Office of the Director of National Intelligence, 'Global Trends 2040: A More Contested World', p. 104.
29 See 'Google Identifies New Malware Linked to Russia-based Hacking Group', Reuters, 7 May 2025, https://www.reuters.com/technology/cybersecurity/google-identifies-new-malware-linked-russia-based-hacking-group-2025-05-07; and Mandiant, 'M-Trends 2025 Report', https://services.google.com/fh/files/misc/m-trends-2025-en.pdf.
30 See Kevin O'Malley, 'Is Moving Operational Technology to the Cloud a Good Idea?', Palo Alto Networks, 2023, https://www.paloaltonetworks.com/cybersecurity-perspectives/is-moving-operational-technology-to-the-cloud-a-good-idea.
31 US Department of Homeland Security, Office of Intelligence and Analysis, 'Homeland Threat Assessment 2025', https://www.dhs.gov/sites/default/files/2024-10/24_0930_ia_24-320-ia-publication-2025-hta-final-30sep24-508.pdf.
32 See Nick Monaco, Scott Minneman and Katie Joseff, 'The Hyperconnected World of 2030–2040', Institute for the Future, November 2019, https://www.iftf.org/projects/the-hyperconnected-world-of-2030-2040/.
33 See Justin Sherman, 'The Era of Supply Chain Spy Wars Is Here', *Foreign Policy*, 10 December 2024, https://foreignpolicy.com/2024/12/10/the-era-of-supply-chain-spy-wars-is-here/.

34 See Joseph Bell et al., 'Future Dynamics of Warfare: Everyone Is a Player, Everything Is a Target, Conflict as a Sandbox', US Department of Defense, 3 September 2024, https://media.defense.gov/2024/Sep/03/2003536124/-1/-1/0/SULLIVAN%20REPORT%20FINAL%201.PDF.

35 US National Intelligence Council, Office of the Director of National Intelligence, 'Global Trends 2040: A More Contested World', p. 63.

36 *Ibid.*, p. 59.

37 See Rebecca Slayton, 'What Is the Cyber Offense–Defense Balance?'.

38 Quoted in Mark Pomerleau, 'New DoD Doctrine Officially Outlines and Defines Expeditionary Cyberspace Operations', *DefenseScoop*, 12 May 2023, https://defensescoop.com/2023/05/12/new-dod-doctrine-officially-outlines-and-defines-expeditionary-cyberspace-operations/.

39 See US Cyber Command, 'USCYBERCOM Unveils AI Roadmap for Cyber Operations', 5 April 2025, https://www.cybercom.mil/Media/News/Article/3905064/uscybercom-unveils-ai-roadmap-for-cyber-operations/.

Thinker, Lawyer, Soldier, Spy: The Makers of Xi Jinping's Grand Strategy

Nadège Rolland

A notable sign of Xi Jinping's consolidated authority within the Chinese Communist Party (CCP) has been the rapid inclusion of his 'thought' within the party canon. Introduced at the 19th national party congress in October 2017 and enshrined in the constitution of the People's Republic a few months later, 'Xi Jinping Thought on Socialism with Chinese Characteristics for a New Era', commonly abbreviated outside China as 'Xi Jinping Thought', reflects the Chinese leader's vision for the future of the party, the country and the Chinese people. As the 2017 CCP report to the national congress asserts, the 'Party leads everything': 'party, government, military, people and education, east, west, south and north'.[1] Accordingly, the party's top leader has some thoughts on everything – diplomacy, the military, literature and art, education, the rule of law, Taiwan, the media and poverty.[2] No matter how wide-ranging Xi's thoughts, however, he is not omniscient. In fact, 'Xi Jinping Thought' is not solely the product of his own brain, recorded in spare moments as he has managed the party, the army and the country, but rather it represents a layered compendium of old and new concepts, formulations and ideas developed over a prolonged period by a hive mind – a large group of theorists and experts who work for the party-state's sprawling knowledge-production apparatus.[3]

After decades of institutionalised collective leadership, one would expect the return to personalistic rule to leave very little room for diverging views,

---

Nadège Rolland is Distinguished Fellow, China Studies, at the National Bureau of Asian Research.

especially as the concentration of power in Xi's hands has been accompanied by an unprecedented anti-corruption campaign used to purge or intimidate potential opposing factions, arrogant cadres or critical voices.[4] Even high-ranking protégés, such as Admiral Miao Hua, a former member of the powerful Central Military Commission, have not been spared the ruthless scalpel of the party's Central Commission for Discipline Inspection.[5] For his third term as supreme ruler, Xi has chosen to surround himself with Politburo members believed to have been chosen primarily for their loyalty rather than on merit.[6] One would expect this to inhibit their ability to speak the truth or to share any original thoughts with the leader. As French Army General Hubert Lyautey reportedly said, 'When heels click at my arrival, I hear brains shutting down'. The enforcement of strict ideological discipline among the lower party ranks might also be expected to discourage genuine debate or the development of alternative views, while enhancing the prospect of groupthink.[7]

Yet Xi – unlike Mao Zedong and Deng Xiaoping, who tended to make decisions alone – values expert knowledge and has urged Chinese intellectuals to participate in policymaking. In that sense, he takes after Jiang Zemin and Hu Jintao, who regularly sought advice from experts drawn from national think tanks and academia, especially on economic and international issues. More often than is generally acknowledged, Xi's agenda builds on and accelerates plans already initiated by his predecessors. This is certainly true of Xi's grand strategy. Most of the concepts in this domain that now bear Xi's imprint emerged within the Chinese strategic community years before he rose to power – in some cases, before the end of the Cold War.

China's strategic thinkers
One can only speculate about the reasons for the inclusion of specific concepts in Xi Jinping Thought. It's possible they are more compatible with Xi's personal vision than that of his predecessors. Their proponents may belong to factions that have lately become more influential within the party-state apparatus. Or they may be the products of exceptionally far-sighted individuals whose early insights now align more closely with China's material power and strategic environment. Whatever the case, it is

worth becoming familiar with some of the thinkers who have contributed to the current leadership's vision of China as a world power with expanded interests and global influence.

The portraits presented here represent only a fraction of a larger group of academics, military and intelligence officers, and bureaucrats who have contributed to the elaboration of China's current grand strategy, as described in my study for the National Bureau of Asian Research, 'Mapping China's Strategic Space'.[8] Although they may employ differing language or approaches, all of these men (female voices are extremely rare in these discussions) share similar views about China's great-power ambitions, which they usually describe in terms echoing those used by Western geopoliticians at the turn of the twentieth century. They portray the state as an organism that must expand to survive, but that must struggle for space in a world characterised by intense competition and hostile attempts to squeeze or choke it. While they have not publicly outlined any intention to achieve conquest by force, they all agree that it is necessary and inevitable that China position itself at the centre of the global system. The first three individuals profiled here have sought to delineate the geographical extent of China's power, whereas the last two are more focused on the ideological underpinnings of a China-led world order.

The military officer
As a member of the general staff in 1987, Senior Colonel Xu Guangyu pondered the implications of the recently defined national strategic goals for the Chinese armed forces. Two years earlier, the Central Military Commission had decided on a major doctrinal shift, instructing the People's Liberation Army (PLA) to move away from planning for a total war against a massive Soviet invasion to prepare instead for conflicts that could break out anywhere on China's periphery. The Chinese military would henceforth need to undertake a momentous transformation to become a force capable of projecting power away from the nation's frontiers. But to what extent, and in which directions?

Xu believed China needed to expand its horizons well beyond its national borders, not only for defensive reasons, but also to ensure China's future development as a great power. The country required 'vital space', he wrote in a *PLA Daily* article published in 1987, to allow it access to crucial resources and to enable its survival.[9] Expansion was in any case the natural consequence of the country's growing might, propelled by scientific and technological advances. If Beijing was to lay the foundations for becoming a global power by 2049, the 100th anniversary of the People's Republic, then expansion across multiple dimensions would be necessary, according to Xu. The country would need to expand its presence in both tangible realms (the high seas and seabeds, polar regions and outer space) and invisible ones (ideology and spheres of influence).

After his retirement from the PLA Air Force in 1994 with the rank of major-general, Xu joined the China Arms Control and Disarmament Association and became a regular commentator on strategic issues for Chinese national television networks. His vision of expanding China's 'strategic space' was ultimately incorporated in the 2013 'Science of Military Strategy', one of the PLA's most authoritative doctrinal publications. The 2015 National Security Law included for the first time a reference to 'outer space, international seabed areas and polar regions' as spaces the Chinese state would explore and use, and where it would seek to preserve 'the security of our nation's activities and assets'.[10]

The international-relations professor
Wang Jisi's contribution to China's grand strategy is most evident in post-2008 discussions that led to the formulation of the Belt and Road plan. He is also believed to have played a crucial role in the development of Hu's 'peaceful rise' theory in the early 2000s, together with Zheng Bijian.[11] The two men were for a short while colleagues at the Central Party School (CPS) and, according to Alex Joske, were close to intelligence and state-security circles at the time.[12] As director of the school's Institute for International Strategic Studies, Wang also worked until 2009 with Xi (who headed the CPS from 2007 to 2012). In addition to working as a professor of international studies at Peking University and publishing widely in US foreign-affairs journals, Wang was a member of the Foreign Policy Advisory Committee of China's Foreign Ministry from 2008 to 2016. During that period, he was involved in

domestic discussions that acknowledged China's growing material power while raising concerns about a perceived intensification of US-led containment efforts and insisting on the need to find a suitable new grand strategy for China. His intellectual leadership is manifest in thought pieces such as 'Marching Westward: The Rebalancing of China's Geostrategy', an essay first published by Peking University in October 2012, which advocates China's investment in its continental backyard to counterbalance the newly announced US maritime 'pivot' to Asia.[13]

Although Wang's idea was widely debated within China's strategic community and supported by PLA heavyweights such as General Peng Guangqian, it was only one of several strategic propositions under discussion at the time. Other academics closer to PLA circles, such as Zhang Wenmu and Ni Lexiong, had for much of the preceding decade been calling for China to become a sea power instead, which would necessitate a significant naval build-up.[14] They envisioned a massive extension of China's ability to project power to far seas, starting with the Indian and Pacific oceans. Meanwhile, a third group of analysts connected to China's intelligence and state-security apparatus were exploring a different proposal for China's expansion, embracing both its maritime and its continental backyards.

By summer 2013, Wang's prescription for China's grand strategy had evolved dramatically. He called for China to be positioned at the centre of an extended territory covering the Eurasian continent, the Western Pacific and the Indian oceans, and including Africa, Europe and the greater Middle East – a vast zone that the 2013 edition of 'Science of Military Strategy' described as 'crucial … in influencing our nation's strategic development and security in the future', and that corresponded with the geography of the yet-to-be-announced Belt and Road Initiative.[15]

The intelligence analyst
In 2004, a group of experts from the 11th bureau of the Ministry of State Security (MSS), better known externally as the China Institutes of Contemporary International Relations (CICIR), were invited to share their thoughts about the geographies of China's expanded power.[16] As Hu was promoting the creation of a 'harmonious world' and giving new missions

to the PLA, China's strategic community was warily observing the 'colour revolutions' unfolding in the former Soviet space, which they saw as the product of US containment manoeuvres. Lu Zhongwei, a Japan expert newly installed as president of CICIR who would become vice-minister of the MSS in 2011; Fu Mengzi, the current vice-president of CICIR who was then director of its Institute of American Studies; and Chen Xiangyang, an analyst then working for CICIR's Security and Strategy Institute who later became director of its World Politics Institute, concurred in their assessment that, instead of focusing narrowly on China's neighbours, Beijing should start working towards the creation of a 'greater periphery' made up of countries that shared interests with and were connected to China by security, economic, trade, energy and cultural ties.

In the decade that followed, Chen regularly called for China to incorporate six subregions (Northeast Asia, Southeast Asia, South Asia, Central Asia, the Middle East and the South Pacific) into its 'greater periphery', and urged China's leadership to design a dedicated strategy to better integrate these areas in support of the country's leading position on the global stage. Yuan Peng, another vice-president of CICIR, described this 'greater periphery' in 2013 as China's gateway to 'dash out of Asia and walk into the world'.[17] In October that year, on the heels of launching the Belt and Road Initiative, Xi convened an inaugural central conference on 'periphery diplomacy'. He stressed that he saw regions bordering China as 'strategically significant' not only because of their geographic proximity, but also because of their political and economic ties with China.[18] Beijing's diplomacy henceforth replaced the traditional term 'neighbourhood' with 'periphery', which implicitly situates China at the core.

The ideologue

China's most notorious 'scholar-official' (a former academic who has joined the party bureaucracy) is undoubtedly Wang Huning, whom Chris Buckley described in the *New York Times* as the CCP's 'most influential ideological adviser in decades'.[19] A former professor of international politics and dean of Fudan University's law school, Wang is currently the fourth-ranking member of the Politburo Standing Committee. He left academia to join the

CCP's Central Policy Research Office (CPRO) in 1995, which he eventually chaired for 18 years, until October 2020. The office is responsible for drafting the party's most important documents and leaders' speeches, and for providing recommendations regarding party construction, ideology and theory. In short, it is the party's core ideological factory. During his time at the CPRO, Wang is believed to have personally helped craft key slogans that defined the successive tenures of Jiang, Hu and Xi.[20] Wang favours a strong, authoritarian state under the unyielding dominance of the party to lead the nation's re-establishment as a great power, in competition with the West. This vision, nurtured at the highest levels of the CCP, is shared by a widening cadre of public intellectuals who support a strong leader, a strong party and a strong country, and serve as 'champions, even official advisers, defending and honing the party's hardening policies'.[21]

The legal scholar
Among the so-called 'statist' intellectuals who favour a strong China, legal scholar Jiang Shigong stands out. An expert on Hong Kong's constitution and legal system, Jiang is a proponent of the superiority of political sovereignty over the rule of law. He is believed to be the author of the June 2014 State Council White Paper on 'The Practice of the "One Country, Two Systems" Policy in the Hong Kong Special Administrative Region', which defends the right of the central government to act in Hong Kong while disregarding any legal restrictions.[22] Together with a growing group of Chinese theorists and legal scholars, Jiang's thought draws heavily from the late German jurist and political theorist Carl Schmitt, a staunch critic of liberalism and parliamentary democracy, and an active supporter of National Socialism.[23]

Jiang's personal influence increased as Xi began his second term as China's supreme leader thanks to the publication of a long essay extolling the historical significance of the 'Xi Jinping era' for the party, the country and humankind.[24] Once the director of the legal research centre of Peking University, Jiang was promoted in October 2023 to vice-president of Minzu University of China (*minzu* means 'nationalities' or 'ethnicities'). Jiang is not a government official in the Western sense: he does not work for a state ministry or commission, nor for a party organ or committee. But he's also not an academic in the Western sense: Minzu University is affiliated with the National Ethnic Affairs Commission, a body under the direct control of the CCP Central Committee's United Front Work Department. Jiang's work has focused not just on domestic but also on international orders – specifically world empires and civilisations – and on redefining political universalism. He has argued that China can serve as a shining alternative to the West and act on behalf of the world as a whole.[25]

Concepts to watch
China's grand strategy is still a work in progress. Having resolved the question of the physical scope of China's strategic space a decade ago, there is still much for Chinese policymakers to discuss regarding how its 'intangible' spaces – the ideological realm and China's sphere of influence as identified four decades ago by Colonel Xu – should be shaped. Many of the concepts that have gained prominence in Xi's 'new era' cluster around two main themes, civilisation and modernity.

These themes reflect the CCP's desire to present itself and its agenda as the only desirable political path for China, and as an inspiring alternative model for the rest of the world – one that is applicable to 'any country that wants to speed up their development while preserving their independence'.[26] The unspoken objective is to perpetuate the party's monopoly on power domestically by refuting the supposedly universal suitability of the liberal-democratic model, which constitutes the ultimate threat to its survival. Whether by design or as an unintended consequence, this foreshadows the creation of a new sphere of influence in which the China model is not only respected but emulated, and from which the West is excluded as irrelevant.

Since 2021, Xi has increasingly pushed the concept of 'Chinese-style modernisation' alongside his promotion of a dialogue among 'civilisations', which the Global Civilization Initiative was founded in early 2023 to encourage.[27] Chinese understandings of both concepts carry at their core a rejection of the West, construed as the source of all ills, while promising a non-Western path exemplified by China's own economic and political achievements. Both are intended to speak to those in non-Western countries, particularly in the developing world, who may not identify with the values that underpin the post-1945 international system.

Party theorists, whose main role is to engage in the exegesis of CCP scriptures, usually define Chinese-style modernity in opposition to its Western nemesis. They assert that whereas capitalist-based modernisation has led to the sins of individualism and hedonism, China's model can deliver common prosperity and a harmonious balance between the material and the spiritual, humanity and nature. Likewise, Chinese and Western civilisations are characterised as fundamentally divergent. The Western approach to modernisation is described as dependent on imperialism, exploitation, oppression and violence. It has shown its limits and failed to deliver on its promises; it belongs to the dustbin of history. By contrast, China's option is presented as a shining vision for a prosperous and peaceful future, having inherited the 'genes' of traditional Chinese culture, which values peace, harmony, benevolence and inclusiveness. This intentional reading of ancient Chinese philosophy and history as intrinsically peaceful is accompanied and supported by the works of a growing cohort of Chinese intellectuals, such as Yan Xuetong, who has elaborated a theory combining material power with 'humane authority' leading to a stable hierarchical order; Qin Yaqing, who explored international relations through a Confucian (also hierarchical) prism; and philosopher Zhao Tingyang, who has been revisiting the traditional concept of *tianxia* ('everything under heaven') as a future alternative 'world society', transcending borders and legitimised by its presumed moral values rather than the ballot box.[28]

A report jointly published in 2024 by the Institute of Party History and Literature and the Xinhua Institute, respectively housed within the CCP Central Committee and the State Council, notes that liberal democracy does not represent the culmination of human evolution, nor the end of history.[29] Rather, China is 'leading the world's new trend of modernization' and is showing the way towards the creation of a 'new form of human civilization'.[30] Such formulations echo the triumphant tone of a speech delivered by Xi in February 2023, in which he claimed that China offers an 'alternative model for developing countries to modernize', and provides a 'Chinese solution for mankind to explore a better social system'. He also debunked the 'myth' that Westernisation is synonymous with modernisation, a point that had been made some years earlier by Samuel Huntington.[31] Such instances of uncanny similarity between Chinese and Western thinking serve as reminders that China's grand strategy continues to draw inspiration from Western ideas, even as the party-state urges its knowledge-production apparatus to create and develop a 'discourse system' that is distinct from Western concepts and practices.

* * *

As challenging as it may be, particularly at a time when Beijing is working to restrict foreign access to information, it is imperative for external observers to continue to track intellectual trends within China's strategic community and to understand the structures and processes that encourage the creation, development and dissemination of intellectual contributions to Chinese policy. Given that some of the men introduced here can be expected to depart the public stage soon due to old age, China watchers will need to identify their successors and wrestle with their ideas. Who will fill the shoes of Wang Jisi or Xu Guangyu, and what do they think about?

Notes

1. China Media Project, 'Observations on the 19th Congress Report', 24 October 2017, https://chinamediaproject.org/2017/10/24/observations-on-the-19th-congress-report/.
2. China Media Project, 'Xi Jinping Thought on Socialism with Chinese Characteristics for a New Era', 27 March 2021, https://chinamediaproject.org/the_ccp_dictionary/xi-jinping-thought-on-socialism-with-chinese-characteristics-for-a-new-era/.
3. Shan Wei, Gu Yongxin and Chen Juan, 'Layering Ideologies from Deng Xiaoping to Xi Jinping: Tracing Ideological Changes of the Communist Party of China Using Text Analysis', *China: An International Journal*, vol. 21, no. 2, May 2023, pp. 26–50.
4. For more on 'personalistic rule' in contemporary China, see Susan L. Shirk, 'China in Xi's "New Era": The Return to Personalistic Rule', *Journal of Democracy*, vol. 29, no. 2, April 2018, pp. 22–36.
5. See Jonathan A. Czin, 'Thoughts on the Political Demise of Miao Hua', Brookings Institution, 18 February 2025, https://www.brookings.edu/articles/thoughts-on-the-political-demise-of-miao-hua/.

6 See Weiyi Cai et al., 'How Xi Returned China to One-man Rule', *New York Times*, 2 September 2023, https://www.nytimes.com/interactive/2023/09/02/world/asia/china-xi-rule.html.

7 See Jacob Stokes, 'Beyond China's Black Box: Five Trends Shaping Beijing's Foreign and Security Policy Decision-making Under Xi Jinping', CNAS, April 2024, https://s3.us-east-1.amazonaws.com/files.cnas.org/documents/BeyondChinasBlackBox_2024_Final.pdf.

8 Nadège Rolland, 'Mapping China's Strategic Space', NBR Special Report No. 111, September 2024, https://strategicspace.nbr.org/mapping-chinas-strategic-space-report/.

9 Xu Guangyu 徐光裕, 'Zhuiqiu heli de sanwei zhanlüe bianjiang' 追求合理的三维战略边疆 [Pursuit of equitable three-dimensional strategic boundaries], *PLA Daily*, 3 April 1987.

10 'National Security Law of the People's Republic of China', 1 July 2015, available from China Law Translate, https://www.chinalawtranslate.com/en/2015nsl/.

11 See Cheng Li, 'A Ladder to Power and Influence: China's Official Think Tanks to Watch', China–US Focus, 14 October 2022, https://www.chinausfocus.com/2022-CPC-congress/a-ladder-to-power-and-influence-chinas-official-think-tanks-to-watch.

12 Alex Joske, *Spies and Lies: How China's Greatest Covert Operations Fooled the World* (Melbourne: Hardie Grant Books, 2022), pp. 139–40.

13 Wang Jisi, 'Marching Westward: The Rebalancing of China's Geostrategy', Institute of International and Strategic Studies, Peking University, International and Strategic Studies Report No. 73, October 2012.

14 See Ralph D. Sawyer, James R. Holmes and Toshi Yoshihara, 'Chinese Naval Strategy in the 21st Century: The Turn to Mahan', *Naval War College Review*, vol. 61, no. 2, Spring 2008, https://digital-commons.usnwc.edu/nwc-review/vol61/iss2/14.

15 Wang Jisi 王缉思, 'Zhongguo de quanqiu dingwei yu diyuanzhengzhi zhanlüe' 中国的全球定位与地缘政治战略 [China's global positioning and geostrategy], Aisixiang, 12 August 2013, https://www.aisixiang.com/data/66458.html; and Chinese Academy of Military Science, Military Strategy Studies Department, 'The Science of Military Strategy (2013 Edition)', December 2013, p. 309, available from US Department of the Air Force, China Aerospace Studies Institute, https://www.airuniversity.af.edu/CASI/Display/Article/2485204/plas-science-of-military-strategy-2013/.

16 Lu Zhongwei et al., 'Jiedu Zhongguo da zhoubian' 解读中国大周边 [Interpreting China's greater periphery], *World Knowledge*, no. 24, 2004, pp. 20–8.

17 Yuan Peng 袁鹏, 'Guanyu xin shiqi Zhongguo da zhoubian zhanlüe de sikao' 关于新时期中国大周边战略的思考 [Reflections on China's periphery strategy in the new era], *Contemporary International Relations*, 2013.

18 'Xi Jinping zai zhoubian waijiao gongzuo zuotan hui shang fabiao zhongyao jianghua' 习近平在周边外交工作座谈会上发表重要讲话 [Xi Jinping delivers an important speech at the conference on periphery diplomacy work], Xinhua, 25 October

2013, http://www.xinhuanet.com//politics/2013-10/25/c_117878897.htm.

19 Chris Buckley, 'The Man Who Shaped China's Strongman Rule Has a New Job: Winning Taiwan', *New York Times*, 26 October 2024, https://www.nytimes.com/2024/10/26/world/asia/china-xi-jinping-adviser-taiwan.html.

20 See Jane Perlez, 'Behind the Scenes, Communist Strategist Presses China's Rise', *New York Times*, 13 November 2017, https://www.nytimes.com/2017/11/13/world/asia/china-xi-jinping-wang-huning.html.

21 Chris Buckley, '"Clean Up This Mess": The Chinese Thinkers Behind Xi's Hard Line', *New York Times*, 3 August 2020, https://www.nytimes.com/2020/08/02/world/asia/china-hong-kong-national-security-law.html.

22 State Council of the People's Republic of China, 'The Practice of the "One Country, Two Systems" Policy in the Hong Kong Special Administrative Region', June 2014, https://english.www.gov.cn/archive/white_paper/2014/08/23/content_281474982986578.htm. See also Sebastian Veg, 'The "Restructuring" of Hong Kong and the Rise of Neostatism', Tocqueville21, 27 June 2020, https://tocqueville21.com/le-club/the-restructuring-of-hong-kong-and-the-rise-of-neostatism/.

23 See Jackson T. Reinhardt, 'Totalitarian Friendship: Carl Schmitt in Contemporary China', *Inquiries Journal*, vol. 12, no. 7, 2020.

24 Jiang Shigong, 'Philosophy and History: Interpreting the "Xi Jinping Era" Through Xi's Report to the Nineteenth National Congress of the CCP', January 2018, available from Reading the China Dream, https://www.readingthechinadream.com/jiang-shigong-philosophy-and-history.html.

25 Jiang Shigong, 'The Internal Logic of Super-sized Political Entities: "Empire" and World Order', April 2019, available from Reading the China Dream, https://www.readingthechinadream.com/jiang-shigong-empire-and-world-order.html.

26 'Socialism with Chinese Characteristics Enters New Era', Xinhua, 18 October 2017, http://www.xinhuanet.com/english/2017-10/18/c_136688475.htm.

27 Deng Xiaoping reportedly first used the phrase in 1983 when meeting a foreign delegation: 'The modernization we are doing is Chinese-style modernization. The socialism we are building is socialism with Chinese characteristics.' See China Media Project Dictionary, 'Chinese-style Modernization', 12 May 2023, https://chinamediaproject.org/the_ccp_dictionary/chinese-style-modernization/.

28 For more details, see Nadège Rolland, 'China's Vision for a New World Order', NBR Special Report, no. 83, January 2020.

29 See Arran Hope, 'Foreign Fixations at the Heart of Chinese-style Modernization', *China Brief*, vol. 24, no. 10, 10 May 2024, https://jamestown.org/program/foreign-fixations-at-the-heart-of-chinese-style-modernization/.

30 See *ibid.*; and David Bandurski, 'New Form of Human Civilization', China Media Project Dictionary, 6 November 2023, https://chinamediaproject.org/the_ccp_dictionary/new-form-of-human-civilization/.

31 For Xi's comments, see Xinlu Liang, 'Xi Jinping Hails China Modernization Miracle as Path for Developing Countries', *South China Morning Post*, 8 February 2023, https://www.scmp.com/news/china/politics/article/3209450/xi-hails-china-modernisation-miracle-path-developing-countries. Samuel Huntington wrote in 1996 that 'modernization … does not necessarily mean Westernization. Non-Western societies can modernize and have modernized without abandoning their own cultures and adopting wholesale Western values, institutions, and practices … In fundamental ways, the world is becoming more modern and less Western.' Samuel P. Huntington, *The Clash of Civilizations and the Remaking of World Order* (New York: Touchstone, 1996), p. 78.

South Korea's Resilient Democracy

Ramon Pacheco Pardo

The shock of the martial-law declaration by Yoon Suk-yeol, then president of South Korea, on 3 December 2024 was met by a swift vote of the National Assembly to overturn it; clear opposition by a large majority of South Koreans; a unanimous vote by judges in the Constitutional Court to uphold Yoon's impeachment; and the resounding victory of opposition candidate Lee Jae-myung in the election on 3 June 2025, exactly six months after Yoon's declaration.[1] History may well record that Yoon's declaration was the last gasp of those who believed that South Koreans prefer authoritarianism over democracy. In the end, South Korea's democracy won. It was a clear victory, leaving no doubt about the resilience of the country's institutional set-up and strong societal support for the democratic rules that have governed the country since October 1987.

True, the martial-law declaration came at a time of growing populism and political polarisation across democratic countries, including those in Asia. Populism in South Korea may not have reached the same levels seen in other countries, but the justification that Yoon offered for his declaration – alleged cooperation between South Korean liberals and North Korea to overthrow the country's democracy – shows that there are South Korean politicians of a populist bent.[2] The strength of the institutional response to Yoon's declaration, however, indicates that South Korean democracy has

---

Ramon Pacheco Pardo is Professor of International Relations and head of the Department of European and International Studies at King's College London; Regional Envoy for East and Southeast Asia, King's College London; and KF-VUB Korea Chair, Brussels School of Governance, Vrije Universiteit Brussel.

matured to the point that no single individual can threaten it. In fact, the peaceful transition of power and the behaviour of the losing party after the 2022 and 2025 elections underscore this point. Back in 2022, Lee lost the election to Yoon by the narrowest margin in South Korean history: a mere 0.7% of the vote separated the two candidates.[3] Lee and the Democratic Party of Korea (DP), however, immediately accepted the result. This time, Lee won by a wide margin: 8.3%. Kim Moon-soo and his People Power Party (PPP) accepted the decision of the South Korean voters without hesitation.[4]

Lee now faces the tasks of healing South Korea's political divide and moving ahead with an ambitious socio-economic agenda, while driving South Korean foreign policy at a time of international turmoil.

An experienced politician

Lee's life story is well known to South Koreans, given his long political career. The fifth of seven siblings, Lee was born in 1963 and sought employment rather than attend middle school to help support his family. While working in a factory, he suffered an accident that permanently damaged his arm. Nevertheless, he was eventually able to finish school and complete a law degree at Chung-Ang University in Seoul. He then worked as a labour lawyer before launching his political career in the 2000s. Lee was first elected mayor of Seongnam, a city located south of Seoul, in 2010, serving until 2018. He then served as the governor of Gyeonggi, the province surrounding Seoul, from 2018 to 2021. Making the jump to national politics, Lee became the DP's presidential candidate in 2022. While this candidacy was unsuccessful, Lee was elected to the National Assembly later that same year.[5] He finally became South Korean president in June 2025.

The new president has shown himself to be a pragmatic politician and a political survivor. During his time as Seongnam mayor and Gyeonggi governor, he adopted policies that many would consider to be leftist, such as offering universal basic income to young people and universal relief grants during the COVID-19 pandemic, while showing his willingness to work with the *chaebol* or big conglomerates that dominate the South Korean economy.[6] In fact, Lee ran for the South Korean presidency on a pro-growth and business-friendly platform, meeting with the president of the Federation of Korean Industries and with several *chaebol* leaders during his campaign. Shortly after becoming president and before attending the G7 summit in Canada, Lee met with *chaebol* leaders once more to pledge business-friendly reforms.[7]

Lee did bring some baggage with him to the presidency. He faces several cases in the South Korean court system dating to his time in Seongnam and Gyeonggi. These cases relate to alleged election interference and corruption.[8] This is the first time that a sitting president has faced court cases in the history of democratic South Korea. The country's presidents are immune from criminal prosecution while in office, except on charges of rebellion or treason. Thus, there is a debate in the South Korean judiciary about whether to pause the cases against Lee until he steps down.[9]

Regardless of his legal troubles, Lee has a strong mandate. The DP now forms a supermajority in the National Assembly, where it holds 171 seats (other liberal parties hold an additional 17 seats) out of 300.[10] With National Assembly elections not due again until spring 2028, Lee will enjoy three years of this supermajority, and could conceivably work with a DP majority for the last two years of his single five-year term as well. Furthermore, the PPP and broader conservative movement will face limitations while in opposition as they seek to rebuild in time for the 2028 National Assembly and 2030 presidential elections.

Differences to overcome

South Korean elections are still won by attracting non-partisan voters, and Lee reached out to them as well as to conservative voters during his campaign. The results of the election suggest that this strategy was at least partially successful, as he performed well in traditional conservative strongholds including Busan, Ulsan and South Gyeongsang Province.[11]

At the same time, Lee is a polarising figure. Throughout his career, he has been outspoken and prone to bombastic remarks. Many conservative and non-partisan voters dislike his style. Meanwhile, his willingness to reach beyond the liberal party and its traditional supporters, such as trade unions, does not sit well with some groups within the liberal movement.[12] It is no secret that many within the DP would have liked to field a different candidate in the 2022 election, before Lee led the party to a strong performance in the 2024 National Assembly elections.[13] While Lee noticeably moderated his style and messaging during the recent presidential election, and faced no strong challenge to his nomination as the DP candidate, there are groups that might seek to undermine his presidency.

There have been calls in South Korea for Lee to heal the country's political divide, but this would be a difficult proposition in any consolidated democracy. Most South Koreans agree that they want their country to remain democratic, and are proud of the way citizens forced the authoritarian regime of the 1980s to transition away from dictatorial rule.[14] However, in a democracy there will inevitably be competing views on policy.[15] Lee, unlike South Korea's pre-democratic rulers, will not be able to coerce agreement from those who oppose him. Nonetheless, Lee could still take certain steps to bridge the gap between liberals and conservatives. To begin with, he could work to pass major legislation with the PPP in areas in which both parties broadly agree, such as the need for government–private sector cooperation to boost growth and innovation. Lee could also reach out to the PPP to tackle what some believe is the judicialisation of South Korean politics, so as to clearly separate the judiciary from political and policymaking processes. He could also engage in regular dialogue with the leaders of the opposition, a practice that Yoon shunned.

If anything, Lee should be careful in the use of his supermajority. Since South Korea transitioned to democracy in 1987, the country's population has been wary of a single individual or party wielding too much power. South Korea has been characterised as having an 'imperial presidency', its president supposedly able to decide and implement policy unopposed.[16] Yet Yoon's time in office showed that, with the possible exception of foreign policy, this was not true. The former president's inability to reach out to the DP-controlled National Assembly or even to the PPP caucus paralysed his domestic-policy agenda. In fact, another justification given by Yoon for his martial-law declaration was the opposition's use of its supermajority to block his legislative agenda.[17]

> *Lee noticeably moderated his style and messaging*

Lee will need to consult with his own party, and voters will probably expect him to reach out to the opposition. Otherwise, he might find that his popularity plunges much as Yoon's did.[18] During his time as leader of the opposition, Lee's critics accused him of using impeachment proceedings against members and appointees of the Yoon government, as well as the judiciary, as a means to impede the normal functioning of South Korean institutions. Lee will need to consider whether launching impeachment proceedings against his political opponents or the judiciary is a wise move, since voters could think that he is simply targeting those with different political views. Furthermore, liberal politicians will not take long to start preparing for the 2028 National Assembly and 2030 presidential elections, when Lee will be obliged to leave office. Ambitious lawmakers seeking to present themselves as the next DP presidential candidate could well assemble an opposition bloc within the liberal caucus.[19]

Lee has proposed reforming the presidential system to allow presidents to serve two four-year terms, as in the United States.[20] The rationale is that this would make presidents more accountable to the people. At the same time, Lee has suggested that the National Assembly should be given a greater voice in the policymaking process.[21] Lee is not the first politician to make these or similar suggestions to address the alleged winner-takes-all mentality that pervades South Korean democracy, and which is perceived to lead to dramatic shifts in policy when a new president takes office.[22] Yet reform has been elusive. Were Lee to pursue this reform without announcing that he would not run for a second term himself, voters could interpret this as self-seeking and turn against him.

Meanwhile, the PPP and the conservative movement more broadly are facing a moment of reckoning. The impeachment of the last two conservative presidents, the wide margin of Kim's loss to Lee in the June election, and heavy defeats in the National Assembly elections of 2020 and 2024 indicate the need for renewal and generational change.[23] Thus, the PPP could decide to support some policies of the Lee government to promote economic growth as a way of showing that it can play a constructive role and will be ready for office by 2028 or 2030. Yet the PPP base voted for Kim as their party's candidate even after he had failed to distance himself from Yoon's deeply unpopular martial-law declaration.[24] It remains to be seen whether PPP leaders can prevent the breakdown of the party, let alone attain stronger electability.

A society in crisis?

Several indicators suggest that South Korea is in a strong economic position. The country maintains high GDP per capita growth rates: as of April 2025, its GDP per capita (purchasing power parity) was higher than that of G7 members Italy, Japan and the United Kingdom.[25] South Korean workers enjoy the highest average salaries among Asia's major economies.[26] As of May 2025, the country's employment rate was the highest on record at almost 70%, and unemployment was below 3%.[27] Youth unemployment is low by global standards, measuring under 7% as of 2024.[28] The country set a new record in the value of its exports in 2024, as well as in inward-investment pledges.[29] Its trade partners are diversified, with China and the US amounting to a similar share, the Association of Southeast Asian Nations (ASEAN) following closely behind, and the European Union and Japan also being strong partners.[30] The South Korean economy is powered by innovation, and its cultural products are popular around the world.[31]

Many countries would be proud of such achievements, but not South Korea. South Korean economic culture is characterised by a perpetual sense of crisis, which has helped to drive growth, but also prevents policymakers, businesspeople and the general population from enjoying the country's success. An incomplete list of the real or imaginary crises that have underpinned South Korea's quest for economic growth includes the Korean War and the threat of new invasions by North Korea in the 1950s and 1960s; the assassination of Park Chung-hee and the country's inability to transition to democracy in the late 1970s and early 1980s; China's opening up in the 1980s and the accompanying fears that South Korea would be unable to compete; and the dread of being sandwiched between low-cost China and high-tech Japan in the 1990s and 2000s. Today, South Korean distress is driven by the idea that the country has reached 'peak Korea', and will henceforth lose its status as a developed, high-tech economy and cultural trendsetter.[32] This is coupled with anxieties about the end of the US-led liberal international order that has served South Korea so well over the decades.

This sense of crisis is not entirely unjustified. The United States under Donald Trump has apparently embraced economic nationalism and begun to use tariffs against its trade partners. China's economy is increasingly tech-driven, and the country is in direct competition with South Korea in sectors such as electric vehicles and electric batteries. North Korea's nuclear and missile programmes pose a constant threat, with implications for South Korean policy and budget decisions.

South Korea faces significant socio-economic issues as well. The era of high GDP growth is most likely over now that the country has achieved a high level of development.[33] This will require some mental adjustment among those accustomed to the high growth rates of previous decades. South Korea has a low birth rate, and even though this started to increase along with marriage rates in 2024, it is still not expected to reach replacement level.[34] The result is that South Korea will have to grapple with an ageing population. This may be offset to some extent by migration, as South Korea becomes more multicultural and marriages with foreign-born spouses become more common, but multiculturalism still needs to be carefully managed.[35]

South Korean policymakers and businesspeople are aware of these pressures, and agree on some of the ways in which they might be addressed. The country has been pushing for trade and investment diversification for well over a decade now. After betting heavily on China as a production base and potential market in the 2000s, South Korean firms started to move to alternative production locations in the 2010s. There has also been a push to open new markets for South Korean products in Latin America, the Middle East and South Asia.[36] And while South Korea is best known for its high-tech and cultural products, its exports encompass a diverse range of sectors, including beauty, cuisine, gaming, tourism and webtoons.[37] Indeed, the latter sector was pioneered by South Korean firms in the early 2000s and has now gone global. Following the Asian Financial Crisis of 1997–98, then-president Kim Dae-jung identified the export of cultural products as a way to support the recovery and diversification of the South Korean economy. Time has shown that this was the right policy, with South Korean cultural products and related industries becoming popular globally since the turn of the twenty-first century.

Closely linked to this internationalisation and diversification is the open innovation model that South Korea has been promoting at least since the 1997–98 crisis. Successive South Korean governments fostered a model in which government, *chaebol* and start-ups work together to benefit from each other's strengths. For example, the government might provide funding for a start-up with an innovative idea that is then mass produced and sold internationally in partnership with a *chaebol*.[38] While some may argue that open innovation only entrenches the advantages of big conglomerates over smaller firms, this model is suitable for a country in which the leading *chaebol* are very unlikely to collapse.

Arguably the biggest domestic problem faced by South Korea are the labour shortages that have plagued the South Korean economy. To address this, South Korean leaders seem to have settled on a three-pronged strategy. Firstly, South Korea is promoting greater labour-force participation, especially among women and the elderly. South Korea's female-employment rate stood at 63.1% at the end of 2024, which is below the Organisation for Economic Co-operation and Development (OECD) average.[39] The days when married women would quit their jobs to raise children are long gone, yet many workers continue to feel unwelcome once they get married or decide to have babies. More could be done to change attitudes and support female workers. Meanwhile, South Korea's effective retirement age is towards the lower end of the OECD average, and the South Korean government is pushing to raise this, and to create more jobs for the elderly.[40]

In addition, South Korea is at the forefront of automating various economic processes. The country has the highest rate of industrial robots per worker in the world – at the end of 2023, there were 1,012 robots per 10,000 employees – placing it well ahead of Singapore, China and Germany, the next three countries on the list.[41] This has helped South Korea to retain factories that otherwise might have been moved to lower-cost locations. The service industry is also undergoing rapid automation.[42] These sectors are typically shunned by South Korean workers, a problem the government believes can be solved by automation.

Finally, the South Korea of today is much more open to migration than the South Korea of 20 years ago. At the end of 2024, migrants represented 5.2% of South Korea's total population, a lower level than that seen in Europe or North America.[43] Yet this surpasses the OECD threshold to be classified as multicultural – a significant development in a country that was among the most homogeneous in the world until the late twentieth century. China, Vietnam, Thailand and other Asian countries account for a significant share of migrants to South Korea, followed by the US, Europe, Canada and Australia.[44] Migrants are mainly divided between those filling white-collar jobs, particularly in *chaebol* and foreign multinational firms, and those taking jobs in factories, health services and the agricultural sector.

As for South Korea's low birth rate, successive South Korean governments have implemented a raft of policies to support new parents.[45] However, the main reason behind the country's low birth rate is a decline in marriages. For young South Koreans, whether to get married and have babies has become a lifestyle choice rather than a near-universal milestone.[46] That more than 95% of babies are born to married parents in South Korea, compared to less than half in Europe or the US, has implications for the country's birth rate.[47] While a large and growing share of South Koreans in their 20s and 30s support parents' choice to have babies outside of wedlock, it remains to be seen whether this will lead to a change in behaviour.[48] The marriage rate is going up, but there seems to be little the government can do to boost the birth rate, given that South Koreans today feel far less pressure than in the past to have children.

> *The marriage rate is going up*

Lee's moderation of his economic platform seems to be a nod to the bipartisan consensus that characterises South Korea's approach to socio-economic policy. Cooperation between the government and the private sector to promote diversified trade and investment has long been a South Korean tool to promote the goal of economic growth. South Korean policymakers and businesspeople understand that working together benefits the country as a whole, and the private sector in particular. Lee has already indicated that he doesn't plan to deviate from this strategy. As a presidential candidate, he made constant references to a pro-growth economic agenda. He courted *chaebol* leaders while also promising to support small and medium-sized enterprises, and start-ups. He has also announced huge investments in high-tech sectors such as artificial intelligence and semiconductors.[49] Lee has also promised to expand the welfare state, including support for new parents, as a means to boost the South Korean labour force. At the same time, he has prioritised negotiations with the Trump administration to reduce or even remove the tariffs on key South Korean sectors, such as vehicles, vehicle parts and steel.[50] He has indicated that he will strive to improve relations with China after they deteriorated during the Yoon presidency, while also seeking to sustain the improvement in South Korea–Japan relations that characterised Yoon's years in office.[51] China continues to be one of South Korea's key economic partners (along with the US), while Japan is one of its top-five trading partners. By following South Korea's time-tested economic recipe and working with as many domestic economic actors and foreign partners as possible, Lee could demonstrate his pragmatism.

Implications for South Korea's foreign policy

Lee's focus on economic growth, coupled with the country's decades-old grand strategy, means that we should expect little change in the foreign policies he inherited from his most recent predecessors, Yoon and Moon Jae-in.[52] These two presidents faced an international environment marked by open Sino-American competition in areas including trade and technology; an assertive China under Xi Jinping; and a more nationalistic US, as seen in the economic policies of the first Trump administration and, to an extent, of the Biden administration.

Yoon and Moon responded to these developments in a similar way. To begin with, they doubled down on the South Korea–US alliance, and on efforts to diversify the economy. Moon agreed to the renegotiation of the South Korea–US free-trade agreement (KORUS), with South Korea being the first country to renegotiate a trade agreement with Trump; signed trade agreements with countries such as Cambodia and Indonesia; and promoted arms exports as a new engine of growth.[53] Yoon encouraged South Korean investment in the US; signed trade agreements with the Gulf Cooperation

Council and the Philippines; and promoted the export of armaments and semiconductors.[54] Both presidents were regularly accompanied by large business delegations during their foreign trips. Less discussed but equally relevant, South Korean firms and universities cultivated ties with their US counterparts in the area of innovation.[55] A prominent example was the decision by LG to cooperate with Boston Dynamics, a humanoid-robotics firm.[56] This is a sector that both the South Korean government and the private sector wish to prioritise.

Neither Yoon nor Moon pursued economic decoupling from China. Although the combined share of South Korean exports going to mainland China and Hong Kong has decreased from a peak of 34.4% in 2018 to 23.7% in 2024, China remains an important production base and export destination for South Korean firms.[57] This is particularly the case for intermediate goods that South Korean firms use in their Chinese factories.[58] Nevertheless, South Korea has been seeking to minimise the riskiness of its exposure to China. In common with the US and its allies and partners, South Korean firms in sectors such as semiconductors, electric vehicles and electric batteries do not produce the latest technologies in China.[59] If forced to choose between China and the US, South Korea's preference for the latter is clear.

Lee may even double down on some of his predecessors' approaches. For example, the Lee government may want to resume formal negotiations to join the Comprehensive and Progressive Agreement for Trans-Pacific Partnership (CPTPP). The Park government refused to join CPTPP negotiations, preferring to focus on free-trade negotiations with China.[60] The Moon government decided to enter negotiations, only to run out of time.[61] The Yoon government did not follow up. Yet the growing inability of the World Trade Organization to set the rules of the game means it would be sensible for South Korea to join alternative agreements. Similarly, Lee may take advantage of South Korea having become the first Asian country to join Europe's flagship innovation initiative, Horizon Europe.[62] The Lee government could encourage South Korean universities and research centres to pursue collaborative projects with their European counterparts. As for the US, Lee is more likely than not to encourage deeper trade, investment and technology ties.

Then there is the issue of North Korea. Relations between South and North Korea stalled during the Yoon government. There were several factors leading to this: the collapse of inter-Korean dialogue towards the end of the Moon government, North Korea's decision to cut ties with the outside world during the COVID-19 pandemic and Yoon's own confrontational approach towards Pyongyang. Lee has promised to restore inter-Korean dialogue and engagement, in cooperation with the US. He has acknowledged, however, that this will be difficult given the current state of inter-Korean relations and North Korea's burgeoning ties with Russia.

*   *   *

Yoon's December 2024 martial-law declaration came as a shock to South Koreans and foreigners alike. Yet it has served to demonstrate that South Korea has a consolidated democracy, with a strong institutional set-up that no individual can realistically hope to subvert. As unwelcome as the declaration was, it should discourage future presidents or others from the idea that they can overturn the democratic system that South Koreans fought so hard to achieve.

Lee has taken office after an unexpectedly decisive electoral win. This gives him a strong mandate, which, coupled with the supermajority that the DP enjoys in the National Assembly, means that the new president has the power to pursue his preferred domestic and foreign-policy agenda at least until National Assembly elections take place in 2028.

Of course, with great power comes great responsibility. South Koreans expect the new president to address a range of short-term and structural issues. These include an unstable international environment, lower GDP growth than in decades past, and low birth rates coupled with the consequence of an ageing population or higher rates of inward migration. South Koreans expect Lee to work together with both the DP's lawmakers in the National Assembly and the conservative opposition, while limiting confrontation with those who think differently from him. In short, voters do not want Lee to continue the approach pursued by Yoon. Lee will need to build on the country's existing strengths, including a robust democracy, a strong and tech-driven economy, diversified economic relations and strong soft-power resources to ensure that the country continues to thrive.

Notes

1. See Ramon Pacheco Pardo, 'Lee Jae-myung's 2025 Presidential Election Victory', Centre for Security, Diplomacy and Strategy, 3 June 2025, https://csds.vub.be/publication/lee-jae-myungs-2025-presidential-election-victory/.
2. See Kim Eun-jung, 'Yoon Declares Emergency Martial Law; Parliament Votes to Lift Decree', Yonhap News, 4 December 2024, https://en.yna.co.kr/view/AEN20241203012155315.
3. Ramon Pacheco Pardo, *Shrimp to Whale: South Korea from the Forgotten War to K-Pop* (London: C. Hurst & Co., 2022), p. 207.
4. See Pacheco Pardo, 'Lee Jae-myung's 2025 Presidential Election Victory'.
5. See Lee Soo-jung, 'A Life Pursuit: Lee Jae-myung's Journey from Factory Worker to Presidential Front-runner', *Korea JoongAng Daily*, 16 May 2025, https://koreajoongangdaily.joins.com/news/2025-05-16/national/politics/A-life-pursuit-Lee-Jaemyungs-journey-from-factory-worker-to-presidential-frontrunner/2307212.
6. See Lee Haye-ah, 'Outspoken and Aggressive, Lee Jae-myung Faces Challenges Head On', Yonhap News, 10 October 2021, https://en.yna.co.kr/view/AEN20211008006400315; and Kelly Casulis Cho, 'Lee Jae-myung Is a Technocrat with Hardscrabble Origins', *New York Times*, 9 March 2022, https://www.nytimes.com/2022/03/08/world/asia/lee-jae-myung-south-korea.html.
7. See Yi Wonju, 'Lee Vows to Lift Unnecessary Regulations, Offer Trade Support for Companies', Yonhap News, 13 June 2025, https://en.yna.co.kr/view/AEN20250613005900315.
8. See 'Legal Challenges Facing South Korea's Incoming President Lee Jae-myung', Reuters, 3 June 2025, https://www.reuters.com/world/asia-pacific/legal-challenges-facing-south-koreas-incoming-president-lee-jae-myung-2025-06-03/.
9. 'South Korea President Lee's Election Law Violation Hearing Postponed Indefinitely, Court Says', Reuters, 9 June 2025, https://www.reuters.com/world/asia-pacific/south-korea-president-lees-election-law-violation-hearing-postponed-indefinitely-2025-06-09/.
10. National Assembly of the Republic of Korea, 'Current Members', https://korea.assembly.go.kr:447/portalEn/assm/mmbrby/memSearch.do?menuNo=1500086.
11. National Election Commission, 'Je21dae daetongryeongseongeo' 제21대 대통령선거 [21st presidential election], http://info.nec.go.kr/.
12. See Gavin Butler and Yuna Ku, 'Lee Jae-myung: How Political Chaos Forged South Korea's New President', BBC News, 27 May 2025, https://www.bbc.co.uk/news/articles/c4gepwxzeqg0.
13. See Josh Smith and Sangmi Cha, 'S. Korea's Lee Wins Ruling Party Primary in Presidential Race

Overshadowed by Scandal', Reuters, 10 October 2021, https://www.reuters.com/world/asia-pacific/skoreas-lee-seeks-primary-win-presidential-race-overshadowed-by-scandal-2021-10-10/; and Kim Eun-jung, 'Ex-DP Chief Wins Sweeping Victory in Primary of Party Leadership on 1st Day', Yonhap News, 20 July 2024, https://en.yna.co.kr/view/AEN20240720001751320.

[14] Pacheco Pardo, *Shrimp to Whale*, ch. 6.

[15] See Victor Cha and Ramon Pacheco Pardo, *Korea: A New History of South and North* (New Haven, CT, and London: Yale University Press, 2023), ch. 6.

[16] Jorg Michael Dostal, 'South Korea: The Lasting Pitfalls of the "Imperial Presidency"', *Political Quarterly*, vol. 94, no. 1, January–March 2023, pp. 57–68.

[17] Kim, 'Yoon Declares Emergency Martial Law; Parliament Votes to Lift Decree'.

[18] See Sarah Kim, 'Yoon's Approval Rating Falls to a Record-low 28 Percent', *Korea JoongAng Daily*, 31 July 2022, https://koreajoongangdaily.joins.com/2022/07/31/national/politics/Korea-Yoon-Sukyeol-approval-rating/20220731150215645.html.

[19] This happened during Lee Myung-bak's government, when Park Geun-hye emerged as the leader of a group within the conservative movement offering views about policy that differed from the government's. See Gi-wook Shin, 'The Election that Could Reorder South Korea's Politics', *Current History*, vol. 111, no. 746, September 2012, pp. 223–8.

[20] Yun Hee-hun and Kim Mi-geon, 'New President Seeks to Rewrite Constitution, Extend Term Limits', *Chosun Daily*, 4 June 2025, https://www.chosun.com/english/national-en/2025/06/04/XQULBMMNB5FWRDKKHH7NBTUHMQ/.

[21] *Ibid.*

[22] See Jorg Michal Dostal, 'South Korean Presidential Politics Turns Liberal: Transformative Change or Business as Usual?', *Political Quarterly*, vol. 88, no. 3, July–September 2017, pp. 480–91. Former president Moon Jae-in is another politician to have made this kind of proposal. See Song Jun-a, 'South Korea's Moon Proposes Shorter Presidency with 2-term Limit', *Financial Times*, 22 March 2018, https://www.ft.com/content/56f4732c-2d8f-11e8-9b4b-bc4b9f08f381.

[23] The key voting constituency of the party generally skews older. See Choi Hye-seung and Kim Mi-geon, 'Lee Jae-myung 51.7%, Kim Moon-soo 39.3% in Presidential Election Exit Polls', *Chosun Daily*, 3 June 2025, https://www.chosun.com/english/national-en/2025/06/03/CALOIJ44XZDBPPI6QAC52XMH2M/.

[24] See Park Boram, 'PPP's Kim Moon-soo Registers Presidential Candidacy with Election Watchdog', Yonhap News, 11 May 2025, https://en.yna.co.kr/view/AEN20250511000500315.

[25] World Bank, 'GDP Per Capita Growth (Annual %) – Korea, Repl.', https://data.worldbank.org/indicator/NY.GDP.PCAP.KD.ZG?locations=KR; and International Monetary Fund, 'World Economic Outlook Database – Gross Domestic Product Per Capita, Constant Prices', April 2025, https://www.imf.org/en/Publications/WEO/weo-database/2025/april/weo-report?c=171

,193,122,124,156,960,423,935,128,939,172,132,134,174,532,176,178,436,136,158,542,941,946,137,546,181,138,196,142,182,359,135,576,936,961,184,144,146,528,112,111,&s=NGDPRPPPPC,&sy=2024&ey=2025&ssm=0&scsm=1&scc=0&ssd=1&ssc=0&sic=0&sort=country&ds=.&br=1.

26 OECD, 'Average Annual Wages', https://www.oecd.org/en/data/indicators/average-annual-wages.html.

27 South Korea Ministry of Economy and Finance, 'Current Employment Situation, May 2025', 11 June 2025, https://english.moef.go.kr/pc/selectTbPressCenterDtl.do?boardCd=N0001&seq=6182.

28 Ibid.; and World Bank, 'Unemployment, Youth Total (% of Total Labor Force Ages 15–24) (Modeled ILO Estimate)', https://data.worldbank.org/indicator/SL.UEM.1524.ZS.

29 Kang Yoon-seung, 'S. Korea's Exports Up 8.2 Pct in 2024 to Fresh Record', Yonhap News, 1 January 2025, https://en.yna.co.kr/view/AEN20250101000400320; and Kang Yoon-seung, 'FDI Pledges to S. Korea Hit Record High in 2024 on Rise in Manufacturing Sector', Yonhap News, 7 January 2025, https://en.yna.co.kr/view/AEN20250107001500320.

30 Korea International Trade Association, 'Export & Import Trends for 2024 & December 2024', 31 January 2025, https://kita.org/kitaTradeReport/kitaTradeReport/kitaTradeReportDetail.do?no=22.

31 See Hoon Sahib Hoo, Youngsun Koh and Anwar Aridi (eds), *Innovative Korea: Leveraging Innovation and Technology for Development* (Washington DC: The World Bank, 2023); and Jake Kwon, 'From Squid Game to Blackpink, How South Korea Became a Cultural Powerhouse', BBC News, 28 December 2024, https://www.bbc.co.uk/news/articles/cz6jynn5w9no.

32 See 'Flood of Warnings on "Peak Korea"', *Dong-A Ilbo*, 3 February 2025, https://www.donga.com/en/article/all/20250203/5428672/1.

33 World Bank, 'GDP Growth (Annual %) – Korea, Rep.', https://data.worldbank.org/indicator/NY.GDP.MKTP.KD.ZG?locations=KR.

34 Kim Han-joo, 'S. Korea's Childbirths Rise for 9th Month in March amid Post-pandemic Marriage Boom', Yonhap News, 28 May 2025, https://en.yna.co.kr/view/AEN20250528003900320.

35 See Lee Joo-hyung and Lee Jae-eun, 'Foreign Residents in Korea Hit Record High, Over Half Earn 2–3 Million Won a Month', *Chosun Daily*, 18 March 2025, https://www.chosun.com/english/national-en/2025/03/18/JLJTCJ2CBRH2JMY4YVCQS6MUAM/; and Darcie Draudt-Vejares, 'Multicultural at the Meso-level: Governing Diversity Within the Family in South Korea', *Pacific Affairs*, vol. 96, no. 4, December 2023, pp. 701–22.

36 See Ramon Pacheco Pardo, *South Korea's Grand Strategy: Making Its Own Destiny* (New York: Columbia University Press, 2023), chs 6 and 7.

37 Korea International Trade Association, 'Export & Import Trends for 2024 & December 2024'.

38 See Robyn Klingler-Vidra and Ramon Pacheco Pardo, *Startup Capitalism: New Approaches to Innovation Strategies in East Asia* (Ithaca, NY: Cornell

University Press, 2025), ch. 3.
39 Chang Dong-woo, 'S. Korea's Female Employment Rate Low Among OECD Nations: Report', Yonhap News, 6 January 2025, https://en.yna.co.kr/view/AEN20250106002100320.
40 OECD, *Pensions at a Glance 2023: OECD and G20 Indicators* (Paris: OECD Publishing, 2023), pp. 42, 118.
41 International Federation of Robotics, 'Global Robot Density in Factories Doubled in Seven Years', 20 November 2024, https://ifr.org/ifr-press-releases/news/global-robot-density-in-factories-doubled-in-seven-years.
42 Joo-Wan Kim, 'Money Pours In for Technology to Reshape Korean Restaurants', *Korea Economic Daily*, 1 April 2024, https://www.kedglobal.com/korean-startups/newsView/ked202404010008.
43 Jung Da-hyun, 'Foreign Residents in Korea Hit All-time High, Account for Over 5% of Population', *Korea Times*, 3 March 2025, https://www.koreatimes.co.kr/southkorea/society/20250303/foreign-residents-in-south-korea-hit-all-time-high-account-for-over-5-of-population.
44 Korean Statistical Information Service, 'International Migration of Foreign by Sex and Citizenship', https://kosis.kr/statHtml/statHtml.do?sso=ok&returnurl=https%3A%2F%2Fkosis.kr%3A443%2FstatHtml%2FstatHtml.do%3Fconn_path%3DI3%26tblId%3DDT_1B81A21%26language%3Den%26orgId%3D101%26.
45 See Choi Jeong-yoon, 'Every Baby in 2024 Comes with W29.6m Cash Support', *Korea Herald*, 22 January 2024, https://www.koreaherald.com/article/3309598.
46 See Yoon Min-sik, 'Only Half of Koreans Believe Marriage Is Essential: Study', *Korea Herald*, 13 November 2024, https://www.koreaherald.com/article/3853832.
47 Son Ji-hyoung, 'South Korea's Birth Rate Rises for First Time in 9 Years', *Korea Herald*, 6 February 2025, https://www.koreaherald.com/article/10429076.
48 Ray Kim and Kim Mi-geon, 'More Young South Koreans Support Nonmarital Childbirth', *Chosun Daily*, 27 December 2024, https://www.chosun.com/english/national-en/2024/12/27/2H5QGYKAWNBMNAQVBORNVCC6RE/.
49 See Lee Jae-lim, 'New President Reiterates Commitment to Korea's Tech Future', *Korean JoongAng Daily*, 4 June 2025, https://koreajoongangdaily.joins.com/news/2025-06-04/business/industry/New-administration-has-massive-implications-for-Koreas-tech-future/2321702.
50 See Joyce Lee, Hyunjoo Jin and Trevor Hunnicutt, 'South Korea's Lee, Trump Agree to Work Towards Swift Tariff Deal, Lee's Office Says', Reuters, 6 June 2025, https://www.reuters.com/world/asia-pacific/trump-south-koreas-new-president-lee-speak-by-phone-lees-office-says-2025-06-06/.
51 See Ramon Pacheco Pardo, 'What to Expect from South Korea's New President', *Foreign Policy*, 5 June 2025, https://foreignpolicy.com/2025/06/05/south-korea-president-election-results-lee-jae-myung-foreign-policy/.
52 For an analysis of South Korea's grand strategy dating back to the 1987 democratic transition, see Pacheco Pardo, *South Korea's Grand Strategy*.

53 See Asia Regional Integration Center, 'Free Trade Agreements', https://aric.adb.org/fta-country; and 'South Korea Wants to Become One of the World's Biggest Arms Exporters', *The Economist*, 12 February 2022, https://www.economist.com/asia/2022/02/12/south-korea-wants-to-become-one-of-the-worlds-biggest-arms-exporters.

54 See Asia Regional Integration Center, 'Free Trade Agreements'; and Lee Hyo-jin, 'Yoon Vows to Expand Support for the Arms Industry', *Korea Times*, 7 December 2023, https://www.koreatimes.co.kr/southkorea/defense/20231207/yoon-vows-to-expand-support-for-arms-industry.

55 See Lee Sung-eun and Jeong Jong-hoon, 'Korea, U.S. to Promote Exchanges and Cooperation', *Korea JoongAng Daily*, 27 April 2023, https://koreajoongangdaily.joins.com/2023/04/27/national/socialAffairs/korea-stem-semiconductor/20230427165159902.html.

56 LG, 'LG Innotek and Boston Dynamics to Create the Next Generation Robot Vision System', 15 May 2025, https://www.lgcorp.com/media/release/28979.

57 Ramon Pacheco Pardo, 'South Korea Has More Leverage over China than You Think', *Foreign Policy*, 10 February 2025, https://foreignpolicy.com/2025/02/10/south-korea-china-economy-diplomacy-trade/?utm_content=gifting&tpcc=gifting_article.

58 *Ibid.*

59 See Eun Kyo Cho and Woojung Shim, 'The Evolving Structure of Korea–China Supply Chains in High-tech Industries and Korea's Response', *KIET Monthly Industrial Economics*, vol. 306, no. 24, 29 March 2024.

60 See Pacheco Pardo, *South Korea's Grand Strategy*, p. 139.

61 *Ibid.*, p. 176.

62 European Commission, 'Republic of Korea to Join Horizon Europe Under Transitional Arrangement', 6 January 2025, https://research-and-innovation.ec.europa.eu/news/all-research-and-innovation-news/republic-korea-join-horizon-europe-under-transitional-arrangement-2025-01-06_en#:~:text=As%20of%201%20January%202025%2C%20the%20Republic%20of,opportunities%20for%20researchers%20and%20unlocking%20potential%20for%20collaboration.

Supply Chains and Southeast Asia: The Sino-American Shadow

Amos Yeo

Southeast Asia is prime geopolitical real estate, at a crossroads of global trade routes. The region has important natural resources, including oil, gas and critical minerals. It also encompasses the Malacca Strait, which channels 30% of the world's trade, and the South China Sea, a potential strategic flashpoint.[1] As a result, Southeast Asia is no stranger to great-power contestation, from European colonisation to the Second World War and the Cold War. In recent years, the region has become a focal point of the United States and China's battle for influence, markets and military advantage. While the rivalry is playing out across all domains – economic, diplomatic, political and military – an area of particular concern to Southeast Asia is that of supply chains.[2]

American efforts

During his first term as US president, Donald Trump stated in an executive order that 'a strong America cannot be dependent on imports from foreign adversaries for the critical minerals that are increasingly necessary to maintain our economic and military strength in the 21st century'.[3] In his second term, heavy tariffs have constituted his primary means of reducing that dependence, the idea being that tariffs will trim the United States' trade deficit and incentivise the reshoring of manufacturing, especially the advanced variety. Trump's tariff policies have,

---

Amos Yeo is an IISS Visiting Fellow and a brigadier general in the Singapore Air Force.

of course, gyrated, and it is not clear where they will end up. But Biden administration incentives, such as those effected by the 2022 CHIPS and Science Act, have produced only small results, given the long lead time for capital investments to yield profits, scepticism about future US policy continuity and high US labour costs.[4]

The US has sought to diversify away from China for resources, especially critical minerals. The Export–Import Bank of the United States and the International Development Finance Corporation have approved projects that boost rare-earth, cobalt, nickel and graphite supply chains.[5] In April 2025, the US and Ukraine signed a deal that gives the US preferential access to Ukraine's critical minerals and natural resources.[6] The US has also imposed export controls to stymie the access of Chinese companies such as Huawei and Semiconductor Manufacturing International Corporation to high-end technologies, notably high-bandwidth chips, graphics-processing units and advanced chip-making tools.[7] These export controls have modestly curtailed Chinese companies' technological advancement.

China's efforts

To reduce its technological reliance on the US and the West more broadly, China has embarked on the Made in China 2025 initiative to strengthen China's high-tech manufacturing base in sectors such as information technology, advanced robotics and artificial intelligence (AI).[8] The programme has borne fruit, as demonstrated by, for instance, the continued viability of the telecommunications company Huawei and the surprising success of AI company DeepSeek despite stringent US sanctions.[9]

More comprehensively, in 2013, China launched the One Belt, One Road initiative, subsequently renamed the Belt and Road Initiative (BRI). Through projects such as the Central Asia–China gas pipeline and the development of Gwadar Port under the China–Pakistan Economic Corridor initiative, China has secured long-term access to energy resources in Central Asia and the Middle East via routes that are less susceptible to disruption by the US military.[10] China has also inked multibillion-dollar deals with Iran and Russia to consolidate access to oil and gas supplies, and made significant inroads into Africa to secure oil, copper, cobalt and other essential minerals.[11]

China is willing to threaten the United States' supply chains, and its primary leverage consists in its reserves and processing capability of critical minerals including rare-earth elements. In response to US sanctions and tariffs, China imposed export controls on gallium and germanium in July 2023; on tungsten, indium, bismuth, tellurium and molybdenum in February 2025; and on samarium, gadolinium, terbium, dysprosium, lutetium, scandium and yttrium in April 2025.

Implications for Southeast Asia

For Southeast Asian states, most of which are small and export-dependent, the challenges of navigating the US–China strategic rivalry would be daunting regardless of who led the United States. Trump's radical and volatile positions on free trade in particular and multilateralism in general have intensified them, raising concerns about the breakdown of the rules-based order and international trading system. Singaporean Prime Minister Lawrence Wong encapsulated their anxieties when he remarked that 'without a rules-based order that treats countries equally, the risks for small states increase exponentially. We face the danger of descending into a world where power dictates justice.'[12]

It appears unlikely that the United States' economic nationalism under Trump will abate. If that is the case, the decoupling of the US and Chinese economies, escalating tariff wars and deglobalisation will hit trade-dependent Southeast Asian economies especially hard. Tariffs pose the greatest economic threat. With the exception of Singapore, Southeast Asian states have large trade surpluses with the United States. They will be subject to tariffs from 25% (Malaysia) to 40% (Laos and Myanmar). Imports from Vietnam will incur 20% tariffs, goods transshipped through Vietnam 40% tariffs.

It remains to be seen if these concessions, alongside Vietnam's potential strategic utility in countering China, will sway the Trump administration, which harbours suspicions about Vietnam's motivations and good faith.[13] Those suspicions extend to other countries in the region. Washington has scrutinised Singapore's potential role as an intermediary in the illegal movement of NVIDIA chips to China that would bypass

US export controls.[14] In turn, Malaysian Prime Minister Anwar Ibrahim has explicitly warned Chinese firms against using Malaysia as a base for rebadging for the purpose of avoiding US tariffs.[15]

In addition to trade, foreign direct investment (FDI) is crucial for Southeast Asia's economic growth and infrastructure development. The US and China are the largest sources of FDI in the region, accounting for $74.4 billion and $17.3bn, respectively, in 2023.[16] The United States' push for onshoring will reduce this flow of American FDI. Structural obstacles to reshoring in the US itself, and the diversion of FDI from China to Southeast Asia, as part of companies' 'China plus one' strategy, are potential mitigating factors.[17] But whether Southeast Asian nations can be 'plus ones' will depend largely on whether they can negotiate reprieves from US tariffs. They will no doubt continue to hedge their bets and attract investment from both the US and China, but at some risk of retaliation from both countries.[18]

Southeast Asian nations will continue to hedge their bets

For Southeast Asian leaders, financing for infrastructure and development projects not only fuels economic growth but also engenders goodwill from local populations.[19] China's BRI continues to be an option for the region to access funds and loans, without the onerous demands that often accompany arrangements with Western governments or institutions. That said, Chinese largesse has recently declined owing to domestic economic impediments and overexposure to developing-world debt.[20] Work on Cambodia's $1.7bn Funan Techo Canal project, launched in November 2024 to much fanfare, has flagged, reportedly due to a lack of Chinese funding.[21] Overall, countries looking to China may be uncomfortable with the BRI's borrowing terms and with US pushback. Panama withdrew from the BRI in February 2025 following strong US pressure.[22]

The Western alternative to the BRI is the Partnership for Global Infrastructure and Investment, under which the US and G7 aim to funnel $600bn into global infrastructure projects by 2027. The Luzon Economic Corridor would see $100bn invested into the Philippines' economy within ten years.[23] Other potential conduits include Indonesia's Nusantara Ring Corridor and Thailand's Eastern Economic Corridor.[24] Southeast Asian states, however, will be concerned over the sustainability of commitments and funding for these projects, given the Trump administration's recent moves to cut foreign aid.

As the US–China rivalry sharpens, each side is paying more attention to the other's investments in third-party countries. Among the ten states of the Association of Southeast Asian Nations (ASEAN), half – Malaysia, Myanmar, Philippines, Singapore and Vietnam[25] – have processes in place to screen foreign investments to safeguard national security and also avoid being inadvertently drawn into the great-power struggle for influence. The remaining five without such mechanisms in place – Brunei, Cambodia, Indonesia, Laos and Thailand[26] – should consider establishing them.

The third area of concern is the control of critical minerals through reserves, processing capacity or both. Indonesia and the Philippines have reserves of nickel as well as significant processing capacities. Vietnam is endowed with tungsten and rare-earth elements, though production and refinement are still in early stages. Malaysia plays a key role in processing rare-earth elements.[27] Indonesia produces two-thirds of the world's mined nickel and nearly half of its refined nickel.[28] It has leveraged its nickel reserves to force investments in downstream processing, most of it from Chinese firms. They now control 75% of Indonesia's nickel-refining capacity, which has increased Western nervousness.[29] A US–Indonesia critical-minerals agreement covering nickel and cobalt was already under negotiation before the 'Liberation Day' tariffs, and negotiations to reduce Indonesia's tariff include consideration of critical minerals.[30]

Finally, the US under Trump will view engagement with Southeast Asia through the lens of great-power competition and, as it did during Trump's first administration, favour bilateral over multilateral engagement. If unopposed, this preference could sideline ASEAN, which the region values as a neutral platform for engaging major powers and as a mechanism for smaller states to amplify their voices. China, for its part, is poised to exploit the void left by the US to deepen its bilateral and multilateral engagement of Southeast Asian countries.[31] These are worrying trends for Southeast Asian policymakers, who have traditionally relied on ASEAN to engage multiple powers simultaneously, and on the US to check growing Chinese influence.

The big picture

The broader question is whether ASEAN countries will be able to continue to avoid choosing sides between the US and China. The Trump administration's dealings with Canada, Mexico and China indicate a Manichaean 'with us or against us' mentality and a determination to link issues such as immigration and illicit drug trafficking to trade. Yet, given its proximity, size and economic ties with the region, China will inevitably play a key role in the destiny of Southeast Asia. China has continued to consolidate its position as ASEAN's largest trading partner.[32] Against the backdrop of the United States' disruption of the global trading system, Beijing has sought to portray itself as a defender of the multilateral rules-based order and economic system.[33] This diplomatic stratagem appears to be paying off. In a 2025 ISEAS–Yusof Ishak Institute poll, 47.7% said that ASEAN should side with China over the US if forced to choose between the two. While slightly lower than the 50.5% of the previous year, this figure remains markedly higher than the 38–43% from 2021–23.[34] Furthermore, the latest poll was conducted in January and February 2025, before Trump's 'Liberation Day' tariffs were announced, and the preference for China surely would have been higher had the poll followed that announcement. Southeast Asian pragmatism in prioritising China's economic heft and regional ties thus appears durable, despite lingering concerns over China's coercive use of economic and military power.[35]

A looming issue for Southeast Asian policymakers is whether the apparent diminution of the United States' commitment to regional stability is temporary or permanent. Some early assessments have emerged. In January, Malaysian Prime Minister Ibrahim said, 'we engage well with the US but it does not engage the region as actively as it did in the past. China in that sense takes a more positive attitude.'[36] On the US tariffs, he remarked that the United States' basis for calculating tariffs is 'fundamentally flawed'.[37] Singaporean Prime Minister Wong lamented that the US tariffs are not 'actions one does to a friend'.[38] Vietnam's trade ministry called the tariffs 'unreasonable'.[39] In October 2024, Indonesia, Malaysia, Thailand and Vietnam became partner countries of the BRICS, signalling openness towards alternatives to US-centric arrangements.[40] In January, Indonesia went one step further and joined the BRICS as its first Southeast Asian member, prompting Western concerns.[41]

The silver lining could be that ASEAN may now be compelled to function as a true bloc and break free of the internal squabbles and paralysis over the non-interference principle that have traditionally kept it from doing so. Its strengths are clear: a large, combined domestic market of 630 million people, a young and dynamic workforce, and stellar economic growth averaging 5% annually.[42] However, ASEAN member states are also remarkably diverse in terms of size, ethnicity, development levels, political systems and degrees of alignment with the US and China. These factors and a rigidly consensus-based decision-making process have precluded the organisation from reaching agreement on contentious issues, particularly those involving China.[43] Much as the threat of US abandonment has galvanised Europeans into stronger collective action, though, ASEAN states may at last be motivated to speak more boldly and work harder towards policy alignment.

At the ASEAN Defence Ministers' Meeting Retreat in February, the ministers agreed to admit Germany and Turkiye to its observer programme, which dissident members had previously blocked.[44] Perhaps most significantly, in response to the US 'Liberation Day' tariffs, the ASEAN economic ministers expeditiously agreed that ASEAN would not impose reciprocal tariffs on the US. These steps, though incremental, are non-trivial in the ASEAN diplomatic context, where words are customarily minced and progress painfully slow. This bodes well for ASEAN's prospective resiliency, as it will come under increasing strain from the US–China rivalry.

ASEAN has identified supply-chain resilience and efficiency as a specific focus of cooperation. The Framework on ASEAN Supply Chain Efficiency and Resilience, published in 2024, goes beyond the usual platitudes about cross-border harmonisation, economic corridors and resilience against future disruptions, articulating specific initiatives and designating lead agencies to establish reserves of specific goods and develop regional production capabilities to address identified capacity gaps.[45] If Southeast Asian states can implement this ambitious framework, supply-chain resilience may empower ASEAN.

* * *

The US–China tussle over supply chains, exacerbated by the US tariffs, presents a significant challenge for Southeast Asian states. They appear capable of withstanding it for several reasons. Firstly, US attitudes and actions towards Southeast Asian states, however damaging, are likely to be tempered by the larger strategic concerns about effectively confronting China. Even under Trump, the US will probably be wary of alienating Southeast Asian states too much and pushing them closer to Beijing. Secondly, strong underlying structural factors – a young and dynamic workforce, a large combined market and increasing integration via the ASEAN Economic Community – will continue to propel the region's economic growth. Thirdly, the region's strategic location, maritime thoroughfares and critical resources afford it agency and leverage. Ultimately, of course, it is up to savvy national leaders and capable officials to step up and steer their countries, as well as ASEAN.

Notes

1. Andrea Willige and Spencer Freingold, 'These Are the World's Most Vital Waterways for Global Trade', World Economic Forum, 15 February 2024, https://www.weforum.org/stories/2024/02/worlds-busiest-ocean-shipping-routes-trade/.
2. The region is defined as the ten nation-states in the Association of Southeast Asian Nations (ASEAN): Brunei Darussalam, Cambodia, Indonesia, Laos, Malaysia, Myanmar, Philippines, Singapore, Thailand and Vietnam.
3. White House, 'Executive Order on Addressing the Threat to the Domestic Supply Chain from Reliance on Critical Minerals from Foreign Adversaries', 30 September 2020, https://trumpwhitehouse.archives.gov/presidential-actions/executive-order-addressing-threat-domestic-supply-chain-reliance-critical-minerals-foreign-adversaries/.
4. See Megan Cerullo, 'These Companies Say They're Investing More in US Manufacturing as Tariffs Go into Effect', CBS News, 30 April 2025, https://www.cbsnews.com/news/us-manufacturing-domestic-tariffs/.
5. See Sydney Tucker, 'Competing for Africa's Resources: How the US and China Invest in Critical Minerals', Stimson Center, 28 February 2025, https://www.stimson.org/2025/competing-for-africas-resources-how-the-us-and-china-invest-in-critical-minerals/.
6. See Sayma Kullab, 'Ukraine and the US Have Finally Signed a Minerals Deal. What Does It Include?', AP News, 1 May 2025, https://apnews.com/article/ukraine-us-rare-earth-minerals-deal-8566241ea0e121a30437d845357055d8.
7. See Bureau of Industry and Security, US Department of Commerce, 'Department of Commerce Implements Controls on Quantum

8   See Andrew Chatzky and James McBride, 'Is "Made in China 2025" a Threat to Global Trade?', Council on Foreign Relations, 13 May 2019, https://www.cfr.org/backgrounder/made-china-2025-threat-global-trade.

9   Huawei surprised the world in 2023 with the launch of the Huawei Mate 60 series, containing a completely Chinese-made chipset. See Jay Liu, 'Rumors Debunked: Who Made the SoC Within Huawei Mate 60 Pro?', *DigitimesAsia*, 4 September 2023, https://www.digitimes.com/news/a20230904PD210/china-ic-design-distribution-ic-manufacturing.html. In January 2025, DeepSeek revealed that its new AI model, which rivals OpenAI's, cost only $6 million to train and was developed using less advanced H800 chips that complied with export restrictions. See Karen Freifeld and Stephen Nellis, 'Nvidia Says DeepSeek Advances Prove Need for More of Its Chips', Reuters, 27 January 2025, https://www.reuters.com/technology/nvidia-says-deepseek-advances-prove-need-more-its-chips-2025-01-27/.

10 See James McBride, 'China's Massive Belt and Road Initiative', Council on Foreign Relations, 3 February 2023, https://www.cfr.org/backgrounder/chinas-massive-belt-and-road-initiative.

11 See Luhn Alec and Terry Macalister, 'Russia Signs 30-year Deal Worth $400bn to Deliver Gas to China', *Guardian*, 30 November 2017, https://www.theguardian.com/world/2014/may/21/russia-30-year-400bn-gas-deal-china; Lina Benabdallah, 'China's Role in Africa's Critical Minerals Landscape: Challenges and Key Opportunities', APRI, 6 September 2024, https://afripoli.org/chinas-role-in-africas-critical-minerals-landscape-challenges-and-key-opportunities; and 'Iran and China Sign 25-year Cooperation Agreement', Reuters, 27 March 2021, https://www.reuters.com/world/china/iran-china-sign-25-year-cooperation-agreement-2021-03-27/.

12 Quoted in Arvind Jayaram, 'Small States Need to Join Hands to Uphold Multilateral System in an Era of Conflict: PM Wong', *Straits Times*, 20 September 2024, https://www.straitstimes.com/world/united-states/small-states-need-to-join-hands-to-uphold-multilateral-system-in-an-era-of-conflict-pm-wong.

13 Trump suggested that a China–Vietnam leaders' meeting was to figure out how to 'screw the United States of America'. On Vietnam's proposed concessions, Senior Counselor for Trade and Manufacturing Peter Navarro said that the zero tariffs offered by Vietnam 'means nothing to us because it's the nontariff cheating that matters'. Quoted in Joshua Kurlantzick, 'Vietnam's Tariff Trouble Just Gets Worse', Council on Foreign Relations, 12 May 2025, https://www.cfr.org/blog/vietnams-tariff-trouble-just-gets-worse.

14 See '3 Men Charged with Fraud, Cases Linked to Alleged Movement of Nvidia Chips', CNA, 28 February 2025, https://www.channelnewsasia.

com/singapore/3-men-charged-fraud-nvidia-chips-singapore-china-deepseek-4964721.

15 See 'Malaysia Warns Chinese Firms from Using It as a Base to "Rebadge" to Avoid US Tariffs', *South China Morning Post*, 2 December 2024, https://www.scmp.com/news/asia/southeast-asia/article/3288972/malaysia-warns-chinese-firms-using-it-base-rebadge-avoid-us-tariffs.

16 See ASEAN, 'ASEAN Investment Report 2024', October 2024, https://asean.org/book/asean-investment-report-2024-asean-economic-community-2025-and-foreign-direct-investment/.

17 See 'The Rise and Rise of "China Plus One" Risk Strategies', *Strategic Risk Global*, 10 September 2024, https://www.strategic-risk-global.com/supply-chain-risk/the-rise-and-rise-of-china-plus-one-risk-strategies/1453004.article.

18 Malaysian Prime Minister Ibrahim's exhortation to a conference of global chipmakers in May 2024 is illustrative: 'I offer our nation as the most neutral and non-aligned location for semiconductor production.' Quoted in Sebastian Strangio, 'Malaysia Unveils Plans to Become Next Global Chip Hub', *Diplomat*, 29 May 2024, https://thediplomat.com/2024/05/malaysia-unveils-plans-to-become-next-global-chip-hub/.

19 See Charles Dunst, 'Battleground Southeast Asia: China's Rise and America's Options', LSE IDEAS, 25 March 2020, https://lseideas.medium.com/battleground-southeast-asia-chinas-rise-and-america-s-options-c5ce81e2880a.

20 See Christina Lu, 'Xi's Belt and Road Is Running Out of Steam', *Foreign Policy*, 8 November 2023, https://foreignpolicy.com/2023/02/13/china-belt-and-road-initiative-infrastructure-development-geopolitics; and Dominic Pino, 'The Belt and Road Initiative Runs into Trouble', *National Review*, 26 September 2022, https://www.nationalreview.com/corner/the-belt-and-road-initiative-runs-into-trouble/.

21 See Francesco Guarascio, 'Cambodia's Flagship Canal in Hot Water as China Funding Dries Up', Reuters, 23 November 2024, https://www.reuters.com/world/asia-pacific/cambodias-flagship-canal-hot-water-china-funding-dries-up-2024-11-21/.

22 See Igor Patrick, 'Panama Formally Exits China's Belt and Road Initiative as US Claims "Victory" in Decision', *South China Morning Post*, 7 February 2025, https://www.scmp.com/news/china/diplomacy/article/3297689/panama-pulls-out-chinas-belt-and-road-initiative-president-mulino-says.

23 See Alvin Camba and Ryan Seay, 'The Luzon Economic Corridor as the United States' Southeast Asian Litmus Test', East Asia Forum, 10 July 2024, https://eastasiaforum.org/2024/07/10/the-luzon-economic-corridor-as-the-united-states-southeast-asian-litmus-test/.

24 See Narupat Rattanakit, 'Strengthening Supply Chains and Engagement: Economic Corridors in Southeast Asia', Center for Strategic and International Studies, 27 January 2025, https://www.csis.org/blogs/new-perspectives-asia/strengthening-supply-chains-and-engagement-economic-corridors-southeast.

25 See, respectively, United Nations Trade and Development, 'Malaysia', 5 April 2023, https://investmentpolicy.unctad.org/investment-policy-monitor/measures/4304/malaysia-announced-the-establishment-of-an-fdi-monitoring-committee; Minn Naing Oo, 'FDI Guide – Myanmar', Allen & Gledhill (Myanmar), 11 March 2025, https://www.ibanet.org/document?id=Tax-Reports-Myanmar-2022; Baker McKenzie, 'Investment Reference Guide – Philippines', 11 March 2025, https://resourcehub.bakermckenzie.com/en/resources/global-private-ma-guide-limited/asia-pacific/philippines/topics/quick-reference-guide; United Nations Trade and Development, 'Singapore', 28 March 2024, https://investmentpolicy.unctad.org/investment-policy-monitor/measures/4459/singapore-introduced-a-screening-regime-for-national-security; and United Nations Development Programme, 'Foreign Investment Screening Instrument', 11 March 2025, https://www.undp.org/sites/g/files/zskgke326/files/2022-11/2.%20The%20Handbook%20of%20FISI_web.pdf.

26 See, respectively, US Department of State, '2023 Investment Climate Statements: Brunei', 11 March 2025, https://www.state.gov/reports/2023-investment-climate-statements/brunei/; Oliver Borgers, 'Foreign Investment Review – Cambodia', Lexology GTDT, 24 January 2023, https://www.tilleke.com/wp-content/uploads/2023/02/2023-Foreign-Investment-Review-Cambodia.pdf; Oscar Damarjati et al., 'Foreign Direct Investment Regimes – Indonesia', ICLG, https://iclg.com/practice-areas/foreign-direct-investment-regimes-laws-and-regulations/indonesia; US Department of State, '2023 Investment Climate Statements: Laos', https://www.state.gov/reports/2023-investment-climate-statements/laos/; and US Department of State, '2023 Investment Climate Statements: Thailand', https://www.state.gov/reports/2023-investment-climate-statements/thailand/.

27 See Han Phoumin, 'ASEAN's Strategic Role in Securing Critical Minerals for Clean Energy and High-tech Futures', Economic Research Institute for ASEAN and East Asia, 16 December 2024, https://www.eria.org/news-and-views/asean-s-strategic-role-in-securing-critical-minerals-for-clean-energy-and-high-tech-futures.

28 See 'Indonesia Nearly Has a Monopoly on Nickel. What Next?', *The Economist*, 9 January 2025, https://www.economist.com/asia/2025/01/09/indonesia-nearly-has-a-monopoly-on-nickel-what-next.

29 'Chinese Firms Control Around 75% of Indonesian Nickel Capacity, Report Finds', Reuters, 5 February 2025, https://www.reuters.com/markets/commodities/chinese-firms-control-around-75-indonesian-nickel-capacity-report-finds-2025-02-05/.

30 See Gayathri Suroyo and Stefanno Sulaiman, 'Indonesia Wants "Fair and Square" Trade in US Tariff Talks', Reuters, 25 April 2025, https://www.reuters.com/markets/asia/indonesia-is-putting-forward-national-interest-us-tariffs-negotiation-minister-2025-04-25/.

31 See James Crabtree, 'U.S.–China–Southeast Asia Relations in a Second Trump Administration', Asia Society, 26 February 2025, https://asiasociety.org/policy-institute/us-china-southeast-asia-relations-second-trump-administration.

32 See ASEAN Secretariat, 'ASEAN Investment Report 2024', October 2024, https://asean.org/wp-content/uploads/2024/10/AIR2024-3.pdf.

33 See Janis Mackey Frayer, Jennifer Jett and Peter Guo, 'As Trump Shakes the International Order, China Casts Itself as a Model of Stability', NBC News, 9 March 2025, https://www.nbcnews.com/news/world/china-beijing-trump-npc-xi-trade-growth-defense-nato-communist-tariffs-rcna195271.

34 See Melody Chan, 'US Regains Edge Over China as Preferred Partner in Southeast Asia: Survey', CNA, 3 April 2025, https://www.channelnewsasia.com/east-asia/iseas-survey-2025-china-us-influence-5037321.

35 See Miranda Jeyaretnam, 'New Southeast Asia Survey Shows Greater Trust in the US than China this Year – But There's a Catch', *Time*, 4 April 2025, https://time.com/7274803/southeast-asia-2025-survey-us-china-trust-asean-iseas-trump/.

36 See Alec Russell and Victor Mallet, 'Global Trade Will Survive "Initial Shock" of Donald Trump's Rule, Says Malaysia PM', *Financial Times*, 20 January 2025, https://www.ft.com/content/1870c45d-aeb8-418c-bfa5-8b2a6becbd7d.

37 See Qistina Sallehuddin, 'US' Basis for Calculating Tariff Fundamentally Flawed, Says Anwar', *New Straits Times*, 6 April 2025, https://www.nst.com.my/news/nation/2025/04/1198036/us-basis-calculating-tariff-fundamentally-flawed-says-anwar.

38 See Lawrence Wong, 'US Tariffs: Safeguarding Singapore in a New and Dangerous Era', *Straits Times*, 8 April 2025, https://www.straitstimes.com/opinion/us-tariffs-safeguarding-singapore-in-a-new-and-dangerous-era.

39 Quoted in Nguyen Xuan Quyn, 'Vietnam Calls Trump Tariffs "Unreasonable" as Trade Talks Start', Bloomberg, 9 May 2025, https://www.bloomberg.com/news/articles/2025-05-09/vietnam-calls-trump-tariff-unreasonable-as-trade-talks-start.

40 See Izaah Aqilah Norman, 'Malaysia, Indonesia, Vietnam and Thailand Become Partner Countries of BRICS', CNA, 24 October 2025, https://www.channelnewsasia.com/asia/malaysia-indonesia-vietnam-thailand-brics-asean-global-south-russia-china-4699841.

41 See Dian Septiari, 'Concern in the West as Indonesia Joins BRICS Bloc as Full Member', *Australian*, 7 January 2025, https://www.theaustralian.com.au/world/concern-in-the-west-as-indonesia-joins-brics-bloc-as-full-member/news-story/d1d06ded0377855795a140758bd8ecd5.

42 World Economic Forum, 'ASEAN', https://www.weforum.org/communities/asean/.

43 For example, participants in the East Asia Summit in 2024 declined to issue a joint declaration following disagreements over

the wording on the South China Sea. See 'East Asia Fails to Adopt South China Sea Statement amid Finger Pointing', Radio Free Asia, 15 October 2024, https://www.rfa.org/english/news/southchinasea/asean-east-asia-summit-china-russia-10152024033408.html.

44 See 'ADMM Agrees to Accept Germany and Türkiye as Observers', BERNAMA, 26 February 2025, http://bernama.com/en/news.php?id=2396863.

45 See ASEAN Secretariat, 'Framework on ASEAN Supply Chain Efficiency and Resilience', 2024, https://asean.org/wp-content/uploads/2024/10/Published-Framework-on-ASEAN-Supply-Chain-Efficiency-and-Resilience-FINAL.pdf.

Copyright © 2025 The International Institute for Strategic Studies

America's 'Ungoverning' in Global Context

Jodi Vittori

'Lenin wanted to destroy the state and that's my goal too ... to bring everything crashing down and destroy all of today's establishment', said Steve Bannon in 2017.[1] In August 2024, Donald Trump himself stated that federal employees were 'destroying this country. They're crooked people, they're dishonest people. They're going to be held accountable.'[2] Before Trump was elected a second time, Russell Vought, who now runs the Office of Management and Budget (OMB), had this to say about federal civil servants: 'When they wake up in the morning, we want them to not want to go to work because they are increasingly viewed as villains.'[3] He was one of the key authors of the Heritage Foundation's Project 2025, which calls for 'dismantling the administrative state' and serves as Trump's blueprint for doing so. Of the 53 executive orders issued in Trump's first week in office in 2025, about two-thirds were sourced in proposals in Project 2025.[4] 'This is the chainsaw for bureaucracy', shouted Elon Musk while waving the power tool at a Conservative Political Action Conference in February 2025.[5]

About 6% of the American federal workforce, or about 130,000 people, had been dismissed by mid-May 2025.[6] Under the direction of the Musk-led Department of Government Efficiency (DOGE), the Office of Personnel Management has been developing software to facilitate

Jodi Vittori is a professor of practice and the co-chair of the Global Politics and Security Concentration of the Master of Science in Foreign Service at Georgetown University, and a non-resident associate fellow with the Centre for Finance and Security at the Royal United Services Institute.

firing people more quickly.[7] Government credit-card spending limits have been decreased to $1, causing chaos across the government, halting essential work and preventing government agencies from procuring basic maintenance and office supplies. Agencies such as the US Agency for International Development (USAID), AmeriCorps and the Consumer Financial Protection Bureau have essentially been eradicated.[8] President Trump's May 2025 budget proposal would slash $135 billion, including extensive cuts to the National Institutes of Health, the Department of Housing and Urban Development, NASA, the State Department, and even law-enforcement agencies.[9] Web pages are being erased, leaving holes in America's official history.[10] Several laws and regulations for thwarting foreign corruption, money laundering and the malign use of cryptocurrency are often no longer enforced, and many charged with enforcing have been fired or reassigned, or quit en masse.[11] Senior military officers have been forced to retire.[12]

The Trump administration is also undermining the government's very ability to fund itself. About 96% of the federal budget is collected via the Internal Revenue Service (IRS), but in two months the IRS lost almost a third of its revenue agents and may lose as many as half of its employees.[13] The IRS offices that have investigated the most abuse-prone taxpayers have been disproportionately cut, and agents have been directed to focus on issues such as immigration. Seven former IRS commissioners have likened this action to taking 'an ax to accounts receivable'.[14] It could leave the US with a tax gap of $2.4 trillion over the next ten years.[15] Meanwhile, Republican tax proposals have raised deficit projections so much that Moody's downgraded the United States' credit rating.[16]

While this across-the-board dismantling of American institutions and the country's fiscal plumbing seems haphazard, confusing and disjointed, there is a term for what is going on: ungoverning. Political theorists Nancy Rosenblum and Russell Muirhead, who coined the term, define ungoverning as an 'attack on the capacity and legitimacy of government, especially the part of the government that goes by the term "administrative state"'.[17] While they consider ungoverning to be atypical – Hugo Chávez's Venezuela being a rare example[18] – it is not as unusual as they attest.

A typology of ungoverning

Governments, especially in democratic states, are compelled to respond to voters' wishes and changing times, and this sometimes requires large-scale reforms. But ungoverning by definition goes beyond extensive policy shifts and targeted reforms, even those involving deep cuts in personnel or the elimination of entire agencies. It is the deliberate and wholesale decimation of state capacity and 'a willful sabotage of the institutions that do the work of government' undertaken 'for reasons unrelated to public welfare'.[19]

Kneecapping public institutions across the board can appear irrational, and often is.[20] But it can also be quite calculated from the standpoint of its perpetrators, even when they exact great costs on those they govern. There are at least five broad and often overlapping reasons short of irrationality that governments might wage war on their own institutions and personnel. To a greater or lesser degree, all apply to the Trump administration.

Ideology

One common reason for ungoverning is that it is part of a regime's larger ideological agenda, usually justified as short-term pain that will produce a utopian result. In Sinclair Lewis's 1935 novel *It Can't Happen Here*, for instance, apologists for a corporatist regime promising a gleaming fascist future argue that you can't make an omelette without breaking some eggs to justify human-rights abuses.[21] Many fascist ideologues, of course, have broken plenty of eggs without ungoverning. Neither Adolf Hitler nor Josef Stalin ungoverned their own countries, even as they eviscerated institutions in the territories they conquered.[22] While these totalitarian regimes may have undertaken the most appalling human-rights and other abuses, and while many of their civil servants (especially under Stalin) were jailed or killed, governing institutions were not themselves dismantled. But other ideological regimes have taken the ungoverning route, often because they believed that the existing system was so corrupt or unmanageable that its violent and sudden destruction was a necessary condition of political rebirth.

In reference to the Soviet Union's treatment of Ukraine and Nazi Germany's treatment of Poland, Timothy Snyder has called this approach 'politics by apocalypse'.[23] An extreme example arose when the communist

Khmer Rouge overthrew the military junta in Cambodia, which was already traumatised and hollowed out by spillover from the Vietnam War, in 1975. Led by Pol Pot, the group renamed the country Democratic Kampuchea and decreed 'Year Zero', when its history would start afresh as an agrarian Maoist utopia. This, he believed, called for the genocidal eradication of corrupt followers of the pre-existing political order. In demolishing Cambodia's social, intellectual, governmental and fiscal infrastructure in favour of rural collectives, the Khmer Rouge systematically murdered up to two million people, or 25% of the population.[24]

While the Taliban's takeover of Afghanistan in the mid-1990s was nowhere near as bloody, it was tantamount to cultural genocide. The group massacred civilians, persecuted religious and ethnic minorities, imposed a strict version of sharia law, shuttered schools for girls, made healthcare substantially unattainable, banned most music and destroyed Buddhist shrines and monuments.[25] Taliban leader Mullah Omar used a tin trunk in his villa as the country's treasury, doling out cash as needed.[26]

Trump's United States, of course, is not broadly comparable with Pol Pot's Kampuchea or the Taliban's Afghanistan. But specific similarities – including the administrative state's rapid demolition and the censorship, and suppression of those who oppose it – are nonetheless disturbing. Furthermore, the most extreme advocates of American ungoverning include far-right 'accelerationists', who seek to hasten the demise of the current governing system to make way for a wholly new one and with whom Trump has at times shown veiled sympathy.[27] There are accelerationists among neo-Nazis, Christian nationalists and 'male supremacists', who all found common cause in the insurrection of 6 January 2021 and believe that 'total collapse must precede any social or political project if they ever hope to reorient society according to their preferred mode of hierarchic organization'.[28] OMB Director Vought is a self-described Christian nationalist.[29] He has clear accelerationist leanings, having claimed during the Biden administration that the country was in the midst of a 'Marxist takeover' and advocated the complete overhaul of the government apparatus to speed its reversal. He considers the domestic situation similar to the one Americans faced in 1776 and 1860.[30]

Crypto-utopians such as Curtis Yarvin preach a variation on accelerationism. In a Substack post from 2022, Yarvin described a 'butterfly revolution' in which Trump supporters would act as a 'regime in internal exile'. Though Trump would nominally remain president, real power would lie in a 'CEO he picks' who would 'run the executive branch without any interference from the Congress or courts, probably also taking over state and local governments. Most existing important institutions, public and private, will be shut down and replaced with new and efficient systems' to create an 'alternative regime', and 'many institutions which are necessary organs of society will have to be destroyed'.[31] Yarvin and other crypto-utopians, including Reid Hoffman and Balaji Srinivasan, contemplate this purge as a means of jump-starting authoritarian governments run by corporations.

If these scenarios sound eerily familiar, it's because they are not altogether hypothetical. An anonymous DOGE adviser reportedly told the *Washington Post* that Yarvin's work was 'the most crisp articulation' of what DOGE has been trying to do.[32] Trump's immediate appointment of Musk, unelected and unconfirmed, as a kind of chief minister to oversee DOGE looked quite a bit like the creation of an unaccountable alternative regime empowered to undermine the old one, and he took considerable steps to advance that objective. With Trump and Musk's falling out, the latter for the moment looks like a disavowed Thomas Cromwell, but he is not likely to suffer Cromwell's fate and could well return to Trump's favour.[33]

Grand corruption

Terms like oligarchy, kleptocracy, state capture and patrimonialism are increasingly becoming a part of the American public discourse. All these terms imply some combination of extremely predatory politicians and other elites engaged in large-scale, systematic corruption. Since the days of Aristotle, oligarchy, whereby the rich are able to rule for their own benefit to the detriment of the many, has been disparaged. An outright kleptocracy – or 'rule by thieves' – is a tightly integrated hierarchy of corrupt networks of elites in political, business, cultural, social and criminal institutions headed by godfather-like figures who engage in unchecked domestic plunder to fuel increasing levels of predatory governance.[34] State capture emphasises the morphing of laws, policies and institutions of the legal state to facilitate that plunder.[35] Meanwhile, the Weberian term 'patrimonialism' references a style of traditional governing wherein the state is considered 'little more than the extended "household" of the ruler', formal bureaucracy is replaced by personalised lines of authority and the country is treated as the private property of the ruler and his family.[36] Whimsical commands proliferate unchecked while the mechanisms of state are disempowered.[37]

However the phenomenon is described, its essence is the dismantling of the instruments of transparency, accountability, good governance and law enforcement to enable grand corruption. It's easy for officials to steer overpriced contracts to cronies when government procurement agencies lack qualified employees to evaluate proposals and award contracts to the most deserving; easier still if law enforcement has been so hobbled that it cannot investigate major corruption, courts are packed with partisan loyalists who won't try those cases that reach them, and the media are too cowed to undertake probing investigations.

Venezuela is considered a prototype of an ungoverning kleptocracy. Once among the richest economies in Latin America, with the most abundant oil reserves on the South American continent, it has suffered economic collapse due to 'rapacious corruption' under Chávez and then Nicolás Maduro.[38] Democracy activist Srdja Popovic describes a 'Maduro Model' of kleptocracy, whereby regimes accept 'economic collapse, endemic violence, mass poverty, and international isolation if that's what it takes to stay in power'.[39]

Anne Applebaum and Fiona Hill have postulated that the United States may be on its way to a full-fledged kleptocracy.[40] Trump is a convicted felon, and his business empire has attracted a rogues' gallery of money launderers and other criminals. His family continues to make lucrative deals with cut-outs for foreign potentates, sometimes behind a veil of shell companies, but often out in the open. Likewise, his cabinet includes a major backer of Tether – the cryptocurrency of choice among terrorists and organised-crime figures – as well as an attorney general who allegedly accepted money from the Donald J. Trump Foundation when she was considering whether to investigate Trump University as a Florida attorney general.[41] Several in Trump's inner circle have engaged in various forms of 'meme coin' and cryptocurrency schemes, which Trump himself used to call a scam.[42] Impropriety is more than merely apparent.

Project 2025 devotes an entire section to undermining American anti-money-laundering and counter-terrorism finance laws, regulations and institutions.[43] Seventeen inspectors general were fired immediately after Trump's 2025 inauguration. On her first day in office, Attorney General Pam Bondi eliminated Task Force KleptoCapture and the Kleptocracy Asset Recovery Initiative, and issued orders to de-prioritise many Foreign Agents Registration Act and Foreign Corrupt Practices Act investigations and prosecutions.[44] In March, the Treasury Department stopped enforcing the law against anonymous shell companies.[45] With loyalists now placed in key law-enforcement agencies such as the FBI and the Securities and Exchange Commission, their career-professional ranks systematically thinned and media oversight suppressed, there now exists a strong enabling environment for kleptocracy in the United States.

Warlordism

Max Weber famously noted that a true state must have an effective monopoly on the legitimate use of violence. But such a monopoly has never been the normal condition under which most people have lived.[46] In some places, states have devolved into agglomerations of tribal leaders, warlords, businesses, organised criminals and politicians competing – often violently – for power and wealth. In these situations, the government pointedly lacks a monopoly on the use of violence. Instead, contending fiefdoms veer towards Thomas Hobbes's nasty, brutish and short dystopia. In attempting to take over the government – or deny it to their rivals – warlords and their ilk engage in forms of ungoverning. Warlordism is often if not usually a product of civil war. Currently, Somalia epitomises it, while Lebanon, Libya, South Sudan and Sudan at times tilt in its direction. All five countries have endured vicious civil wars.

While civil war in the United States still seems fairly unlikely, the possibility has undoubtedly become more salient over the past decade.[47] In September 2019, during his first impeachment, Trump himself retweeted a remark by a Fox News commentator that the impeachment would 'cause a

Civil War-like fracture in this Nation from which our Country would never heal'.[48] The Oath Keepers at the time also noted that the US was 'on the verge of a HOT civil war'.[49]

The notion that warlordism as such would precede or follow the outbreak of civil war in the United States, however, has not explicitly come up. And it's not clear that militias or national organisations like the Oath Keepers, the Proud Boys and the Three Percenters are precursors to warlord fiefdoms. That said, certain techno-utopian proposals made by Trump supporters would constitute self-regulated communities with exclusive territories. The Freedom Cities Coalition, for example, wants to create privately funded and corporately governed societies with integrated cryptocurrencies so that people can 'exit' from their current governing system and choose from a marketplace of alternatives to liberal Western democracy. These would essentially take the form of special economic zones where national regulatory rules and legalities did not apply, which would lead to, among other things, technological innovation.[50]

A version of one of these 'start-up cities' called Próspera was founded in 2017 in Honduras. It boasted low taxes, few regulations and limited transparency or oversight for corporate governance, but attracted only 79 full-time residents and a host of legal issues.[51] But the concept is gaining new interest, and Trump and several of his prominent backers – including tech billionaires Peter Thiel, Joe Lonsdale and Marc Andreessen – support it. In a 2024 campaign statement, Trump advocated chartering up to ten new 'freedom cities', presumably carved out of federally owned land.[52] How governing rules would be established and enforced, and leaders chosen, remains fuzzy. But one critic, Gil Duran, notes that one feature is clear: 'These are going to be cities without workers' rights. These are going to be cities where the owners of the city, the corporations, the billionaires have all the power and everyone else has no power.'[53]

The Constitutional Sheriffs movement, long associated with the far right, also advocates something akin to pseudo-feudal states. It holds that county governments should have the authority to determine whether a law is constitutional within their jurisdictions without deference to the US Supreme Court. Thus, constitutional sheriffs often refuse to implement laws they disagree with, especially gun laws. Richard Mack – one of the movement's leading promoters, a former Arizona sheriff and member of the Oath Keepers – wrote a foreword for one of white-supremacist Randy Weaver's books about the 1992 Ruby Ridge, Idaho, stand-off, which has long been a cause célèbre of the far right.[54] Investigative journalist Jessica Pishko estimates that perhaps 300 of the 3,000 sheriffs in the US are associated with the Constitutional Sheriffs movement, but no solid numbers have been uncovered.[55]

Neither the Constitutional Sheriffs movement nor the Network State movement explicitly advocate civil war. To make either work, however, would require the significant weakening of the federal state, if not wholesale ungoverning.

Coup-proofing

Leaders who seek to stay in office indefinitely and fear being ousted will minimise potential domestic threats to their rule, even at the expense of homeland defence and law enforcement. This is known as coup-proofing. It is common in personalistic regimes or military dictatorships.[56] Owing to their special competence in using coercion, militaries are effective instruments of regime change. Thus, leaders fearing coups may engage in coup-proofing by deliberately kneecapping their militaries.[57]

A hallmark of this practice is undermining merit-based promotions of qualified personnel and instead elevating political loyalists, epitomised by the South Vietnamese government during the early years of the Vietnam War.[58] It prioritised loyalty – sometimes incompetent loyalty – in its senior military leadership to minimise chances of a coup. As early as 1957, the head of the US Military Assistance Advisory Group noted that in the South Vietnamese military 'officers who are performing their duties efficiently are relieved and transferred to other duties'.[59] Throughout US involvement in the war, American observers noted that Saigon's premium on loyalty and the ongoing incompetence and corruption of senior leaders severely undermined the fighting ability of South Vietnamese forces against North Vietnam.[60] In post-Saddam Hussein, US-occupied Iraq, American officials conceived of de-Ba'athification, though it proved problematic for other reasons, as a form of externally imposed coup-proofing. Saddam's Ba'athification of his government, of course, had itself constituted more successful coup-proofing.

More than once, Trump has mentioned running again in 2028 despite being constitutionally prohibited from doing so – maybe facetiously, maybe not.[61] And he has shown signs of coup-proofing. He has prized loyalty over experience in appointing palpably unqualified people to key security and intelligence positions, most notably Pete Hegseth as secretary of defense, Tulsi Gabbard as director of national intelligence and Kash Patel as director of the FBI. Trump has also continually destabilised civil–military relations by purging senior military officers, baselessly threatening to prosecute his former chairman of the Joint Chiefs of Staff (JCS) for treason and encouraging military personnel to boo former president Joe Biden at a June 2025 rally. Perhaps most tellingly, he pulled a former three-star general out of retirement and personally expedited his promotion to four-star rank so that he would qualify to become JCS chairman, whereupon his appointment was confirmed.[62] The president has considered issuing an executive order establishing a 'warrior board' composed of hand-picked retired officials to select military officers for promotion, supplanting the apolitical and rigorous intramural processes that the military branches have developed over decades.[63]

Mental instability

In some highly personalistic regimes, ungoverning may be a result of their leaders' mental problems. One of the most flagrant examples was Uganda under Idi Amin, who was widely believed to be a schizophrenic, a sadist and a cannibal. Henry Kissinger observed that he simply eliminated the leadership of entire groups 'with little regard for the consequences of wiping out the economic and intellectual backbone of the country'.[64] In particular, he expelled from the country all Asians of Indian descent with British passports in 1972 – he claimed on account of a dream he had. Because they were integral to the economy, Uganda suffered a severe economic downturn from which it did not recover for over a decade.[65]

Recent scholarship has questioned whether Amin was as crazy as he appeared. Mark Leopold concludes that 'he was not a cannibal, and did not have his wives murdered or keep heads in his fridge. He did not expel

Uganda's Asians because of a dream he had, nor because of racist attitudes towards them. He was probably not responsible for half a million deaths, nor anything like the figure.'[66] The head of the East Africa desk in the United Kingdom's Foreign and Commonwealth Office, notes Leopold, reported that he was 'not mad' and 'always found a logic, and often a craftiness and even astuteness, behind his actions'.[67] Amin may have been undertaking a political tactic known as 'dead-catting', whereby one eager to divert attention from bigger problems might throw a metaphorical dead cat on the table so that the cat was all anyone could talk about.[68] Furthermore, outré public statements that sounded stupid or insane to foreigners and educated Ugandans 'were interpreted by many in Uganda itself as the behavior of a strong, powerful man'.[69] They also made local elites and foreign leaders inclined to underestimate Amin.[70]

The safest assessment is that Amin was mentally unbalanced but sometimes might have instrumentalised his craziness calculatedly. Trump's mental issues clearly aren't comparable to Amin's. While Trump has shown clear mental decline in rambling, disjointed speeches full of non sequiturs, it is possible that at times he is dead-catting. In 2024, he characterised his speeches as 'the weave' – an intentional intertwining of stories that emerges as a coherent theme by the time he is finished.[71] He has also claimed that his policies, such as brinkmanship with North Korea, were deliberately unpredictable as opposed to incoherent – a version of the 'madman' theory associated with Richard Nixon's idea of somehow convincing the North Vietnamese that he was 'obsessed with Communism', unrestrainable 'when he is angry' and might even resort to nuclear weapons to end the war.[72] In defending economically damaging tariffs, Treasury Secretary Scott Bessent has said that 'President Trump creates what I would call strategic uncertainty in the negotiations'.[73] *New York Times* reporting has suggested that his talk about a third term is a form of dead-catting.[74]

Whether genuine impairment or political artifice, Trump's apparent eccentricity is a tool of ungoverning. Previous American instances of executive impairment – Woodrow Wilson's stroke, John F. Kennedy's use of pharmaceuticals, Ronald Reagan's Alzheimer's disease, Joe Biden's decline – were troubling, but those presidents were, to varying degrees, insulated by the competent advisers and professionalised bureaucracies that surrounded them. In the present case, these features are lacking or simply absent. Musk was reportedly using a cornucopia of drugs while in charge of DOGE.[75] Hegseth appears to have had serious problems with alcoholism, domestic abuse and sexual misconduct.[76] Patel has promoted a number of conspiracy theories, including QAnon's bizarre and unfounded notion that prominent Democrats are part of a cabal of paedophiles.[77] Moreover, in gutting the administrative state, Trump has wilfully degraded the institutional means of moderating his and his principals' excesses that previous presidents enjoyed, conducting official business via unfiltered 'truths' and 'tweets'. This too is a species of ungoverning.

*   *   *

It is unclear how far the ungoverning of the United States will go. Lawsuits by states and civil-society groups have blunted a number of Trump's efforts. Growing popular protests, a troubled economy and general discomfort with his tilt towards autocracy may motivate Congress – especially if the midterm elections improve Democrats' standing – to reassert its constitutional responsibilities and prerogatives. Furthermore, the United States has a venerable and venerated Constitution, a highly professionalised military and a fundamentally strong economy. Although Trump's machinations have shaken all three edifices, they remain potential sources of political resilience. In shrinking, denaturing and corrupting the federal workforce, however, the Trump administration has already dismantled the administrative state to a significant degree. Even if his efforts ceased immediately, American civil servants were offered their old jobs back and withheld funding were restored, some of the damage done to American democratic and economic institutions could be irreversible.

What is unprecedented and alarming about the ungoverning that Trump has unleashed is that it is occurring in a mature democracy with putatively entrenched governmental structures. The underlying political motivations – dashed economic expectations of the white working class, latent racism and xenophobia, broader culture wars between 'woke' and more conventional types – are fairly clear at this point. Nevertheless, Trump's seizure and command of the process have been shocking and traumatic. Explicitly or implicitly, he has effectively instrumentalised all five means of ungoverning discussed here: ideology, corruption, warlordism, coup-proofing and mental instability, real or perceived. The partisan and cynically compliant Republican congressional majorities, of course, bear major responsibility for facilitating state capture, as does a Supreme Court skewed to the right and apparently intent on according the president unprecedented executive authority that disparages the separation of powers.

The warlordist dimension of Trump's agenda is probably negligible. Extremist ideology and the mental instability of elected leaders are difficult for democracies to systemically preclude; just ask, say, Germany and the Philippines, respectively. The protection of democracies against corruption and coup-proofing may be more feasible by virtue of the substantially bipartisan nature of the standards that govern self-dealing and civil–military relations, respectively. Even so, Trump's ongoing self-aggrandisement through his office and his controversial deployment of the National Guard and active-duty military for domestic law enforcement have shown that these standards too are vulnerable. Should Congress and the courts resolve these issues against the Trump administration, they would go some distance in stopping the rot of executive nihilism via ungoverning. The fact remains, as Stephen Hanson and Jeffrey Kopstein point out, that there is a broad movement against modern administrative states.[78] Trump has now normalised – for some even valorised – ungoverning in established democracies. More should be anticipated.

Notes

[1] Quoted in Victor Sebestyen, 'Bannon Says He's a Leninist: That Could Explain the White House's New Tactics', *Guardian*, 6 February 2017, https://www.theguardian.com/commentisfree/2017/feb/06/lenin-white-house-steve-bannon.

[2] Quoted in Erich Wagner, 'Trump Calls Federal Workforce "Crooked", Vows to Hold Them "Accountable"', *Government Executive*, 18 August 2024, https://www.govexec.com/workforce/2024/08/trump-calls-federal-workforce-crooked-vows-hold-them-accountable/399138/.

[3] Quoted in Molly Redden, Andy Kroll and Nick Surgey, '"Put Them in Trauma": Inside a Key MAGA

Leader's Plans for a New Trump Agenda', ProPublica, 28 October 2024, https://www.propublica.org/article/video-donald-trump-russ-vought-center-renewing-america-maga.

4   See Steve Contorno and Casey Tolan, 'Trump Said He Hadn't Read Project 2025 – But Most of His Early Executive Orders Overlap with Its Proposals', CNN, 31 January 2025, https://www.cnn.com/2025/01/31/politics/trump-policy-project-2025-executive-orders-invs/index.html.

5   Quoted in Adriana Gomez Licon, 'Musk Waves a Chainsaw and Charms Conservatives Talking Up Trump's Cost-cutting Efforts', Associated Press, 21 February 2025, https://apnews.com/article/musk-chainsaw-trump-doge-6568e9e0cfc42ad6cdcfd58a409eb312.

6   William Wan and Hannah Natanson, 'White House Officials Wanted to Put Federal Workers "in Trauma." It's Working', *Washington Post*, 20 May 2025, https://www.washingtonpost.com/investigations/2025/05/20/federal-workers-trump-mental-health/.

7   See Alexandra Alper, 'Exclusive: DOGE-led Software Revamp to Speed US Job Cuts Even as Musk Steps Back', Reuters, 8 May 2025, https://www.reuters.com/business/world-at-work/doge-led-software-revamp-speed-us-job-cuts-even-musk-steps-back-2025-05-08/.

8   See Anastasia Obis, 'DoD's Purchase Card Freeze, Travel Pause Create More Uncertainty for Civilian Workforce', 14 March 2025, https://federalnewsnetwork.com/defense-main/2025/03/dods-purchase-card-freeze-travel-pause-create-more-uncertainty-for-civilian-workforce/.

9   See Andrea Shalal, James Oliphant and Bo Erickson, 'Trump Proposes $163 Billion Cut to US Budget that Slashes Domestic Spending', Reuters, 2 May 2025, https://www.reuters.com/world/us/trump-unveils-federal-budget-blueprint-2025-05-02/.

10 See Chris Baraniuk, 'Inside the Desperate Rush to Save Decades of US Scientific Data from Deletion', 23 April 2025, https://www.bbc.com/future/article/20250422-usa-scientists-race-to-save-climate-data-before-its-deleted-by-the-trump-administration; and Curtis Bunn, 'Historical Figures Cut from Military Websites While Others Are Restored Following "DEI" Ban', NBC News, 22 March 2025, https://www.nbcnews.com/news/nbcblk/historic-figures-cut-military-websites-others-are-restored-dei-ban-rcna197336.

11 See 'The Crypto Industry Is Suddenly at the Heart of American Politics', *The Economist*, 15 May 2025, https://www.economist.com/briefing/2025/05/15/the-crypto-industry-is-suddenly-at-the-heart-of-american-politics; and Jodi Vittori, 'Another Anti-corruption Pillar Crumbles', *Foreign Policy*, 14 May 2025, https://foreignpolicy.com/2025/04/07/cta-trump-anti-corruption-regulatory-chaos/.

12 See Lindsay Cohn, 'Trump's Military Purge Spells Trouble for Democracy and Defense', *Lawfare*, 27 February 2025, https://www.lawfaremedia.org/article/trump-s-military-purge-spells-trouble-for-democracy-and-defense.

13 Andrew Duehren, 'Trump Administration Pushes to Slash I.R.S.

Work Force in Half', *New York Times*, 4 March 2025, https://www.nytimes.com/2025/03/04/us/politics/irs-job-cuts.html; and Vanessa Williamson and Ellis Chen, 'What's Going On at the IRS?', *Lawfare*, 13 May 2025, https://www.lawfaremedia.org/article/what-s-going-on-at-the-irs.

14 Lawrence Gibbs et al., 'Trump Just Fired 6,700 I.R.S. Workers in the Middle of Tax Season. That's a Huge Mistake', *New York Times*, 24 February 2025, https://www.nytimes.com/2025/02/24/opinion/irs-taxes-trump.html.

15 Williamson and Chen, 'What's Going On at the IRS?'.

16 Moody's Ratings, 'Rating Action: Moody's Ratings Downgrades United States Ratings to Aa1 from Aaa; Changes Outlook to Stable', 16 May 2025, https://ratings.moodys.com/ratings-news/443154.

17 Nancy L. Rosenblum and Russell Muirhead, *Ungoverning: The Attack on the Administrative State and the Politics of Chaos* (Princeton, NJ: Princeton University Press, 2024), p. 1.

18 Ibid., p. 4.

19 Ibid., pp. 4, 6.

20 Ibid., p. 4.

21 Senator John Kennedy used the metaphor to justify the chaos caused by the Trump administration's dismemberment of USAID. See Presley Bo Tyler, '"I Like Omelets Better than Sex." Sen. John Kennedy with Strange Fox Interview Talking USAID', Yahoo News, 4 February 2025, https://www.yahoo.com/news/omelets-better-sex-sen-john-181158371.html.

22 See Timothy Snyder, *Black Earth: The Holocaust as History and Warning* (New York: Tim Duggan Books, 2015).

23 Ibid., p. 335.

24 See Alexander Laban Hinton, *Why Did They Kill? Cambodia in the Shadow of Genocide* (Berkeley, CA: University of California Press, 2004), pp. 7–8.

25 See Ahmed Rashid, *Taliban: The Power of Militant Islam in Afghanistan and Beyond* (London: I.B. Tauris & Company, 2010), p. 106.

26 Ibid., pp. 24–5.

27 See Cynthia Miller-Idriss, *Hate in the Homeland: The New Global Far Right* (Princeton, NJ: Princeton University Press, 2020), pp. 14–15.

28 Kristina Hummel, 'Uniting for Total Collapse: The January 6 Boost to Accelerationism', Combating Terrorism Center, 27 April 2021, https://ctc.westpoint.edu/uniting-for-total-collapse-the-january-6-boost-to-accelerationism/.

29 See 'Russ Vought: Donald Trump's Holy Warrior', *The Economist*, 3 January 2025, https://www.economist.com/united-states/2025/01/03/russ-vought-donald-trumps-holy-warrior.

30 Redden, Kroll and Surgey, '"Put Them in Trauma"'.

31 Curtis Yarvin, 'Curtsyarvn', *ND's Newsletter*, Substack, 18 April 2022, https://nd8ed.substack.com/p/curtsyarvn.

32 See Peter Jamison and Elizabeth Dwoskin, 'Curtis Yarvin Helped Inspire DOGE. Now He Scorns It', *Washington Post*, 8 May 2025, https://www.washingtonpost.com/politics/2025/05/08/curtis-yarvin-doge-musk-thiel/.

33 See David Streitfeld, 'Elon Musk and Donald Trump Are Splitsville, Until They Aren't', *New York Times*, 6 June 2025, https://www.nytimes.

com/2025/06/06/technology/elon-musk-trump-feud.html.

34 Jodi Vittori, 'Is America a Kleptocracy?', *Foreign Policy*, Spring 2025, https://foreignpolicy.com/2025/03/25/america-kleptocracy-trump-musk-corruption/.

35 See Daniel Kaufmann, 'State Capture: Data and What It Means for Anti-corruption Efforts', Results for Development, 27 June 2024, https://r4d.org/blog/state-capture-matters-challenging-corruption-new-dataset/.

36 Jonathan Rauch, 'One Word Describes Trump', *Atlantic*, 24 February 2025, https://www.theatlantic.com/ideas/archive/2025/02/corruption-trump-administration/681794/.

37 See Stephen E. Hanson and Jeffrey S. Kopstein, *The Assault on the State: How the Global Attack on Modern Government Endangers Our Future* (Cambridge: Polity Press, 2024), pp. 6–7.

38 See Anne Applebaum, *Autocracy, Inc: The Dictators Who Want to Run the World* (New York: Doubleday, 2024), p. 37; and 'US Accuses Venezuela's Leader of Operating "a Kleptocracy"', Voice of America, 10 September 2018, https://www.voanews.com/a/us-accuses-venezuela-s-leader-of-operating-a-kleptocracy-/4565912.html.

39 Applebaum, *Autocracy, Inc.*, p. 12.

40 See Anne Applebaum, 'Kleptocracy, Inc.', *Atlantic*, 14 April 2025, https://www.theatlantic.com/ideas/archive/2025/04/trump-kleptocracy-autocracy-inc/682281/; and Maura Reynolds, '"Everything Is Subservient to the Big Guy": Fiona Hill on Trump and America's Emerging Oligarchy', *Politico*, 28 October 2024, https://www.politico.com/news/magazine/2024/10/28/fiona-hill-explains-trump-musk-putin-00185820.

41 See Zeke Faux and Todd Gillespie, 'Commerce Nominee Lutnick Is Backer of Outlaws' Favorite Cryptocurrency', Bloomberg, 18 January 2025, https://www.bloomberg.com/news/features/2025-01-18/trump-commerce-nominee-lutnick-is-backer-of-outlaws-favorite-cryptocurrency; and Citizens for Responsibility and Ethics in Washington (CREW), 'The Trump Foundation–Pam Bondi Scandal', 4 November 2016, https://www.citizensforethics.org/reports-investigations/crew-investigations/the-trump-foundation-pam-bondi-scandal/.

42 See Joel Khalili, 'The First Bitcoin President? Tracing Trump's Crypto Connections', *Wired*, 16 January 2025, https://www.wired.com/story/mapping-donald-trump-crypto-connections/.

43 See William L. Walton, Stephen Moore and David R. Burton, 'Department of the Treasury', in Project 2025, *Mandate for Leadership: The Conservative Promise* (Washington DC: Heritage Foundation, 2023), pp. 706–8, https://static.project2025.org/2025_MandateForLeadership_FULL.pdf.

44 See Transparency International, 'Attorney General Memorandum Redirects U.S. Anti-corruption Efforts Raising Questions and Concerns', 6 February 2025, https://us.transparency.org/news/attorney-general-memorandum-raises-questions-around-enforcement-of-transnational-anti-corruption-laws/.

45 See Vittori, 'Another Anti-corruption Pillar Crumbles'.

46 See Douglass North, John Joseph Wallis and Barry Weingast, *Violence and Social Orders: A Conceptual Framework for Interpreting Recorded History* (New York: Cambridge University Press, 2009).

47 See, for example, Stephen Marche, *The Next Civil War: Dispatches from the American Future* (New York: Avid Reader Press, 2022); Jeff Sharlet, *The Undertow: Scenes from a Slow Civil War* (New York: W. W. Norton & Co., 2023); Steven Simon and Jonathan Stevenson, 'These Disunited States', *New York Review of Books*, vol. 69, no. 14, 22 September 2022, pp. 51–4; and Barbara F. Walter, *How Civil Wars Start – and How to Stop Them* (New York: Crown, 2022).

48 See Maegan Vazquez, 'Trump Circulates Quote Invoking "Civil War-like Fracture" if He's Removed from Office', CNN, 30 September 2019, https://www.cnn.com/2019/09/30/politics/donald-trump-civil-war-impeachment.

49 Quoted in Alexander Laban Hinton, *It Can Happen Here: White Power and the Rising Threat of Genocide in the US*, reprint edition (New York: NYU Press, 2022), pp. 162, 163.

50 See Caroline Haskins, '"Startup Nation" Groups Say They're Meeting Trump Officials to Push for Deregulated "Freedom Cities"', *Wired*, 7 March 2025, https://www.wired.com/story/startup-nations-donald-trump-legislation/.

51 See Lucas Ropek, 'Worst New Trend of 2024: Techno-colonialism and the Network State Movement', Gizmodo, 27 December 2024, https://gizmodo.com/worst-new-trend-of-2024-techno-colonialism-and-the-network-state-movement-2000525617; and Oliver Wainwright, 'Seasteading – A Vanity Project for the Rich or the Future of Humanity?', *Guardian*, 24 June 2020, https://www.theguardian.com/environment/2020/jun/24/seasteading-a-vanity-project-for-the-rich-or-the-future-of-humanity.

52 See 'JUST IN: Trump Proposes Building Ten New US "Freedom Cities", Offering "Baby Bonuses"', Forbes Breaking News, 3 March 2023, https://www.youtube.com/watch?v=dJA_GBhCGgE.

53 Quoted in Haskins, '"Startup Nation" Groups Say They're Meeting Trump Officials to Push for Deregulated "Freedom Cities"'.

54 See Southern Poverty Law Center, 'Constitutional Sheriffs', 2023, https://www.splcenter.org/resources/extremist-files/constitutional-sheriffs/.

55 See Jessica Pishko, *The Highest Law in the Land: How the Unchecked Power of Sheriffs Threatens Democracy* (New York: Dutton, 2024).

56 See Caitlin Talmadge, *The Dictator's Army: Battlefield Effectiveness in Authoritarian Regimes* (Ithaca, NY: Cornell University Press, 2015), pp. 20–1.

57 See *ibid.*, pp. 14–16.

58 See *ibid.*, p. 54.

59 Quoted in *ibid.*, p. 54.

60 *Ibid.*, pp. 54–66.

61 See, for example, Erica L. Green, 'Trump Says He's "Not Joking" About Seeking a Third Term in Defiance of Constitution', *New York Times*, 30 March 2025 (updated 2 April 2025), https://www.nytimes.com/2025/03/30/us/trump-third-term.html.

62 See Steven Simon and Jonathan Stevenson, 'What Trump Could Do to the U.S. Military', *New York Times*, 12 December 2024, https://www.nytimes.com/2024/12/12/opinion/donald-trump-us-military.html.
63 See Vivian Salama, Nancy A. Youssef and Lara Seligman, 'Trump Draft Executive Order Would Create Board to Purge Generals', *Wall Street Journal*, 12 November 2024, https://www.wsj.com/politics/national-security/trump-draft-executive-order-would-create-board-to-purge-generals-7ebaa606?gaa.
64 Henry Kissinger, 'Memorandum from the President's Assistant for National Security Affairs (Kissinger) to President Nixon', 1 November 1972, https://history.state.gov/historicaldocuments/frus1969-76ve05p1/d261.
65 See Mark Leopold, *Idi Amin: The Story of Africa's Icon of Evil* (New Haven, CT: Yale University Press, 2021), pp. 229–35.
66 Ibid., p. 314.
67 Ibid., p. 310.
68 See, for example, David Smith, 'Boris Johnson's Dead Cat Tactics on Tax and a No-deal Brexit', *The Times*, 15 June 2019, https://www.thetimes.com/uk/politics/article/boris-johnsons-dead-cat-tactics-on-tax-and-a-no-deal-brexit-qthllcn9f.
69 Leopold, *Idi Amin*, p. 298.
70 See *ibid.*, p. 300.
71 See Bill Barrow, 'Inside "the Weave": How Donald Trump's Rhetoric Has Grown Darker and Windier', Associated Press, 30 October 2024, https://www.ap.org/news-highlights/spotlights/2024/inside-the-weave-how-donald-trumps-rhetoric-has-grown-darker-and-windier/.
72 Robert Dallek, *Nixon and Kissinger: Partners in Power* (London: Penguin, 2008), p. 106. See also Daniel W. Drezner, 'Does the Madman Theory Actually Work?', *Foreign Policy*, 7 January 2025, https://foreignpolicy.com/2025/01/07/madman-theory-international-relations-unpredictability/; and Jonathan Stevenson, 'The Madness Behind Trump's "Madman" Strategy', *New York Times*, 26 October 2017, https://www.nytimes.com/2017/10/26/opinion/the-madness-behind-trumps-madman-strategy.html.
73 'WATCH: Bessent Defends Trump's "Strategic Uncertainty", Says Certainty "Not Necessarily a Good Thing in Negotiating"', PBS News, 28 April 2025, https://www.pbs.org/newshour/politics/watch-bessent-defends-trumps-strategic-uncertainty-says-certainty-not-necessarily-a-good-thing-in-negotiating.
74 See Tyler Pager, 'The Strategy Behind Trump's Repeated Musings About a Third Term', *New York Times*, 31 March 2025 (updated 1 April 2025), https://www.nytimes.com/2025/03/31/us/politics/trump-third-term.html.
75 See Kirsten Grind, 'On the Campaign Trail, Elon Musk Juggled Drugs and Family Drama', *New York Times*, 30 May 2025, https://www.nytimes.com/2025/05/30/us/elon-musk-drugs-children-trump.html.
76 See Deirdre Walsh, 'Pete Hegseth Faces New Allegations of Alcohol Abuse and Misconduct', NPR, 22 January 2025, https://www.npr.org/2025/01/22/nx-s1-5270033/

pete-hegseth-faces-new-allegations-of-alcohol-abuse-and-misconduct.

77 See David Corn, 'How Kash Patel, Trump's FBI Pick, Embraced the Unhinged QAnon Movement', *Mother Jones*, 1 December 2024, https://www.motherjones.com/politics/2024/12/kash-patel-qanon-trump-fbi/.

78 See Hanson and Kopstein, *The Assault on the State*, p. 6.

A 'Reverse Kissinger'? Why Trump's Anti-China Rapprochement with Russia Is Likely to Fail

Geraint Hughes and Zeno Leoni

In late October 2024, during an interview with Tucker Carlson, Donald Trump argued that he wanted to 'un-unite' Russia and China.[1] He made similar remarks following his return to the Oval Office in March 2025, when he maintained that '[as] a student of history, which I am – and I've watched it all – the first thing you learn is you don't want Russia and China to get together'.[2] Readers of this journal may question the current US president's commitment to self-education – particularly in a discipline as contested as history – but his long-standing admiration for his Russian counterpart, Vladimir Putin; his officials' contempt for European allies; the administration's questioning of US defence aid to Ukraine (as shown by Trump's and Vice President JD Vance's public confrontation with Ukrainian President Volodymyr Zelenskyy on 28 February); Trump's claims that he can negotiate an end to the Russo-Ukrainian war, even if this involves compelling Kyiv to accede to some of Moscow's demands; and his interest in a rapprochement between the United States and Russia are all a matter of record.[3]

The Trump administration's Russia policy has not only ignited a continent-wide dialogue about Europe's future without the US as a security provider, but it has also contributed to speculation that the

---

Geraint Hughes is a Reader in Diplomatic and Military History at King's College London. His latest book is *Britain and the Dhofar War in Oman, 1963–1976: A Covert War in Arabia* (Springer Nature, 2024). **Zeno Leoni** is a Lecturer in Defence Studies at King's College London. His latest book is *A New Cold War: US–China Relations in the 21st Century* (Bristol University Press, 2024).

White House might pursue a '1972 moment' with Moscow, resembling former president Richard Nixon's visit to China in February 1972. The visit represented a significant systemic change that ultimately contributed to the end of the Cold War, a development that Stephen Kotkin suggests holds more weight than the events of 1989.[4] While the prospects of such a 'grand bargain' today have been critiqued by sceptics, others have speculated that a US effort at a 'reverse Kissinger' (a reference to Nixon's national security advisor, and then secretary of state, Henry Kissinger) could break up the 'no limits' partnership between Moscow and Beijing, and provide the possible beginning of a stable 'new world order'.[5] The argument here is that Trump is pursuing a 'new kind of diplomacy' with the aim of building a '"concert" system akin to the one that shaped Europe during the nineteenth century'.[6]

These discussions are part of a growing debate about the potential re-emergence of geopolitical blocs and the Sino-Russian alliance.[7] The idea of a US–Russia rapprochement has raised considerable alarm among European leaders, who remain apprehensive about the possibility that this would lead to the end of NATO and their abandonment.[8] This situation has not only generated a renewed emphasis on military build-up, but also prompted questions about whether Brussels should adopt a more cooperative approach with China, which would not be illogical in the wake of a US–Russia reconciliation.[9]

Taking up Trump's challenge to study the history, this article questions the viability of a reverse Kissinger. Shifts in alliances and diplomatic rapprochements have, to be fair, been a fundamental aspect of international relations, and a decrease in tensions between the US and Russia is theoretically possible in the context of US–China rivalry. Nevertheless, the notion that the US could woo the Russian Federation just as Nixon did with China 53 years ago, thereby counterbalancing Chinese power, is unwarranted, drawing on misplaced historical analogising. Overestimating the possible outcomes of US–Russia discussions heightens the dangers associated with rapid and chaotic rearmament in Europe, and also signifies a failure to recognise the intricacies of the ongoing geopolitical shift in contrast to – in hindsight – the less complicated landscape of the Cold War.

Shifting alliances in history

Colin Krainin has described the history of international politics as being 'littered with rapid revisions' to alliances.[10] In a contribution to this journal on why alliances end (or change), Stephen Walt argued that because being part of a pact has costs, 'states will be reluctant to bear these costs if the alliance no longer serves a useful purpose'.[11] According to Walt, alliance dynamics could be transformed in a changing international environment with new security threats if a pact declined in strength or credibility, or due to domestic politics.[12] One of the most striking instances is the Diplomatic Revolution of 1756, often referred to as the *renversement des alliances*. For centuries, the rivalry between France and the Habsburg dynasty was 'axiomatic', as both sought to assert their dominance in Christian Europe.[13] On 1 May 1756, France entered into various treaties with Austria, which primarily guaranteed the latter's neutrality in the impending conflict between France and Britain, resulting in a 'defensive alliance'.[14] Central to this change were several issues highlighted by Walt, including the strained relations between Britain and Austria, as London expressed disappointment that Vienna had consistently failed to maintain its military commitments, alongside the emergence of Prussia as a significant new threat to the Habsburgs. This not only signalled a diplomatic realignment across Europe, but it also set the stage for the Seven Years' War (1756–63).

The Diplomatic Revolution is just one of several alliance shifts seen in history, some of which had significant systemic effects. For example, in 1915, Italy left the Triple Alliance and aligned itself with Britain, France and Russia, primarily due to concerns over territorial conflicts with Austria-Hungary.[15] Although not formally allied, Nazi Germany and the Soviet Union entered the Molotov–Ribbentrop non-aggression pact in 1939, which they exploited to partition Eastern Europe into spheres of influence. This pact was ultimately violated by Germany during *Operation Barbarossa*.[16] The conclusion of the Second World War resulted in a formal alliance between the US and Japan in 1951, a partnership that would have seemed impossible just a few years earlier.[17] Similarly, after the revolutions of 1989–91, former Warsaw Pact states such as Poland and the three newly independent Baltic states actively sought membership of NATO. In these cases, domestic political change (the end of communism and the transition to democracy) and fears of renewed Russian dominance influenced the decision-making of NATO applicants from 1997 to 2004.[18] If one bears in mind that Estonia, Latvia and Lithuania's annexation by the Soviet Union was due to the Molotov–Ribbentrop pact, then one can see a direct link between the 'diplomatic revolutions' of 1939 and those that followed the end of the Cold War.

US perspectives on Russia

As Charles Kupchan wrote about the expansion of NATO in the post-Cold War years, 'enemies [can] become friends'.[19] Therefore, a rapprochement between the United States and Moscow might not be surprising, particularly as such an idea predates the second Trump administration. Kissinger himself supported a more amicable relationship with Russia following the conclusion of the Cold War, while the international-relations scholar John J. Mearsheimer argued for years that the US will 'someday need Russia's help containing a rising China'.[20]

The emergence of China has certainly altered the geostrategic priorities of the United States over the past 20 years, particularly following Barack Obama's 'pivot to Asia' strategy, which necessitated the resolution of various disputes, including with Moscow in Eastern Europe and Tehran in the Middle East. Supporters of both the 44th and 45th/47th presidents may be incensed by the comparison, but it is worth recalling that both Obama and Trump aimed to engage with Russia to foster opportunities for collaboration. The former envisaged a 'reset' of the relationship between the United States and Russia, dispatching then-secretary of state Hillary Clinton to Moscow in March 2009, with the objectives of enhancing collaboration on arms control and the global financial crisis, and persuading the Russians to cancel an air-defence contract in Iran.[21] In turn, the Obama administration backed Russia's accession to the World Trade Organization and established the US–Russia Bilateral Presidential Commission, while the US government halted the deployment of missile-defence systems in Poland and the Czech Republic. This ultimately resulted in Russia's abstention from United Nations Security Council Resolution 1973 in April 2011, facilitating military intervention in Libya.[22] Perhaps most importantly, Obama was hesitant about providing military assistance to Ukraine after the takeover of Crimea in February–March 2014, although he subsequently launched the European Deterrence Initiative (EDI) in an effort to reassure NATO allies that the US still had a stake in their security.[23]

During his first presidency, Trump articulated a consistent perspective on Russia that favoured rapprochement. He emphasised the need to respect Russia for its role in the Second World War, and asserted that fostering a positive relationship with Russia was in the interest of the United States. 'I just want to have this country be safe', he said, noting that 'Russia and the United States control 90% of the nuclear weapons in the world'.[24] Asked whether he believed that the US and Russia were 'chief adversaries', Trump answered by saying: 'I don't wanna even use the word adversary, we can all work together, we can do great, everybody can do well and we can live in peace.'[25] Nevertheless, he increased funding for the EDI, raising it from the $5.2 billion allocated under Obama to $17.2bn, demonstrating that US foreign policy may not be the product solely of the president's will, but of mediated interests.[26]

Members of Trump's current team have conveyed comparable sentiments, although they have also expressed a more explicit commitment to NATO than Trump himself. In February 2025, US Secretary of State Marco Rubio, US national security advisor Mike Waltz, and Trump's special envoy and negotiator Steve Witkoff made individual statements emphasising the potential benefits that a peace agreement between Russia and Ukraine could offer to the United States' relationship with Moscow.[27] This did not necessarily mean, however, that a diplomatic manoeuvre comparable to that executed by Nixon and Kissinger was on the way.

The 1972 rapprochement

After the establishment of the People's Republic of China in October 1949, successive US administrations adopted a policy combining military containment with efforts at diplomatic isolation, reflecting the view that 'Red China' was run by an illegitimate regime, and that the *de jure* government of China could be found in Taiwan. The US and China fought each other directly during the Korean War (1950–53), and came close to confrontation during the Taiwan crises of 1955 and 1958, as well as during the Vietnam War. Yet by the end of the 1960s, Nixon and Kissinger had several reasons to change course.[28]

Firstly, the US needed to end its disastrous embroilment in Vietnam. Nixon had pledged during the 1968 presidential election to achieve a negotiated settlement that would enable a US troop withdrawal. A second reason was the emergence of the 'triangular diplomacy' concept, whereby the Soviet Union and China would compete with each other to seek better relations with the US while trying to avoid being the odd man out in the great-power competition among the three countries. Nixon and his national security advisor believed that this would encourage both Mao Zedong and Leonid Brezhnev to enable peace negotiations with North Vietnam that would allow for a face-saving US withdrawal.[29] The third reason concerned Kissinger's own views on the global balance of power – deriving from his doctoral studies at Harvard on nineteenth-century European power politics – and his belief that China was an essential part of it. The *existence* of the People's Republic was not an inherent problem for US national interests, he believed; only its *hostility* towards the West was. A rapprochement with Mao would therefore be strategically beneficial for the US, minimising the risks of great-power confrontation and a third world war, not least by providing Washington with a means of counterbalancing Moscow.[30] This perspective was also reflected in Nixon's October 1967 remark that 'we simply cannot afford to leave China forever outside the family of nations'.[31]

The fourth reason involved the president's self-perception that he had a gift for statecraft that traditional foreign-policy elites, whom he associated with his political foes, did not possess. In Congress (1947–53) and as Dwight D. Eisenhower's vice president (1953–61), Nixon had established himself as an anti-communist hawk, particularly towards Beijing, and these credentials helped protect him from attack by the political right for either compromising national security or being 'soft' on China. Nixon therefore believed that he could achieve a diplomatic triumph that none of his predecessors could have managed. While the origins of the phrase 'only Nixon could go to China' can be traced to one of his Democratic opponents, it was a statement that the president himself subscribed to.[32]

Nixon and Kissinger's overtures to Beijing would have failed, however, had it not been for Mao's own reassessment of Chinese national strategy. In March 1969, the Sino-Soviet split turned bloody, with a battle over the disputed island of Zhenbao/Damansky leading to a series of border clashes. Rumours that Moscow was considering a pre-emptive nuclear strike panicked the Chinese leadership, and Beijing began to envisage an all-out war with the Soviet Union rather than the US.[33] For Mao, China's northern neighbour had become the main enemy, and it made strategic sense to seek rapprochement with the Americans.[34] This thinking set the stage for Nixon's groundbreaking visit to Beijing in February 1972.

Furthermore, and with the obvious exception of Taiwan, US allies either welcomed or acquiesced in Nixon's overtures to China. Even the British – as the United States' most loyal allies – had maintained diplomatic ties with the People's Republic since January 1950, and had their own opening to Beijing with the visit by Alec Douglas-Home, then foreign secretary, in October–November 1972.[35] Both the Western Europeans and the Japanese had long regarded the United States' refusal to recognise the People's Republic as absurd, and the reversal of this policy as long overdue.

Challenges to a US–Russia rapprochement

Any effort at a 'reverse Kissinger' would confront stark differences between the favourable conditions of 1972 and the realities of today. The first concerns the current state of Sino-Russian relations, compared to the early 1970s. Despite Chinese leader Xi Jinping's rhetoric on the 'long-standing friendship' between the two powers, Russia was as complicit as other external aggressors in what Beijing terms its 'century of humiliation', carrying out territorial annexations during the nineteenth century and anti-Chinese atrocities such as the Blagoveshchensk massacres of July 1900.[36] By the time Nixon and Kissinger were making their overtures to Mao, Soviet and Chinese soldiers were killing each other in border clashes. Today, by contrast, Russian armed forces and China's People's Liberation Army conduct joint military exercises. Although Mark Galeotti has argued that the policymaking elite in Moscow privately regard the People's Republic as a long-term threat to national security, neither China nor Russia shows any inclination to return to an armed stand-off on their frontiers.[37] And whatever private tensions may have emerged between Putin and Xi over the Ukraine war, the countries' bilateral relations are a long way from the border fighting of 1969.[38]

Secondly, Mao made a major policy concession over the course of 1969–72, which was to abandon his global revolutionary agenda in the interests of normalisation with the US and other Western powers. Chinese foreign policy in the 1960s involved backing far-left insurgent movements across the world, and during the height of the Vietnam War in 1965–68, Beijing urged Hanoi to ignore calls for peace negotiations and to fight the 'people's war' against the Americans to the end. This revisionist international agenda was gradually abandoned from the early 1970s in favour of a less radical and more conciliatory foreign policy towards the West – a prime example being the change in tone in Sino-British discussions over the future of Hong Kong.[39] In contrast, there is little sign that Putin's Russia is prepared to reverse its hostility towards NATO members, or to compromise on its maximalist objectives in Ukraine.[40] America's quagmire in Vietnam was a stimulus to Sino-American reconciliation, but there are no indications that Russia's far more costly and bloody military adventure in Ukraine has forced its president to seek a diplomatic way out.[41]

Finally, although Nixon's rapprochement with Beijing ended the United States' policy of treating Taiwan as the 'legitimate' Chinese state, his administration did not completely abandon the island, and its successors continued to arm it. Mao tacitly accepted that the US–Taiwanese relationship would continue, albeit in a more muted form. In contrast, it is hard to see how an implicit bargain between Trump and Putin would work without significant concessions from the United States, which might include ceding not only Ukraine, but also NATO's eastern member states, to Russia's sphere of influence.[42]

* * *

Nixon's visit to Beijing and the ensuing Sino-American *entente* took advantage of a rift that was fully developed between the Soviet Union and the People's Republic. It would be much harder to prise the Russians and Chinese apart today.

Trump's misconceived diplomatic approach towards Russia has created anxiety among European leaders. While this may encourage them to greater defence spending and multilateral cooperation – which Trump and his officials see as beneficial to US interests – it may also undermine NATO's cohesion and lead America's allies not only to doubt the reliability, credibility and dependability of the US defence commitment to Europe, but also to lose faith in the competence of US policymaking more generally. A more rational and historically grounded examination of Trump's current outreach to Russia suggests that it will be exploited to maximum diplomatic effect by Putin, with consequences not just for Europe, but also for US national-security interests as the transatlantic alliance is weakened and the relationship between Eurasia's two chief autocrats is strengthened.[43]

The Trump administration is already discovering the difficulties of translating the president's declared wishes to end the Russo-Ukrainian war into diplomatic practice.[44] Wider geopolitical and structural factors in the current international system suggest that attempts to entice Putin away from Xi will likewise end in failure.

Notes

[1] 'Former President Trump Campaigns with Tucker Carlson in Glendale', C-Span, 31 October 2024, https://www.c-span.org/program/campaign-2024/former-president-trump-campaigns-with-tucker-carlson-in-glendale-arizona/651374.

[2] Kate Sullivan, 'Trump Says US Doesn't Want Russia, China Moving Closer Together', Bloomberg, 19 March 2025, https://www.bloomberg.com/news/articles/2025-03-19/trump-says-us-doesn-t-want-russia-china-moving-closer-together.

[3] See David A. Graham, 'Donald Trump's Narrative of the Life of Frederick Douglass', *Atlantic*, 1 February 2017, https://www.theatlantic.com/politics/archive/2017/02/frederick-douglass-trump/515292/; Hal Brands and Jeremi Suri (eds), *The Power of the Past: History and Statecraft* (Washington DC: Brookings Institution Press, 2016); Jeffrey Goldberg, 'The Trump Administration Accidentally Texted Me Its War Plans', *Atlantic*, 24 March 2025, https://www.theatlantic.com/politics/archive/2025/03/trump-administration-accidentally-texted-me-its-war-plans/682151/; and 'Zelensky Told to Leave White House After Angry Spat with Trump and Vance', BBC News, 27 February 2025, https://www.bbc.co.uk/news/live/c625ex282zzt.

4   Stephen Kotkin, 'The Cold War Never Ended: Ukraine, the China Challenge, and the Revival of the West', *Foreign Affairs*, vol. 101, no. 3, May/June 2022, p. 67.
5   See Michael McFaul and Evan S. Medeiros, 'China and Russia Will Not Be Split', *Foreign Affairs*, 4 April 2025, https://www.foreignaffairs.com/united-states/china-and-russia-will-not-be-split; A. Wess Mitchell, 'The Return of Great-power Diplomacy', *Foreign Affairs*, May/June 2025, https://www.foreignaffairs.com/united-states/return-great-power-diplomacy-strategy-wess-mitchell; Jianli Yang, 'The Myth of a "Reverse Kissinger": Why Aligning with Russia to Counter China Is a Strategic Illusion', *Diplomat*, 21 February 2025, https://thediplomat.com/2025/02/the-myth-of-a-reverse-kissinger-why-aligning-with-russia-to-counter-china-is-a-strategic-illusion/; Nathaniel Reynolds, 'Russia Is Playing Along with Trump's Hopes for a Rapprochement', Carnegie Endowment for Peace, 15 April 2025, https://carnegieendowment.org/emissary/2025/04/putin-trump-russia-goals-opportunity-ukraine?lang=en; Christian Caryl, 'A Grand Bargain with Russia Would Be a Disaster', *Foreign Policy*, 20 February 2025, https://foreignpolicy.com/2025/02/20/trump-china-russia-grand-bargain-nixon/; and Allan Little, 'Trump Has Blown Up the World Order – and Left Europe's Leaders Scrabbling', BBC News, 26 March 2025, https://www.bbc.co.uk/news/articles/c2er9j83x0z0.
6   Stacie E. Goddard, 'The Rise and Fall of Great-power Competition', *Foreign Affairs*, May/June 2025, https://www.foreignaffairs.com/united-states/rise-and-fall-great-power-competition.
7   See Christopher S. Chivvis and Jack Keating, 'How Evil? Deconstructing the New Russia–China–Iran–North Korea Axis', *Survival*, vol. 66, no. 6, December 2024–January 2025, pp. 51–66; and Zeno Leoni and Sarah Tzinieris, 'The Return of Geopolitical Blocs', *Survival*, vol. 66, no. 2, April–May 2024, pp. 37–54.
8   See Henry Foy and Gideon Rachman, 'EU Readies "Plan B" Should Donald Trump Walk Away from Ukraine Talks', *Financial Times*, 30 April 2025, https://www.ft.com/content/1f4ba00b-9e90-4c9b-be6b-e57efaf1e9d5; and Claire Mills, 'Ukraine and Russia: A Shift in US Policy', House of Commons Library, 3 April 2025, p. 6, https://researchbriefings.files.parliament.uk/documents/CBP-10218/CBP-10218.pdf.
9   See Josef Bouska, 'Russian Roulette – Trump Is Losing Europe and Strengthening China Instead of Isolating It', *Newsweek*, 5 May 2025, https://www.newsweek.com/russian-roulettetrump-losing-europe-strengthening-china-instead-isolating-it-opinion-2039537.
10 Colin Krainin, 'Alliance Dynamics in the Shadow of Shifting Power', *International Studies Quarterly*, vol. 65, no. 4, December 2021, pp. 905–18.
11 Stephen M. Walt, 'Why Alliances Endure or Collapse', *Survival*, vol. 39, no. 1, February–March 1997, p. 158.
12 *Ibid.*, pp. 160–3.
13 David Bayne Horn, 'The Diplomatic Revolution', in J.O. Lindsay (ed.), *The New Cambridge Modern History*,

Volume 7: *The Old Regime, 1713–63* (New York: Cambridge University Press, 1957), p. 440.
14 Randall Lesaffer, 'The Diplomatic Revolution: The First Alliance of Versailles (1756)', Oxford Public International Law, https://opil.ouplaw.com/page/539.
15 See Nicola Labanca, 'The Italian Front', in Jay Winter (ed.), *The Cambridge History of the First World War, Volume I: Global War* (Cambridge: Cambridge University Press, 2013), pp. 269–70.
16 See Roger Moorhouse, *The Devil's Alliance: Hitler's Pact with Stalin, 1939–1941* (London: Vintage, 2014).
17 See Melvyn P. Leffler, *A Preponderance of Power: National Security, the Truman Administration, and the Cold War* (Stanford, CA: Stanford University Press, 1992), pp. 463–9.
18 See M.E. Sarotte, 'How to Enlarge NATO: The Debate Inside the Clinton Administration, 1993–95', *International Security*, vol. 44, no. 1, 2019, pp. 7–41.
19 Charles Kupchan, *How Enemies Become Friends: The Sources of Stable Peace* (Princeton, NJ: Princeton University Press, 2010).
20 See Michael Rubin and Ivana Stradner, 'Henry Kissinger's Long History of Appeasing Dictatorships', American Enterprise Institute, 9 June 2022, https://www.aei.org/op-eds/henry-kissingers-long-history-of-appeasing-dictatorships/; and John J. Mearsheimer, 'Why the Ukraine Crisis Is the West's Fault: The Liberal Delusions that Provoked Putin', *Foreign Affairs*, vol. 93, no. 5, September/October 2014, p. 89.
21 See Angela Stent, 'US–Russia Relations in the Second Obama Administration', *Survival*, vol. 54, no. 6, December 2012–January 2013, pp. 126–7.
22 See Ruth Deyermond, 'The Republican Challenge to Obama's Russia Policy', *Survival*, vol. 54, no. 5, October–November 2012, pp. 70–1; and Douglas J. Feith and Seth Cropsey, 'How the Russian "Reset" Explains Obama's Foreign Policy', *Foreign Policy*, 16 October 2012, https://foreignpolicy.com/2012/10/16/how-the-russian-reset-explains-obamas-foreign-policy/.
23 See Adrian Karatnycky, 'The Long, Destructive Shadow of Obama's Russia Doctrine', *Foreign Policy*, 11 July 2023, https://foreignpolicy.com/2023/07/11/obama-russia-ukraine-war-putin-2014-crimea-georgia-biden/.
24 'Trump: I'm Not Pro-Russia, I Just Want Our Country Safe', *Tucker Carlson Tonight*, Fox News, 10 September 2020, https://video.foxnews.com/v/5810471499001#sp=show-clips.
25 *Ibid*.
26 David Welna, 'Under Trump, NATO Nations Get More U.S. Troops and Military Spending', NPR, 3 December 2019, https://www.npr.org/2019/12/03/784444270/under-trump-nato-nations-get-more-u-s-troops-and-military-spending?t=1588851629769.
27 See Keith Johnson, 'Trump's Proposed Economic Rapprochement with Russia Is Wrongheaded', *Foreign Policy*, 26 February 2025, https://foreignpolicy.com/2025/02/26/trump-russia-putin-sanctions-ukraine-war/.
28 See the introduction to William Burr (ed.), *The Kissinger Transcripts:*

The Top-secret Talks with Beijing and Moscow (New York: W. W. Norton and Company, 1999), pp. 1–26.

29 See Jussi Hanhimaki, 'Selling the "Decent Interval": Kissinger, Triangular Diplomacy, and the End of the Vietnam War, 1971–1973', *Diplomacy and Statecraft*, vol. 14, no. 1, 2003, pp. 159–94.

30 See Robert Dallek, *Nixon and Kissinger: Partners in Power* (London: Penguin 2008), pp. 45–6.

31 Richard Nixon, 'Asia After Vietnam', *Foreign Affairs*, vol. 46, no. 1, 1967, p. 121. Nixon's perspective was also informed by an economic agenda: the opening up of the Chinese market to the global economy was to produce a true change in the world order. See Zeno Leoni, *Grand Strategy and the Rise of China* (Newcastle-upon-Tyne: Agenda Publishing, 2023), pp. 29–46.

32 Senator Mike Mansfield used the phrase in an interview with *US News & World Report* in 1971. 'A Size-up of President Nixon: Interview with Mike Mansfield, Senate Democratic Leader', *US News & World Report*, 6 December 1971.

33 See Raymond Garthoff, *Détente and Confrontation: American–Soviet Relations from Nixon to Reagan*, 2nd ed. (Washington DC: Brookings Institution Press, 1994), pp. 230–1, 237–8; and Covell F. Meyskens, *Mao's Third Front: The Militarization of Cold War China* (Cambridge: Cambridge University Press, 2020).

34 See Chen Jian and David L. Wilson (eds), '"All Under the Heaven Is Great Chaos": Beijing, the Sino-Soviet Border Clashes, and the Turn Towards Sino-American Rapprochement, 1968–69', *Cold War International History Project Bulletin*, no. 11, Winter 1998, pp. 155–75.

35 See Chi-kwan Mark, *The Everyday Cold War: Britain and China, 1950–1972* (London: Bloomsbury, 2019).

36 See 'Xi Hails "Confident" China–Russia Ties as Putin Welcomes "Dear Friend" to Kremlin', *Guardian*, 8 May 2025, https://www.theguardian.com/world/2025/may/08/xi-jinping-vladimir-putin-china-russia-kremlin; and Robert Bickers, *The Scramble for China: Foreign Devils in the Qing Empire* (London: Penguin, 2012), pp. 154, 348.

37 See Mark A. Green, 'China and Russia: Quietly Going Steady', Wilson Center, 29 October 2024, https://www.wilsoncenter.org/blog-post/china-and-russia-quietly-going-steady; and Mark Galeotti, *Putin's Wars: From Chechnya to Ukraine* (London: Osprey Books, 2022), pp. 337–41.

38 See Sergei Radchenko, 'Driving a Wedge Between China and Russia Won't Work', *War on the Rocks*, 24 August 2021, https://warontherocks.com/2021/08/driving-a-wedge-between-china-and-russia-wont-work/.

39 See Robert Bickers, *Out of China: How the Chinese Ended the Era of Western Domination* (London: Penguin, 2018), pp. 350–66.

40 See Lawrence Freedman, 'Strategic Fanaticism: Vladimir Putin and Ukraine', in Hal Brands (ed.), *War in Ukraine: Conflict, Strategy, and the Return of a Fractured World* (Baltimore, MD: Johns Hopkins University Press, 2024), pp. 55–70.

41 See Center for Strategic and International Studies, 'The State of Russia–Ukraine Negotiations

with Michael Kimmage', 2 May 2025, https://www.youtube.com/watch?v=T1JV6aaDgjc.

42 Prior to the Russian invasion of Ukraine, Moscow issued a draft agreement with the US and NATO which demanded a withdrawal of allied forces from Poland and the Baltic states. See Steven Pifer, 'Russia's Draft Agreements with NATO and the United States: Intended for Rejection?', Brookings, 21 December 2021, https://www.brookings.edu/articles/russias-draft-agreements-with-nato-and-the-united-states-intended-for-rejection/.

43 See Erik Jones, 'Transatlantic Rupture: Legitimacy, Integration and Security', *Survival*, vol. 67, no. 2, April–May 2025, pp. 69–84.

44 See 'Zelensky Challenges Putin to Meet Him After Trump Demands Ukraine–Russia Talks', BBC News, 11 May 2025, https://www.bbc.co.uk/news/articles/ckgxrmolnego.

Review Essay

Angela Merkel: A Status Quo Leader in a Revisionist Era

Hanns W. Maull

Freedom: Memoirs 1954–2021
Angela Merkel with Beate Baumann. New York: St. Martin's Press, 2024. $40.00. 720 pp.

Russian prime minister Vladimir Putin kept his host, German chancellor Angela Merkel, and her other guests waiting for almost an hour. The setting was the 2007 G8 summit at Heiligendamm, a German resort on the shores of the Baltic Sea, and the eight leaders were to have an informal outdoor aperitif before dinner. Merkel relates her feelings about Putin's behaviour at the time in her memoirs, one of the very few instances where she allows herself emotion: 'Outwardly, I was having a relaxed chat with the others; inwardly, I was seething' (p. 355). When he finally joined the group, Putin blamed Merkel for the delay. She had, upon his request, sent to his room a crate of his favourite Radeberger beer, which he had come to know and appreciate during his time as a KGB officer in Dresden. He simply had to sample it, and that had kept him away.

Merkel had no illusions about Putin. During their first official encounter as the leaders of Russia and Germany in January 2006, he had presented her with a large stuffed dog: a not-so-subtle hint that he was aware of her fear of dogs (she had been bitten by one). When she visited him in Sochi in January 2007, he tried to scare her by having his huge black Labrador Koni

---

Hanns W. Maull is Senior Distinguished Fellow at the German Institute for International and Security Affairs (SWP) and Adjunct Professor for International Relations and Strategic Studies at Johns Hopkins University, School of Advanced International Studies (SAIS) Europe.

sniff around her, in front of the photographers and camera crews. In both instances, Merkel reminded herself of a maxim of the British royal family: 'never explain, never complain' (pp. 355–60).

Perhaps she should have complained. When she left office on 8 December 2021, she was still widely revered and admired. She had led four governments and held the office of chancellor for 16 years, almost as long as her mentor Helmut Kohl, and much longer than any other chancellor in the history of the Federal Republic.[1] She had appeared several times on the cover of *Time* magazine, which named her 'Person of the Year 2015' as 'Europe's most powerful leader'.[2] By late February 2022, however, her reputation was plummeting as Putin launched his war against Ukraine, prompting Merkel's successor, Olaf Scholz, to cancel Nord Stream 2, Germany's controversial natural-gas project with Russia, and announce a *Zeitenwende* (turning point) in German foreign and security policy.[3]

Eastern illusions

Blaming Merkel for Berlin's misconceived Russia policy is somewhat unfair. She had inherited that policy from her Social Democratic predecessor, Gerhard Schröder, who later joined the board of Gazprom and became a lobbyist for Putin in Germany. Moreover, much of that policy was carried forward by Frank-Walter Steinmeier – Merkel's Social Democratic foreign minister, a long-time collaborator of Schröder's and now federal president – and his mostly Social Democratic successors. The policy rested on profoundly distorted perceptions of Russia under Putin, harboured by both the foreign-policy establishment in Berlin and the German people, particularly in the former East Germany, where many Germans carry complicated emotional baggage related to their convoluted shared history with what was once the Soviet Union. An extensive Russian influence operation in Germany, built from the KGB playbook that Putin knew well, burnished these perceptions.[4]

Merkel did not share those misperceptions and emotions. Yet she not only allowed policies based on them to continue but also, with Nord

Stream 2, doubled down on the bet on Russia. Notwithstanding misgivings about Putin, she shared the hope that Russia eventually could be moulded into a constructive partner through what Steinmeier called a 'modernization partnership' with Germany.[5] In her memoirs, Merkel justifies her decision to green-light Nord Stream 2 in 2015, 18 months after the Russian invasion and annexation of Crimea, with her success in getting Gazprom to accept a follow-up transit agreement with Ukraine to offset its exclusion from Nord Stream 2 (pp. 585–6). She does not explicitly defend the project on the grounds that it was purely commercial, as she had before 2022. Yet she does say that she did not want to increase the cost of energy to German industry and consumers, and therefore saw no alternative to imports of cheap Russian gas.

Merkel's critics also blamed her for the fate of Ukraine. At the NATO summit in Bucharest in 2008, she and French president Nicolas Sarkozy had blocked a US proposal to offer Ukraine and Georgia Membership Action Plans that would have set them on an almost irreversible path to NATO membership. Merkel describes the summit, her role in it and the reasoning behind her position in considerable detail (pp. 423–8). There is a whiff of appeasement in her arguments: while she was under no illusions about Putin and his revisionist ambitions, she did not want to provoke him. But it is hard to disagree with her assessment that a Membership Action Plan for Ukraine would not unequivocally have constituted a more effective deterrent during the years of implementation than the compromise formula of eventual membership, which the summit adopted (p. 438).

The West's response to Russia's invasion and annexation of Crimea in February 2014 represented an important turning point – 'a breath of cold war' (p. 468). In her extensive account of Western efforts to contain and roll back Russia's aggression, she describes the issue of arming Ukraine, which Germany refused to do, as a 'dilemma' (p. 465). Despite the compulsion to help Ukraine defend itself against Russia, sending arms might have strengthened forces within the Ukrainian government that 'hoped only for a military solution' (p. 465). In this context, Merkel also deals with Germany's commitment to increasing its defence spending from 1.15% to 2% of GDP in line with the target agreed at the NATO summit in Wales in September

2014. She presents the gradual increases from 2015 onward as a success, and blames her coalition partners for dragging their feet and perpetuating capability gaps.[6] At the same time, she registers deep discomfort with anything related to military force and war that extends to her recollections about Germany's participation in NATO's Afghanistan mission; she mentions the 59 German soldiers and three policemen who died there, among them an officer who had served in her security detail. Her alternative to arming Ukraine was to try to constrain Putin through the Minsk negotiation process. But Putin was not interested in compromise. As Merkel acknowledges, 'Minsk was dead in the water' (p. 673).[7]

Friction elsewhere

After Russia, the second and related major challenge of Merkel's chancellorship was Germany's relationship with the United States. It lies at the core of Germany's security, which ultimately rests on the transatlantic alliance and America's extended nuclear guarantees. During her time in office, Merkel dealt with four American presidents. With respect to two of them, George W. Bush and Barack Obama, her memoirs suggest personal bonds and mutual sympathy. Bush, during the election campaign in 2000, had singled out China as the new strategic competitor.[8] While 9/11 and his 'global war on terror' diverted America's attention away from China, Obama refocused it with the 'pivot to Asia'. Yet there is nothing in her memoirs to indicate that Merkel fully appreciated the underlying structural problem within the alliance that these two presidents had made clear: the shift of America's strategic focus from the Atlantic to the Indo-Pacific.

The other problem involving America was crumbling domestic political support for the alliance and increasing uncertainty over the reliability of US commitments to the defence of Europe. Donald Trump amplified both factors. During Merkel's first encounter with him at the White House on 17 March 2017, Trump ostentatiously and deliberately refused to shake hands with her in front of the media, instead haranguing her for the alleged sins of Germany and the debts it owed the US. It was hardly surprising, therefore, that Merkel 'felt uneasy' when she returned home. With typical reserve but unmistakable conviction, she subsequently expressed her discomfort publicly in a Bavarian beer garden, commenting that 'the times when we could rely completely on others are somewhat over'. Her conclusion that Europeans therefore 'really need to take our fate in our own hands', however, did not result in any significant follow-up (p. 567).[9]

Germany's relationship with China gets rather short shrift in Merkel's memoirs. She briefly mentions her reception of the Dalai Lama in Berlin in 2007, but not the fury about this in Beijing and its repercussions for bilateral relations (she never met with him again). She does recall being awed by the signs of China's dramatic economic advance during her official visit to China in 2010 and explicitly describes her China policy as continuing Schröder's (pp. 561–4). The result was an ever-closer bilateral commercial relationship that created another huge, politically risky economic dependency. Fuelled by cheap energy from Russian natural gas, German corporate behemoths first focused their exports and then their foreign direct investments on China. This brought huge short-term profits but also enabled China to develop its own industrial base on the back of German know-how. By the end of Merkel's chancellorship, Chinese corporations were ready to challenge Germany's major industries across the board, from automobiles to machine tools, with their equally advanced or even superior yet much cheaper products in the Chinese market, third markets and sometimes even in Germany itself, as in the case of electric vehicles.[10]

Lastly, Merkel had to manage two major European crises, one involving the euro in 2010 and the other involving migration in 2015. In both instances, she dominated European crisis management, and her memoir deals with both problems at considerable length (pp. 386–420, 471–510). She succeeded in keeping the euro intact and the European Union together, though European Central Bank (ECB) president Mario Draghi's famous statement that the ECB would intervene to stabilise the euro in foreign-exchange markets with 'whatever it takes' was probably the decisive factor as to the euro. Nevertheless, underlying structural issues remained unaddressed. Merkel steadfastly refused to accept collective European debt vehicles and an integrated European banking market, thus limiting the means by which the euro could compete with the dollar and European economies could mobilise the huge amounts needed for investment.[11] Nor have solutions materialised to the problems of collectively securing Europe's porous external borders and reconciling the demographic need for immigrant labour with the sociopolitical challenges of integration. In Germany, Merkel is blamed for the rise of the Alternative für Deutschland party. The party was propelled by the euro crisis and galvanised by the 2015 influx of migrants, which also accelerated its shift towards populist extremism.

These crises were expressions of deeper structural tensions within the European project caused by Europe's declining competitiveness, the rise of China and the strains of globalisation. EU institutions had not been designed for 28 member states (since reduced to 27) and were increasingly displaying signs of dysfunction. The European project thus had to be reconceived from the bottom up. Yet Merkel had never been a European supranationalist in the vein of Kohl or Konrad Adenauer. Early in her chancellorship, she made it clear that her preferred approach to European issues was the so-called 'union method', which put the Council of Ministers, and thus the member-state governments, at the centre of decision-making. This bound her to working towards compromises within the existing structures of the EU, however sclerotic they had become.[12]

The limits of compromise

The former chancellor justifiably presents herself as a masterful practitioner of the politics of compromise. Her ability to assess the circumstances at hand and coolly and rationally explore possible options comes across strongly, as does her profound commitment to liberal democracy. The title of her memoirs references this normative compass. Freedom, of course, is not a strategy. Nowhere in the book does Merkel describe what she wanted to achieve in office other than solving the problem of the day. There is no project, no path laid out towards a larger objective. Tellingly, she describes her thoughts upon the parliamentary vote that made her chancellor on 22 November 2005 thus: 'First. I was first' (p. 288). At two sentences and four words, it is the shortest paragraph in the whole memoir. She does describe the sense of elevation she felt when she sat down – alone, since her cabinet had not yet been appointed – for the first time on the government benches in the Bundestag: 'I felt it: you have done something special, as a woman and as an East German' (p. 289). She wanted to be the boss. That was her project.

Still, there was surely some strategy behind her reflections and actions, decipherable by reading between the lines. This strategy was simply to keep things as they were, as much as possible. Germany, its post-war redemption complete, was now a country of liberty, prosperity, openness and tolerance, in which to take pride. And it had achieved this status without any recourse to force, through soft power. The country was still to an extent divided between east and west, to be sure, and Merkel was concerned about that. Still, what she centrally wanted to uphold and defend was the Federal Republic that unification had realised. In this sense, Angela Merkel very much was the chancellor the Germans wanted and deserved, for most shared the desire to hang on to what they had without significant resort to military power.

In the end, she deceived the Germans, and perhaps also herself, in insisting that this was possible.[13] During her 16 years at the helm, Germany's European and international environment was traumatised by historical forces of great consequence: the return of Russian imperialism, the rise of populism and the crisis of American democracy, the arrival of China as an industrial juggernaut. In retrospect, Merkel's politics of compromise around the status quo, highly effective in the moment, merely postponed the day of reckoning. By 2021, Germany's industrial base had become hollowed out by over-reliance on the Chinese market, its energy supplies dangerously dependent on Russia and its security compromised by uncertainty about America's future. Merely trying to hang on to what Germany had achieved, it turned out, was not enough.

Notes

[1] She missed Kohl's record by nine days.
[2] See Nancy Gibbs, 'The Choice', *Time*, 31 December 2015, https://time.com/time-person-of-the-year-2015-angela-merkel-choice/. She beat Donald Trump, who was also on the shortlist.
[3] See Olaf Scholz, 'Speech to the Bundestag', 27 February 2022, https://www.bundesregierung.de/breg-en/service/archive/policy-statement-by-olaf-scholz-chancellor-of-the-federal-republic-of-germany-and-member-of-the-german-bundestag-27-february-2022-in-berlin-2008378. See also Olaf Scholz, 'The Global Zeitenwende: How to Avoid a New Cold War in a Multipolar Era', *Foreign Affairs*, vol. 102, no. 1, January/February 2023, pp. 22–38. For an excellent analysis of efforts to implement *Zeitenwende*, see Molly O'Neal, '*Zeitenwende*, Europe and Germany's Culture of Restraint', *International Spectator*, vol. 59, no. 2, June 2024, pp. 1–17.

4   See Reinhard Bingener and Markus Wehner, *Die Moskau-Connection, Das Schröder-Netzwerk und Deutschlands Weg in die Abhängigkeit* (Munich: C.H. Beck, 2023); and Arndt Freytag von Loringhoven and Leon Erlenhorst, *Putins Angriff auf Deutschland, Desinformation, Propaganda, Cyberattacken* (Berlin: Econ, 2024).

5   See Stephen H. Szabo, 'Germany's Commercial Realism and the Russia Problem', *Survival*, vol. 56, no. 5, October–November 2014, pp. 117–28; and Andreas Umland, 'Germany's Russia Policy in Light of the Ukraine Conflict: Interdependence Theory and Ostpolitik', *Orbis*, vol. 66, no. 1, Winter 2022, pp. 78–94.

6   By the time Merkel stepped down, Germany's defence expenditure stood at 1.45% of GDP, according to NATO statistics. See NATO, 'Defence Expenditure of NATO Countries (2014–2024)', https://www.nato.int/nato_static_fl2014/assets/pdf/2024/6/pdf/240617-def-exp-2024-en.pdf.

7   See Hugo von Essen and Andreas Umland, 'Russlands diktierter Nicht-Frieden im Donbas 2014–2022: Warum die Minsker Abkommen von Anbeginn zum Scheitern verurteilt waren', *SIRIUS: Zeitschrift für Strategische Analysen*, vol. 6, no. 3, 2022, pp. 282–92.

8   See Richard Baum, 'From "Strategic Partners" to "Strategic Competitors": George W. Bush and the Politics of US China Policy', *Journal of East Asian Studies*, vol. 1, no. 2, August 2001, pp. 191–220.

9   See Annett Meiritz, Anne Reimann and Severin Weiland, 'Merkels Bierzeltrede, Jeder Satz ein Treffer', *Der Spiegel*, 29 May 2017, https://www.spiegel.de/politik/deutschland/angela-merkel-das-bedeutet-ihre-bierzelt-rede-ueber-donald-trump-a-1149649.html. Author's translation.

10 See Andreas Fulda, *Germany and China: How Entanglement Undermines Freedom, Prosperity and Security* (London: Bloomsbury, 2024); and Wolfgang Münchau, *Kaput: The End of the German Miracle* (London: Swift Press, 2024), ch. 4.

11 See European Commission, 'The Future of European Competitiveness, Part A: A Competitiveness Strategy for Europe' ('Draghi Report'), September 2024, pp. 63–6, https://commission.europa.eu/document/download/97e481fd-2dc3-412d-be4c-f152a8232961_en?filename=The%20future%20of%20European%20competitiveness%20_%20A%20competitiveness%20strategy%20for%20Europe.pdf.

12 See Angela Merkel, 'Rede von Bundeskanzlerin Merkel anlässlich der Eröffnung des 61. akademischen Jahres des Europakollegs Brügge', College of Europe, Bruges, 2 October 2010, https://www.coleurope.eu/sites/default/files/speech-files/rede_merkel_europakolleg_bruegge_0.pdf. See also Lucas Schramm and Wolfgang Wessels, 'Das europapolitische Erbe Angela Merkels: Krisen, Führung, Vorbild', *Integration*, vol. 45, no. 1, January 2022, pp. 1–19.

13 One of the most astute analyses of Merkel's record as chancellor is Eckart Lohse, *Die Täuschung: Angela Merkel und ihre Deutschen* (Munich: dtv, 2024).

Book Reviews

Russia and Eurasia
Angela Stent

The Illegals: Russia's Most Audacious Spies and the Plot to Infiltrate the West
Shaun Walker. London: Profile Books, 2025. £22.00. 433 pp.

In August 2024, Vladimir Putin stood on the tarmac at Vnukovo Airport in Moscow to greet a group of returning spies after a prisoner swap. 'Buenas noches', he said, as he handed a bunch of flowers to a mother and her daughter. The family was returning from Slovenia, where the parents had posed as Argentinians, speaking Spanish to their children, who knew no Russian. In reality, they were 'illegals', Russians sent to spy abroad, adopting personas that enabled them to blend into the local population and disguise their Russian origins.

In this gripping, impressive and meticulously researched book, Shaun Walker chronicles the century-old Soviet and post-Soviet illegals programme, a unique form of espionage that Russia has perfected. These were not spies operating under diplomatic cover. They were a separate caste known only to their handlers in Moscow and in-country.

Vladimir Lenin created the illegals programme, based on his pre-revolutionary experiences of living in different countries under a variety of aliases and personas. Throughout the Soviet period, official spies were supplemented by illegals, who underwent years of rigorous training to enable them to live and work in Western societies without being detected. One of the illegals, posing as a Costa Rican diplomat in Yugoslavia, was sent to assassinate Josip Broz Tito, whom Josef Stalin detested. He succeeded in gaining Tito's trust but, shortly before he was to have killed him, Stalin died and the assassination was called off.

Walker has interviewed a number of graduates of the illegals programme, including one of the families who were part of a 2010 US–Russian spy exchange. Elena Vavilova and Andrey Bezrukov were recruited as students in the Siberian city of Tomsk. After several years of arduous training, during which they moulded their language, identities and mannerisms into those of a Canadian couple, they settled in Toronto as Tracey Foley and Donald Heathfield and had two children. They subsequently moved to Cambridge, Massachusetts, outwardly living the life of a typical American family. Unbeknownst to them, however, one of the three people in Russia's Foreign Intelligence Service (SVR) who knew all the details of the illegals programme was also working for the Americans. He gave their information to the FBI, which monitored them for a decade before arresting them. Today, Bezrukov advises Igor Sechin, a close ally of Putin's, and works as a professor at the Moscow State Institute of International Relations (MGIMO), giving lectures with titles like 'Inside the American Mind'.

Being an illegal was very challenging. Leading a double life under the constant fear of arrest led a considerable number of spies to succumb to depression, alcoholism and, in some cases, suicide. When they returned to Russia after years of absence, it was often difficult to adapt to a country which they barely knew.

Walker concludes by asking whether the illegals programme was worth it. According to him, 'the available evidence suggests that, for all the ambition, the programme routinely failed to deliver. For every illegal who achieved something useful for Moscow, there were a dozen living frustrated lives that bore little espionage fruit' (p. 350).

Perfect Storm: Russia's Failed Economic Opening, the Hurricane of War and Sanctions, and the Uncertain Future
Thane Gustafson. Oxford: Oxford University Press, 2025.
£22.99. 328 pp.

Thane Gustafson's insightful book is 'an attempt to tell the broader story of Russia's flawed opening to the West in its economic, technological and social dimensions, and the roles these played in its ultimate failure' (p. 1). He explains how both sides' unrealistic expectations for economic cooperation after 1991 contributed to the deterioration of overall ties between the West and Russia, culminating in the 2022 invasion of Ukraine.

When the Soviet Union imploded – an event that coincided with the US-driven rise of neo-liberal globalisation – Western businesses enthusiastically flocked to Russia, attracted by the large market of 148 million potential consumers emerging from 70 years of scarcity under a command economy. Russians too were eager to introduce Western market-style reforms, yet had little idea how to accomplish that. In the chaos of the post-Soviet years, Russia's transition to a market economy was uneven at best, 'shambolic' at worst (p. 50). Moreover, the enormous gap between Russian and Western cultural and political traditions, and understandings of how to conduct business – particularly the role of institutions and laws as opposed to informal networks (*krugovye poruki*) – soured ties between people in the Western and Russian private sectors.

Whereas Russians initially viewed the Westerners in their country fairly positively, the West regarded the Russians who flocked to 'Londongrad' and other Western capitals negatively. Over time, mutual resentment grew, exacerbated by the growing presence of Russian organised crime in Europe and the United States. Gustafson argues that Russia's integration into the global financial system was the most successful of its endeavours, while the arrival of oligarchs and the Russian mafia, and the haemorrhage of capital out of Russia, were overwhelmingly negative for Russia's economic development. Russia's opening 'proved to be flawed and fragile' (p. 80).

Vladimir Putin publicly supported the key features of a market economy during his first two terms, including privatisation, protection of property rights and open international trade. But after his return to the Kremlin in 2012, his attitudes toward both free-market capitalism and Western businesses in Russia soured, mirroring the emergence of his more aggressive geopolitical goals. After 2014, argues Gustafson, his economic policies were dominated by hostility toward the West and his growing obsession with Ukraine.

After Russia's invasion of Ukraine, Russia's integration into the global financial system ended, and rafts of Western sanctions were imposed. Gustafson provides an extensive explanation of how the sanctions worked and why they did not have the impact that the West hoped they would. Russia's response to these sanctions, he argues, has been 'vigorous, creative and on the whole effective in restabilizing the economy' (p. 171).

Gustafson ends his account of Russia's failed opening to the West on a surprisingly optimistic note. He believes that, once Putin has left the Kremlin, the next generation of leaders will be open to a dialogue with the West, and that ties will improve. He might be right, but this assumes that Putin's legacy will be more ephemeral than many believe.

Memory Makers: The Politics of the Past in Putin's Russia
Jade McGlynn. London: Bloomsbury Academic, 2023.
£20.00. 234 pp.

In the 1990s, Boris Yeltsin created a commission to define a new, post-communist, unifying Russian national identity. The attempt failed and, when Vladimir Putin came to power, he took it upon himself to try again and redeem Russia's past from the Soviet collapse. He has succeeded in doing that, as Jade McGlynn explains in this innovative, deeply researched book, by rewriting history to promote Russia's identity as an eternally victorious, indestructible great power. To reject this version of history is to open oneself to state-sponsored invective and possible arrest.

The new Russian identity centres on a cult of the Second World War, intended to bolster Putin's legitimacy and justify Russia's invasion of Ukraine to 'denazify' the country. Russia, Putin claims, will defeat Ukraine just as it defeated Germany. In his version of the 'Great Patriotic War', the Soviet Union did not invade Poland on 17 September 1939, Lend-Lease did not exist, and the Soviets defeated the Nazis single-handedly, with the United States and United Kingdom playing only minor roles. There is no mention of the fact that the Nazi–Soviet pact facilitated the German invasion, or that the Soviets occupied the Baltic states and then Eastern Europe.

A key figure in the propagation of memory politics is Vladimir Medinsky, who is also Putin's envoy to negotiations with Ukraine. His Russian Military Historical Society produces the textbooks to indoctrinate children with a 'correct' version of history that has accompanied the reintroduction of the Soviet-style Russian Schoolchildren's Movement dedicated to creating a new generation of patriots eager to fight for the Motherland.

As minister of culture, Medinsky was obsessed with protecting Russia from cultural infection by the West. He claims that the West has not been objective in its assessment of Russian history. But, as McGlynn points out, his own career path raises questions about his motivations. While working on his two doctoral theses, he ran a major public-relations firm representing the MMM pyramid scheme in which millions of Russians lost their savings.

McGlynn shows how the state has appropriated grassroots movements to amplify its patriotic message. The Immortal Regiment started when ordinary Russians began marching on Victory Day (9 May) carrying portraits of their relatives who fought in the Second World War. The Kremlin saw that this had great propaganda value, and in 2015 officials launched a 'hostile takeover' (p. 152) of the movement, holding their own, competing Immortal Regiment parade in Moscow to commemorate the 70th anniversary of the end of the war. The have continued to do so since then.

McGlynn predicts that the government and media's memory wars and memory diplomacy will become more extreme as the war with Ukraine continues. 'Russia', she concludes, 'will never be at peace with its neighbors until it can be at peace with itself and its history' (p. 2). Its war against Ukraine suggests that it will take generations for Russia to come to terms with its true history.

Our Dear Friends in Moscow: The Inside Story of a Broken Generation
Andrei Soldatov and Irina Borogan. New York: PublicAffairs, 2025. $30.00. 320 pp.

In 2000, the year that Vladimir Putin first came to power, a group of young Russian journalists met up, hopeful for a better European future. They worked together and kept in touch through much of Putin's 25-year rule. By the time of the full-scale invasion of Ukraine in 2022, however, most had parted company. The majority had become enthusiastic supporters of the Russian president's war against Ukraine and antipathy toward the West. Investigative journalists Andrei Soldatov and Irina Borogan, by contrast, strongly opposed Putin and the war, and had been exiled to London. In this engrossing memoir, they follow the personal trajectories of their colleagues, examining choices they made as Putin's regime became increasingly repressive.

The journalists, mostly the scions of elite Soviet families, had come of age between the fall of the Berlin Wall and Putin's ascent to power. They were working at *Izvestia*, which, at the beginning of Putin's term, was still an independent newspaper. Putin soon began to force Yeltsin-era oligarchs to give up their media empires, but the authors believed that the internet would give them the freedom to express ideas without fearing reprisals. They launched a website called 'Agentura' (ring of spies) dedicated to exploring the Russian intelligence and security services. But they soon discovered that 'the FSB [Federal Security Service] had openly set its sights on building a full-scale propaganda and disinformation machine with the help of newspapers' (p. 250).

They subsequently lost their jobs at *Izvestia*, going on to work for a number of different publications and encountering increasing pressure from the authorities – and then from their editors – when their reporting was too critical of the government. This was particularly true when they covered the terrorist attacks in a Moscow theatre in 2002 and at a school in Beslan, North Ossetia, in 2004, where the casualty numbers were far greater than they needed to have been because of the incompetence or callousness of the authorities. After the murder of the pioneering journalist Anna Politkovskaya in 2006, Soldatov and Borogan concluded that any illusions they had harboured as liberals about the possibility of coexistence with Putin had disappeared.

After Russia's victory over Georgia in 2008, their friends were enthusiastic: 'Russia had rediscovered its swagger', they believed (p. 168). To the authors' dismay, they watched as members of their group became increasingly nationalistic and anti-Western, eager to reverse what they viewed as Russia's humiliation after the Soviet collapse, which they blamed on the West. The opening ceremonies for the 2014 Sochi Winter Olympics captured these sentiments. The introductory performance, entitled 'Dreams of Russia', omitted any material on the Gorbachev era and the post-1991 period. Designed to present Russia's glorious history, it really depicted 'dreams of the Russian empire and the Soviet Union' (p. 216).

In September 2020, the authors were forced to leave Russia or face arrest for their writings on the security services. Soldatov's father, a pioneer of the Russian internet and former government minister, was subsequently arrested and imprisoned. Their hopes for a freer, non-imperial Russia were postponed indefinitely.

Odyssey Moscow: One American's Journey from Russia Optimist to Prisoner of the State
Michael Calvey. Cheltenham: The History Press, 2025.
£22.00. 255 pp.

In February 2019, Michael Calvey, a prominent and enthusiastic American investor in Russia, was roused from his bed in Moscow in the early morning hours, arrested and taken for interrogation. He had been engaged in a long-running business dispute with his Russian partner, who had connections to the security services. Calvey was subsequently tried, found guilty, jailed and eventually released as Russia began its full-scale invasion of Ukraine. In this riveting account, he highlights the arbitrary and corrupt nature of the Russian legal system, and the sub-optimal conditions he experienced in jail – as well as the camaraderie and generosity of his Russian cellmates.

Calvey arrived in Russia in the early 1990s and, in those freewheeling days of emerging capitalism in the 'Wild East', he launched the Baring Vostok private-equity firm, which invested across a broad range of industries. Despite the challenges of operating in the new Russian market, Calvey became a high-profile investor committed to remaining in Russia. As the 2000s wore on, however, he noticed 'disturbing clouds on the horizon': 'There was a sense that the security structures of the Putin government had become insatiable monsters, even worse than the oligarchs in the 1990s' (p. 128). In the early 2010s, Baring Vostok invested in Vostochny Bank, and eventually Calvey decided to merge his company with the bank. An ensuing shareholder conflict with one of his partners led to his arrest and imprisonment, approved at the highest levels and apparently initiated by the FSB. After all, a business dispute would normally be resolved in a civil, not a criminal, trial. His subsequent ordeal raised serious questions about the wisdom of investing in Russia.

There is a 99.8% conviction rate for criminal trials in Russia, and Calvey's high-profile trial was no exception. In a judicial system that still resembles the

Soviet system, it was clear that the initial guilty verdict – and subsequent rejection of his appeal – had been written in advance of his trial. Likewise, when he was subsequently released to serve the rest of his sentence under house arrest, he understood that the order had come from the Kremlin.

Calvey was jailed in Moscow's Matrosskaya Tishina prison, otherwise known as 'Kremlin Central' because of the high-profile prisoners there. Despite the prison's harsh conditions, Calvey came to appreciate his cellmates, who treated him with respect and empathy. 'My seven comrades', he writes, 'are among the bravest and most decent guys I have ever met' (p. 51). A firm believer in capitalism, he adds: 'I soon came to believe that prison is probably an environment where communism actually works better than the alternatives' (p. 53).

Calvey admits that, when Putin first came to power, he welcomed his centralisation of power and reining in of the oligarchs. But the rise of Putin's *siloviki* (officials with a security background) created a 'cynical and remorseless system' (p. 232). Yet Calvey remains optimistic about a post-Putin Russia, envisioning a younger generation that will seek better relations with the West.

Cyber Security and Emerging Technologies
Melissa K. Griffith

House of Huawei: The Secret History of China's Most Powerful Company
Eva Dou. New York: Portfolio, 2025. $34.00. 448 pp.

Few companies symbolise China's technological rise and the intensifying US–China rivalry like Huawei. Founded in 1987, this Chinese company has become a lightning rod for geopolitical controversy, finding itself embroiled in intellectual-property disputes, sweeping export controls and human-rights debates across the Middle East and Asia-Pacific. Yet for many, the inner workings and personalities behind this telecom giant – one of China's largest private conglomerates – remain a mystery. Who is Ren Zhengfei, Huawei's enigmatic founder? Is Huawei a typical private company, or does it operate as a strategic extension of the Chinese state? And how did it grow from a modest importer of telephone switches into a global powerhouse employing over 200,000 people in more than 170 countries, with annual revenues approaching $100 billion?

Eva Dou, a technology reporter for the *Washington Post*, draws on meticulous research to unpack Huawei's meteoric ascent and the controversies that continue to dog it, both at home and around the world. Her book sets Ren's journey and the company's founding against the backdrop of China's turbulent twentieth-century history, encompassing the Second World War, Mao Zedong's Great Leap Forward and Cultural Revolution, and the dawn of market reforms. Huawei's notorious 'wolf warrior' culture – marked by relentless hours and unwavering loyalty – set it apart even in China's famously demanding tech sector. A company that started off importing and reverse-engineering telephone switches quickly capitalised on China's demand for connectivity, going on to power the communications networks underpinning Beijing's 2008 Summer Olympics. Today, it operates the highest 5G base station in the world (sitting at an altitude of 6,500 metres on the slopes of Mt Everest), and lies at the heart of China's telecommunication and artificial-intelligence (AI) ambitions at home and abroad.

Dou skilfully recounts Huawei's relentless efforts to dominate global network-communication systems without resorting to sensationalism. However, readers looking for in-depth analysis of Huawei's current projects in data centres, generative AI and robotics will need to look elsewhere. The book's focus is on the company's history, and the road ahead is largely unexplored.

Nevertheless, *House of Huawei* offers a timely, clear and undeniably worrying account of a company whose development reveals much about the intricate nature of modern geopolitics, and China's strategic and technological ascent. It is a must-read for Huawei novices and experts alike.

Rethinking Cyber Warfare: The International Relations of Digital Disruption
R. David Edelman. Oxford: Oxford University Press, 2024.
£32.99. 416 pp.

Are we any closer to understanding or preventing major cyber attacks than we were during the 2007 Russian distributed denial-of-service attacks on Estonia? For R. David Edelman, the answer, if not a resounding no, is that we are not nearly close enough.

When Edelman began exploring state-on-state cyber conflict in the early 2000s, such attacks were mostly theoretical. Today, cyber attacks are ubiquitous and constant. Yet no states are engaged in a full-fledged cyber war, which remains an unlikely prospect. What has restrained, or might restrain, a state's use of cyber attacks, despite the clear strategic advantages they confer?

Drawing on two decades as both a researcher and practitioner in national security, Edelman urges a fundamental rethink of how we view cyber conflict, or more specifically cyber attacks, defined as significant operations designed to deny, degrade, destroy or disrupt both digital and physical systems. Drawing on academic theory as well as a rich history of policy efforts and interventions, he systematically examines the effectiveness of three traditional tools of restraint – deterrence, international law and humanitarian considerations – in the context of cyber attacks.

Edelman finds the first tool, deterrence, largely ineffective. The usual problems – attribution, signalling failures and the lack of clear rules – make rational calculations difficult. As a result, states have shifted toward 'structural deterrence' in an effort to shape the international environment through alliances. While this approach shows some promise, Edelman argues it is still not enough. Similarly, international law, especially the principles of *jus ad bellum* that govern the initiation of war, also falls short, with existing laws doing little to restrain state cyber behaviour. However, the author notes that a more robust international legal framework could offer future benefits, pointing to a potential role for the United Nations and national efforts in this respect.

For Edelman, it is the third category, normative restraint – specifically humanitarian considerations – that holds the most promise. He advocates for a 'cyber-attack taboo', akin to the prohibitions against chemical weapons, rooted in humanitarian norms. While establishing such a taboo would be a challenging process that would likely take years, Edelman argues that it could emerge from a growing informal consensus around protecting civilians and critical infrastructure.

Rethinking Cyber Warfare is a rigorous, interdisciplinary work aimed at, and best suited for, academics. While this may limit the book's potential audience, Edelman's strength lies in his ability to weave together real-world insights and academic theory. Whether readers ultimately agree or disagree with him on the viability of different strategies for restraining offensive cyber operations between states, he delivers a sobering assessment: despite years of debate and escalating cyber threats, the world remains ill-prepared to restrain state-led cyber attacks. His call for normative restraint offers, for him, a glimmer of hope, but the road ahead promises to be a long one, and the stakes are only getting higher.

AI Snake Oil: What Artificial Intelligence Can Do, What It Can't, and How to Tell the Difference
Arvind Narayanan and Sayash Kapoor. Princeton, NJ:
Princeton University Press, 2024. £20.00/$24.95. 360 pp.

'Artificial intelligence' (AI) is a topic of debate both within national-security institutions and across dining-room tables. It sits at the heart of US–China tensions, intellectual-property concerns and deliberations over technology in the classroom. For some, it sparks existential dread. For others, it promises boundless opportunities. AI is everywhere, and yet despite all the hype, it is poorly understood.

Building off the success of their newsletter (which bears the same name as their book), two Princeton computer scientists, Arvind Narayanan and Sayash Kapoor, direct their expertise at demystifying AI. From debates around existential risks to the hype machine itself, they offer readers a deeply accessible dive into the technologies that underpin modern AI.

First and foremost, 'AI' is not a monolith. Instead, it is an umbrella term currently encompassing two main types of loosely related technologies: predictive AI and generative AI. In the first half of the book, the authors caution against conflating these technologies, noting that 'painting AI with a single brush is tempting but flawed' (p. 12). Both present their own challenges and opportunities. Both sit at different levels of maturity. Generative AI, according to the authors, has made significant advances, but remains immature, unreliable and vulnerable to misuse, all while being enveloped in hype and fear. Predictive AI, on the other hand, is already widely deployed by corporations and governments, even though it has yet to be shown that even sophisticated algorithms can reliably forecast the future.

Given the state of the technologies in question, what explains the pervasive hype that surrounds them? In chapter seven, Narayanan and Kapoor divide the contemporary hype machine into three core groups: companies with commercial incentives to exaggerate AI's capabilities; researchers whose careers are tied to citation metrics but whose findings face a reproducibility crisis; and journalists, who often lack technical expertise and time, and therefore tend to amplify sensational claims. Combined with the inherent cognitive biases that make humans susceptible to hype, these forces, according to the authors, create a self-reinforcing cycle that is unique to AI, even when compared to other heavily hyped technologies. While the convergence of these four factors is both plausible and deserving of further study, this section also stands out as the most speculative, without the same level of rigorous, structured research underpinning prior chapters.

AI Snake Oil's greatest strength lies in its clear examination of the technologies themselves and the risks they pose – including a sceptical assessment of ongoing concerns about existential risks. It offers readers a comprehensive introduction to the technologies underpinning AI, their real-world applications, the genuine risks and ethical dilemmas posed by their rapid advancement, and ideas on where we should go from here. This is an exceptionally accessible introduction and a masterful contribution to the debates surrounding one of the defining technologies of our era.

Asia-Pacific
Lanxin Xiang

On Xi Jinping: How Xi's Marxist Nationalism Is Shaping China and the World
Kevin Rudd. Oxford: Oxford University Press, 2025. £26.99. 624 pp.

In this extremely ambitious book, author Kevin Rudd, formerly prime minister of Australia, claims to have discovered a coherent ideology in Xi Jinping's thinking and behaviour yesterday, today and tomorrow – an ideology that he says will determine China's future for years to come. Not even George F. Kennan, the 'father' of the United States' containment policy during the Cold War, was quite this daring when analysing the Soviet Union. *On Xi Jinping* seems to employ the 'simplify, then exaggerate' approach.

Rudd claims that his book does not simply provide an ideological interpretation of the decade that has just passed – the first decade of Xi's rule, between the 18th party congress in 2012 and the 20th congress in 2022 – but also offers 'a level of ideological insight into the critical period that lies ahead, one I have long called the "decade of living dangerously" between 2022 and 2032'. This, according to Rudd, 'is when Xi hopes China will surpass the US economy as the world's largest and become the predominant military power in the region'. The author also explores how Xi's 'ideological framework' might influence any future decision to 'return Taiwan to Chinese sovereignty by armed force' (p. 11). His main argument is that 'Xi has reified the role of ideology in general in the Communist Party as a means of enhancing personal and party control, [party] political legitimacy, and as a mechanism for foreshadowing broad policy change across the Chinese system' (p. 14). He describes Xi's 'intellectual framework' as consisting of 'dialectical materialism, historical materialism, and a Chinese nationalist equivalent of "manifest destiny"' (p. 12).

A clue to the source of Rudd's thinking can be found in the dedication of the book to his college mentor, Pierre Ryckmans (also known as Simon Leys), whose books on Mao Zedong's China, such as *Chinese Shadows* (1974), were known for using a single concept, 'Maoism', and often a single event to attack anything he did not like about China at the time. This approach was deeply rooted in the traditions of Western sinology, which used Montesquieu's ideas to delegitimate China's political system and Max Weber's sociological arguments to denigrate China's originality in managing its economy. Weber attributed China's failure to develop industrial power to Confucianism and the absence of the 'Protestant spirit', seen as essential for successful capitalism. Such essentialising assumptions are part of the reason that Western sinologists have failed to explain, let alone come to terms with, China's rapid rise.

Rudd may have intended for his book to serve as a guide for Western governments looking to develop a new containment policy against China, yet it comes at the very moment when the liberal-democratic West is sinking. Many of the accusations that are levelled at Xi and his alleged 'Marxist–Leninist nationalism', such as disrupting the global economy, supporting an aggressive Vladimir Putin or making expansionist territorial claims, could just as easily be laid at the feet of Donald Trump, the supposed 'leader of the free world'. No one would accuse Trump of being a Marxist–Leninist, however, suggesting that ideology may be less important than Rudd believes.

Pacific Power Paradox: American Statecraft and the Fate of the Asian Peace
Van Jackson. New Haven, CT: Yale University Press, 2023.
$35.00. 312 pp.

Van Jackson has produced a powerful and cogent argument about the much-misunderstood role of the United States in maintaining peace in the Asia-Pacific. He is particularly troubled by the fact that 'nobody in Washington … [thinks] about the absence of war' in the region 'as anything more than a by-product of American hegemony' (p. vii). He challenges the long-held view that America has been a 'beneficent "Pacific power"', arguing that while it has sometimes served as a 'firefighter' in the region, it has also acted as an 'arsonist and an impediment to more durable forms of security' (p. xv).

Nevertheless, many Asian leaders also believe the US presence in the region is crucial for peace, partly because of the United States' forward military deployment there, but more importantly because of the benefits they receive from the US-led international system, which allows them to enjoy growth through economic interdependence. Some have explained Asian peace using a 'developmental state' argument, which holds that decision-makers have sidestepped conflict because it is inconsistent with their economically centred political identity. 'From this vantage point, economic interdependence works by buying states out of conflict' (p. 17). As soon as this interdependence is undermined, however, Asian nations face the challenge of resolving their regional disputes without the input of the United States – a prospect that seems only too likely under Donald Trump's presidency.

The solution to Sino-US rivalry, according to Jackson, lies in adopting a different approach that rejects American primacy, but he has noted that most policymakers in Washington still advocate for 'competitive coexistence' or 'congagement' (a portmanteau of 'containment' and 'engagement'), which continue to assume American primacy. He has written in his newsletter, *Un-diplomatic*, that even though a new Cold War in which adversaries talk to each other is preferable to a Cold War without direct communications … zero-sum statecraft is a dead end. Any policy agenda premised on a net-antagonistic relationship between the great powers facilitates a process of hawkish outbidding within domestic politics, and as we have seen the past decade, that divides America rather than unites it.

In his book, he writes that 'maintaining peace through deterrence is hopeless because at the best it buys some time for a status that is essentially an "organized peacelessness"' (p. 11). But precisely because the United States is divided internally, China is one of the few issues on which a 'bipartisan consensus' can still be assembled. Jackson warns this will make it difficult to steer the country off the path that ends in a Sino-American showdown.

World to Come: The Return of Trump and the End of the Old Order
Mathew Burrows and Josef Braml. London: Brixton Ink, 2025.
£12.99. 160 pp.

Authors Mathew Burrows and Josef Braml have both had distinguished careers in transatlantic relations. They are deeply worried about the failure of US and European Union leaders to grasp the significant changes of the last decade, with EU leaders being even slower than their American counterparts to understand their magnitude. The most important of these concerns the rise of China. According to the authors, US protectionist policies have had the effects of increasing competition from China and undercutting the open marketplace that Europe has relied on for its economic growth (p. 53). In its industrial strategy, China has set the goal of achieving global market leadership and determining international standards in ten value-added, intensive industrial sectors. Europe faces a slow decline unless it can catch up and start competing with China and the United States (pp. 54–5).

Not too long ago, leading commentators were talking about 'Chimerica' – how China and the United States could create a super economy by joining together in a mutually dependent system. Around two-fifths of global economic growth during the 2000s was the result of surging exports from China, which quadrupled its GDP, imported Western technology and created tens of millions of manufacturing jobs for the rural poor. But economists soon coined a new term, 'China shock', to describe how roughly 2m US jobs were lost due to increased Chinese imports. The authors note that this number wouldn't necessarily be unusual in a labour market that typically experiences 'about 60 million job separations' per year. What was different about the China shock was that many displaced workers did not find new employment (p. 57). Meanwhile, easy credit in the United States facilitated by Chinese purchases of US debt meant that many Americans went on a 'spending spree, including buying houses they could not afford' (p. 57).

Of course, China is not solely to blame for the loss of manufacturing jobs in the US – the authors note that manufacturing employment has been 'falling sharply in all high income economies, including in Japan and Germany' (p. 58). Technological innovation and automation account for at least some of these job losses. So why has Chimerica given way to US–China rivalry in every domain? The authors believe that scapegoating is a more successful strategy in domestic politics than encouraging self-reflection. Barack Obama had a plan to put the US at the centre of two large regional trading networks, one connecting the United States to Europe in the Transatlantic Trade and Investment Partnership (TTIP), the other with Asia in the Trans-Pacific Partnership (TPP). 'Both the Democratic Party's progressive left and Trump killed the effort', say the authors (pp. 58–60). While China has been engaging globally, the United States has been gradually closing its doors to the rest of the world since the 2007–08 financial crisis.

Burrows and Braml write that, 'with the United States turning inward – a process that predates Trump – China has now an opportunity to fill a vacuum, creating with others a multipolar world'. Beijing, they say, is 'taking advantage of Washington's strategic narrow-mindedness' by making an increasing number of countries and regions around the world more dependent on China through trade and investment (p. 63). The authors warn that transatlantic efforts to limit this growth and global influence have little chance of success.

Accidental Tyrant: The Life of Kim Il-sung
Fyodor Tertitskiy. London: C. Hurst & Co., 2025. £25.00. 352 pp.

This biography of Kim Il-sung, the founder of the Kim dynasty in North Korea, raises the interesting question of whether Kim's rise to supreme power in North Korea was inevitable. It also asks whether North Korea's social context was bound to give rise to such an inhumane system. Author Fyodor Tertitskiy responds in the negative to both questions, concluding that Kim's ascension to power was not preordained. 'Only a sequence of improbable coincidences allowed him to leverage his political acumen and become and remain the unopposed leader of North Korea', he writes (p. 3).

Kim's family emigrated from Korea to China during his youth, where he joined the Chinese Communist Party and participated in guerrilla warfare against the Japanese. The biggest factor contributing to his emergence as North Korean leader following the Second World War was that, unlike in the other countries that fell into the Soviet sphere after the war, there was no obvious candidate to lead North Korea. Bulgaria, for example, had Georgi Dimitrov, the former chief of the Comintern; Czechoslovakia had Klement Gottwald, who had led the Communist Party of Czechoslovakia from 1929; and Yugoslavia had Josip Broz Tito, who had led the Partisans resistance movement against the German occupation. In Korea, however, Moscow had to look harder to find a new leader.

At the time of the Japanese surrender in September 1945, Kim was serving as a battalion commander for a Korean detachment of the Soviet Red Army, having fled from China to the Soviet Union in 1940. Although his name did not appear on the first list drawn up by the Soviet military command of potential Korean leaders, he eventually emerged as a compromise candidate during a turf war in Moscow between Lavrentiy Beria, the head of the secret police, and the military leadership. Tertitskiy vividly describes the chaos as Soviet authorities scrambled to arrange a grand debut for their puppet leader. Even Kim's outfit proved difficult: because he was being presented as a national hero in the fight against the Japanese, he could not wear a Soviet military uniform, but finding a suitable Western suit presented its own challenge. Kim's name was not known to the Koreans who had lived under the Japanese colonial government, and his limited ability in the Korean language (he was more fluent in Chinese) meant that his inaugural speech had to be written by the Soviets and rehearsed many times (p. 60).

Nevertheless, Kim managed to mould himself into an effective dictator, both by managing internal factional fights and by manipulating his most important neighbours, the Soviet Union and China – both of which created problems for his rule. In the 1950s, Nikita Khrushchev's de-Stalinisation campaign undermined the legitimacy of communist rule, while Mao Zedong's Cultural Revolution in the late 1960s, an unprecedented event in the communist world, threatened to create chaos for Kim's regime. Tertitskiy writes:

> Mao asserted that the leadership of the party – apart from his infallible self, of course – had become corrupt and called on the revolutionary masses – particularly young men and women – to 'bombard the headquarters' … This was definitely not the way Kim Il-sung envisioned running a country. His rule prioritised rigid order, not controlled chaos. Terror was to be carried out by the secret police, not an angry mob. (p. 157)

Seeking to distance himself from both Moscow and Beijing, Kim began to promote the concept of 'Juche', which stressed national independence, as a superior ideology to Marxism–Leninism and Mao Zedong Thought. The author concludes, however, that Kim's loyalty 'was not to an ideology or a specific group but rather to himself. His ego and his cult had a mutually amplifying effect that eventually led the Great Leader to completely cease believing that he might be wrong on any issue' (p. 231).

Never Turn Back: China and the Forbidden History of the 1980s
Julian Gewirtz. Cambridge, MA: Harvard University Press, 2022. £27.95/$32.95. 432 pp.

Julian Gewirtz has produced an interesting account of the political and social-economic debates that informed policymaking in China in the 1980s, a period characterised by openness after the reforms launched by Deng Xiaoping in the late 1970s, but which ended tragically with the brutal events in Tiananmen Square in 1989.

The author has done impressive research using original materials, and his approach differs from many other accounts of the same period. He explains that, 'instead of the factional model of competition over raw political power that has predominated in the scholarship on the period', his own book 'foregrounds the informality and variability of political alignments. It argues for the importance of the ideas and beliefs of key actors in the Chinese system and emphasizes how discourse shapes policy outcomes' (pp. 6–7).

Thus, *Never Turn Back* is essentially a study of the most important 'liberal' politicians and intellectual elites in China at the time, especially party leaders Hu Yaobang and Zhao Ziyang, whose contributions have been effectively erased by the Chinese Communist Party since 1989. As Gewirtz points out, recent efforts by Chinese leader Xi Jinping to combat 'historical nihilism' do not mean that the facts of the 1980s are being restored, but rather that Beijing is targeting any works of history seen to undermine the party's legitimacy or contradict the 'official narrative' (p. 9).

According to the author, the fundamental question faced by Chinese elites in the 1980s was how to modernise (p. 3). Answering this question inevitably meant scrutinising the country's decision-making procedures and political system. The official line was that China needed to pursue 'Four Modernizations', a set of economic-development goals for China focusing on agriculture, industry, science and technology, and national defence. But the country's decision-making system was so inefficient that the possibility of a 'fifth' modernisation – political reform – was also raised.

For Deng, however, political reform would violate his 'Four Cardinal Principles' emphasising the inviolability of the country's communist dictatorship. Hence, Gewirtz writes, more enlightened leaders such as Hu and Zhao found their imaginations shackled by the party elders. Ultimately, their efforts to encourage reform would end in tragedy.

Closing Argument

Predicates and Consequences of the Attack on Iran

Dana H. Allin and Jonathan Stevenson

I

On 12 May 2007, US president George W. Bush and his national-security principals met to consider an Israeli request for US weapons deliveries that would help the Jewish state in an attack on Iran's nuclear facilities. In the White House there was disagreement: Dick Cheney, the vice president, supported Israel's request; secretary of defense Robert Gates wanted the president to deny it. Cheney could point to the apparent successes of Israel's attacks on nuclear reactors in Syria a few months earlier and in Iraq in 1981. Gates, preoccupied with the predicaments US troops faced in Afghanistan and Iraq, urged restraint based on the general proposition that when 'you find yourself in a hole, the first thing to do is stop digging'.[1] Gates won the argument: Bush not only turned down the equipment request, but also signalled sharply that Israel should hold fire.[2]

Tension between the United States and Israel recurred with greater acrimony a few years later. Barack Obama had entered the White House convinced that it was time for a 'new beginning' in America's approach to and relationship with the Muslim societies of the Middle East.[3] This entailed, inter alia, an American demand that Israel freeze construction of settlements in the occupied West Bank, which the new administration considered, along with Palestinian terrorism, to be the major obstacle to a workable two-state settlement of the Israeli–Palestinian conflict. But there

---

Dana H. Allin is an IISS Senior Fellow and Editor of *Survival*. **Jonathan Stevenson** is an IISS Senior Fellow and Managing Editor of *Survival*.

was also a new government in Israel. Ehud Olmert, a centrist who had made a genuine and significant effort towards peace with the Palestinians, was succeeded in late March 2009 – two months after Obama took office – by Benjamin Netanyahu, who fiercely resisted not just the settlements freeze but the entire Obama world view, including a future Palestinian state roughly outside the lines of Israel's pre-1967 borders.

The debate about how to handle Iran's nuclear programme overlay the disagreement about how to deal with the Palestinians. Obama did believe that both problems called for assertive diplomacy and, in the case of Iran, implicit military threats. But Israelis – especially those on the right – tended to view Iran, which supplied money and weapons to Hamas and Palestinian Islamic Jihad, as the ultimate cause of Palestinian unrest. The Israelis weren't imagining Iranian hostility, nor were they crazy to fear what an Iranian clerical regime that condemned the idea of a Jewish state might do about it if it acquired nuclear weapons.

Many Israelis disliked Obama and feared his diplomacy. From our perspective – we are both Americans – their antagonism seemed suspicious and unsavoury. But their underlying focus had to be taken seriously. Some 13 years ago, as the Israeli government was again agitating for military action against Iran and threatening to go it alone, one of us used this space to explore Israel's and the United States' divergent perceptions:

> Israel's political leadership paints a picture of self-contained air-strikes without a hugely damaging blowback. The picture is plausible. But one reason Washington doesn't believe it is that Washington has a much broader stake in the rules of international order. This statement may sound odd to those who look at America as the archetype of a superpower bull in the world's china shop. And it is true that the United States is generally inclined to a flexible reading of international law when it comes to judging its own use of force. Nonetheless, America sees itself – and has reason to see itself – as a main pillar of world order, with responsibilities that include, but certainly go far beyond, preventing Iran from developing a nuclear weapon. America's own excursion into preventive war is recent and regretted. The current administration can count many ways that US power was depleted

through preventive action against an Iraqi threat that turned out to be more distant and hypothetical than claimed at the time.[4]

In his subsequent campaign to stymie Obama's diplomatic efforts to contain Iran's nuclear ambitions through an arms-control agreement, Netanyahu went to another well of hostility to America's first black president: the US Republican Party. Netanyahu's 3 March 2015 speech warning a joint session of Congress of a 'bad deal' that would 'all but guarantee' a nuclear-armed Iran was an undisguised attack on the administration and a key moment in the partisan polarisation of US support for Israel.[5] In the event, Netanyahu failed and Obama's preference for pressure and diplomacy succeeded.

Amid the wreckage of international diplomacy, comity and order in 2025, it is truly astonishing to look back just ten years. In 2015, major state powers and international organisations – notably China, France, Germany, Russia, the United Kingdom, the United States, the United Nations and the European Union – cohered as a genuine 'international community' regarding, at least, the imperatives of non-proliferation. Led by the United States under Obama, negotiators achieved the breakthrough agreement known as the Joint Comprehensive Plan of Action (JCPOA) in 2015. In essence, the deal lifted debilitating sanctions on Iran in exchange for its forbearance on uranium enrichment and submission to monitoring and inspections.

It was, in fact, an extremely good deal from any reasonable American or indeed Israeli perspective, involving the substantial removal of enriched uranium from Iran, limits on its stockpile, a cap on enrichment purity – translating to a breakout time for Iran to produce enough fissile material for a nuclear weapon of at least one year versus a matter of weeks in 2025 – and the most intrusive international monitoring programme ever established.[6] While critics pointed to sunset provisions they considered too lax and the fact that the JCPOA did not address Iran's missile programme or its destabilising regional activities through the 'axis of resistance', the US intelligence community and the International Atomic Energy Agency consistently assessed that the Iranians were complying with the agreement – in other words, that it was working for its primary intended purpose.

Aside from his later effort to subvert the process of American democracy, the most consequential act of Donald Trump's first term was probably his 2018 abrogation of the JCPOA. It is difficult to view its abandonment despite Iran's substantial compliance as anything other than an act of wilful political vandalism directed against Obama's legacy. As Mark Fitzpatrick emphasises in this issue, its consequences – a steep increase in Iran's stockpile of enriched uranium and an inferred decrease in its breakout time – were certainly main predicates for Israel's *Operation Rising Lion*, as it styled the attacks of June 2025.[7] Additional predicates were Hamas's harrowing massacres of 7 October 2023 followed by Israel's brutal war of collective punishment against Palestinians in Gaza. Israel extended the Gaza war beyond any apparent strategic rationale or humanitarian decency, planting the strong suspicion, substantiated by a recent *New York Times* investigation, that Netanyahu perpetuated it to ensure his own political survival.[8] The war's continuation also allowed Israel to widen the war to Lebanon, where it devastated Hizbullah with unexpected ease, and to Iran itself, as Israel demonstrated and stunningly exploited the superiority of its intelligence, air defences and airpower.

What is abundantly clear is that Israel's urgency in June 2025 had very little to do with an imminent threat and much more to do with two temporary windows of opportunity: its own overwhelming strategic superiority, which might over time have eroded as Iran rebuilt its air defences, and the possibility that this American president, unlike his predecessors, would not intercede to stop Israeli action.

II

Indeed, nine days into Israel's campaign, Trump ordered US bombers to join the attack on three main nuclear sites, whereupon Netanyahu promptly nominated Trump for the Nobel Peace Prize. Having finally succeeded in bringing the substantial weight of US military power into action against Iran's nuclear facilities, the Israeli prime minister may well feel that he deserves a prize himself. In any event, the episode seems likely to further contort American politics regarding the problem of Israel.

Liberals in general have not been terribly critical of Trump's march to war at Israel's behest. While a few progressives called for his impeachment, Democrats for the most part shilly-shallied between meek caution and bland approval.[9] The tepidness of their reactions is hardly puzzling. To be sure, many American liberals perceived the Biden administration as acquiescing to Netanyahu's inhumane and likely unlawful measures in the Gaza war, and would not blanch at excoriations of Trump for similarly backing Israeli maximalism with respect to Iran.[10] On the domestic front, however, Trump has equated sharp criticism of Israel with anti-Semitism writ large and used it as a pretext for disempowering American institutions of higher education – notably Columbia and Harvard universities – and thereby weakening a major source of resistance to his authoritarian agenda. In effect, he is daring his political opponents to take anti-Israeli positions.

The European reaction broadly mirrored the Democrats' ambivalence. French President Emmanuel Macron, for instance, mused that while there was 'no legal framework' to support striking Iran's nuclear sites, there was 'legitimacy' in doing so. German Chancellor Friedrich Merz leaned farther forward, lauding the Trump administration for doing the West's 'dirty work'.[11] NATO Secretary General Mark Rutte, previewing wider genuflection following the NATO summit, was fawning to the point of sycophancy.[12]

While obsequious backslapping and even grudging approval will buoy Trump's spirit, militarily re-immersing the United States in the Middle East carries serious domestic and strategic risks for him. In the United States, the case for focusing on Asia within the Trump administration will persist, and America First champions will reiterate that going to war at all was unwise. In the region, as Hasan T. Alhasan and Wolf-Christian Paes argue in this issue, Arab Gulf states, encouraged by American efforts to normalise relations between them and Israel by way of the Abraham Accords and other initiatives, now see medium-term prospects for their fruition evaporating due to Israel's unending war in Gaza, its attacks on Iran and the United States' failure to restrain them.[13] Riyadh wanted to peacefully contain Iran, which even in the face of Israel's abuses of Palestinians in Gaza lodged its displeasure weakly, mainly through proxies. From the Arab Gulf states' perspective, the regional players were, however messily, sorting out their own problems, and war in lieu of diplomacy was unwelcome and unnecessary.[14]

Israel's air campaign included targeted assassinations of political and military leaders, as well as nuclear scientists. Although regime change from the air seemed like a dubious proposition – and, even if possible, raised the question of whether a worse regime or dangerous power vacuum might follow – Netanyahu suggested that it was one of the goals.[15] Trump, of course, had long railed against regime-change efforts by the United States, so his alignment with Israel's campaign was, in this respect, an anomaly. He may have solved the problem, however, through a characteristic detachment from reality. The US strikes had 'obliterated' Iran's nuclear facilities, he announced, dismissing intelligence estimates to the contrary.[16] It is possible that Trump's implicit insistence on 'one and done' has quelled Israel's regime-change ambitions for the time being, though probably not for the long run.

III

In 2003, when opposition to Britain's joining the United States' invasion of Iraq led Robin Cook, then leader of the House of Commons, to resign from the government, he warned his colleagues of second-order consequences:

> The reality is that Britain is being asked to embark on a war without agreement in any of the international bodies of which we are a leading partner – not NATO, not the European Union and, now, not the Security Council. To end up in such diplomatic weakness is a serious reverse. Only a year ago, we and the United States were part of a coalition against terrorism that was wider and more diverse than I would ever have imagined possible. History will be astonished at the diplomatic miscalculations that led so quickly to the disintegration of that powerful coalition. The US can afford to go it alone, but Britain is not a superpower. Our interests are best protected not by unilateral action but by multilateral agreement and a world order governed by rules. Yet tonight the international partnerships

most important to us are weakened: the European Union is divided; the Security Council is in stalemate. Those are heavy casualties of a war in which a shot has yet to be fired.[17]

Soon afterwards, as coalition forces rolled through Iraq and Iraqis joyfully toppled Saddam Hussein's statue, it looked as though Cook might have been too pessimistic. In the fullness of time, of course, it became clear that he was not.

It remains conceivable that the 12-day war of June 2025 will in fact end up deterring Iran from reconstituting its nuclear programme and pursuing nuclear weapons. Iran, knowing it will be hammered again and again, might now seek a lasting diplomatic solution.[18] The empirical ingredients of such an eventuality, systematically detailed in Fabian Hinz's article, are Israel's substantial neutralisation of Iran's regional axis of resistance over the course of 2024, its thorough degradation of Iran's missile assets and Iran's resulting post-conflict quiescence.[19] As he argues, it will take some time for Iran to revise its shattered missile strategy, re-establish its deterrent and a degree of operational freedom of action, and pose a formidable regional threat again.

Moreover, Israel's decimation of the axis of resistance and establishment of regional military superiority that includes its operational sway in Iranian airspace, in theory, point to a more peaceful trajectory. Certainly, Iran's kabuki retaliation against US forces in Qatar reveals a regime that knows it is cornered for now. The aforementioned contributors to this issue, however, expect Iran to bide its time and reconstitute both its military assets and its nuclear programme.

As Fitzpatrick's article lays out, the Trump administration's claims that the US strikes visited terminal damage on Iran's nuclear capabilities lack credibility. Fitzpatrick also notes that Iran had already produced and apparently secured from attack enough enriched uranium to make several nuclear bombs. Israeli as well as American intelligence sources have confirmed that at least some of that enriched uranium remains intact.[20] Iran is thus left with a reasonable technical basis for reconstituting its nuclear programme on some level and, given Israel's now unambiguous intention to forcibly suppress it and the United States' loose yet palpable commitment to support such efforts, ample psychological grounds as well. Fitzpatrick's well-founded fear is that a cycle of short but high-intensity wars initiated by Israel will ensue, perpetuating instability while still culminating in a nuclear Iran.

Such a scenario could present Trump with a Hobson's choice of entering an inevitably unpopular 'forever war' of the kind he has pledged to avoid, or declaring victory and standing pat regardless of facts on the ground to the contrary. The Biden administration's inability to control Israel's conduct of the Gaza war demonstrated that America's return to the Middle East as an authoritative regional arbiter was infeasible; US frustration with Iran would presumably drive home the point to Trump as well. And the pledge of America First looms. Yet failure to decisively end Iran's nuclear programme by force would bolster perceptions of the United States' and especially Trump's fecklessness, given that he scuppered a sound deal in 2018, tried in vain to revive it in 2025 and then undertook an unsuccessful military adventure. Regional players would be left with a more unstable and unpredictable Iran to handle with less US help, and the rest of the world with a US government more clueless about constructive intervention and unmindful of the world order that, generations ago, it helped to build.

Notes

[1] Robert M. Gates, *Duty: Memoirs of a Secretary at War* (New York: Alfred A. Knopf, 2014), p. 182.

[2] See Dana H. Allin and Steven N. Simon, *Our Separate Ways: The Struggle for the Future of the U.S.–Israel Alliance* (New York: PublicAffairs, 2016), p. 158.

[3] Obama White House, 'The President's Speech in Cairo: A New Beginning', 4 June 2009, https://obamawhitehouse.archives.gov/issues/foreign-policy/presidents-speech-cairo-a-new-beginning.

[4] Dana H. Allin, 'Rumours of War', *Survival*, vol. 54, no. 2, April–May 2012, pp. 211–20.

[5] See, for example, Peter Baker, 'In Congress, Netanyahu Faults "Bad Deal" on Iran Nuclear Program', *New York Times*, 3 March 2025, https://www.nytimes.com/2015/03/04/world/middleeast/netanyahu-congress-iran-israel-speech.html.

[6] See 'Joint Comprehensive Plan of Action', Vienna, 14 July 2015, https://2009-2017.state.gov/documents/organization/245317.

pdf; and Center for Arms Control and Non-Proliferation, 'The Iran Deal, Then and Now', updated June 2025, https://armscontrolcenter.org/wp-content/uploads/2021/03/The-Iran-Deal-Then-and-Now-June-2025-Fact-Sheet.pdf.

7   Mark Fitzpatrick, 'Attacking Iran and Tempting Fate', *Survival*, vol. 67, no. 4, August–September 2025, pp. 7–24.

8   See Patrick Kingsley, Ronen Bergman and Natan Odenheimer, 'How Netanyahu Prolonged the War in Gaza to Stay in Power', *New York Times*, 11 July 2025, https://www.nytimes.com/2025/07/11/magazine/benjamin-netanyahu-gaza-war.html.

9   See, for example, Elena Schneider and Nicholas Wu, 'Dems Struggle to Respond as Trump's Iran Strikes Sow Chaos', *Politico*, 24 June 2025, https://www.politico.com/news/2025/06/24/democrat-response-trump-iran-strikes-00422403.

10 See Steven Simon, 'After Gaza: American Liberals and Israel', *Survival*, vol. 67, no. 1, February–March 2025, pp. 143–58.

11 Quoted in Clea Caulcutt, 'Macron: US Strikes on Iran Aren't Legal', *Politico*, 23 June 2025, https://www.politico.eu/article/emmanuel-macron-iran-israel-us-legal-war-mena/.

12 See Lulu Garcia-Navarro, 'The Interview: The Head of NATO Thinks President Trump "Deserves All the Praise"', *New York Times*, 5 July 2025, https://www.nytimes.com/2025/07/05/magazine/mark-rutte-interview.html; and Will Weissert, '"Dear Donald." Trump Posts Fawning Private Text from NATO Chief on Social Media', Associated Press, 24 June 2025, https://apnews.com/article/trump-rutte-text-message-nato-signal-6263810ac3ca77a5bf7366499f51c772.

13 Hasan T. Alhasan and Wolf-Christian Paes, 'Israel's Perilous Revisionism', *Survival*, vol. 67, no. 4, August–September 2025, pp. 25–32.

14 See Steven Simon and Jonathan Stevenson, 'The Middle East Is Still Post-American', *Foreign Affairs*, 9 April 2024, https://www.foreignaffairs.com/israel/middle-east-still-post-american.

15 See, for example, Michael Crowley, '"Regime Change"? Questions About Israel's Iran Goal Pressure Trump', *New York Times*, 17 June 2025, https://www.nytimes.com/2025/06/17/us/politics/regime-change-israel-iran-trump.html. John Bolton, one of Trump's national security advisors in his first term, has urged the current administration to pursue it. See John Bolton, 'Trump's Work in Iran Has Only Begun', *New York Times*, 3 July 2025, https://www.nytimes.com/2025/07/03/opinion/bolton-iran-nuclear.html.

16 See Missy Ryan and Ashley Parker, 'The One-and-done Doctrine', *Atlantic*, 29 June 2025, https://www.theatlantic.com/politics/archive/2025/06/trump-military-iran-nuclear/683348/; and Gregory Svirnovskiy, 'Trump Continues to Project Optimism that Strikes on Iran "Obliterated" Its Nuclear Program', *Politico*, 29 June 2025, https://www.politico.com/news/2025/06/29/trump-iran-strikes-obliterated-00431729.

17 Robin Cook, 'Personal Statement', UK Parliament, 17 March 2003, https://publications.parliament.uk/pa/

cm200203/cmhansrd/vo030317/
debtext/30317-33.htm.

18 See, for instance, Yegeneh Torbati, 'Iran Sees Chance for Nuclear Deal with U.S. Even After Attacks', *Washington Post*, 13 July 2025, https://www.washingtonpost.com/world/2025/07/13/iran-nuclear-negotiations-pezeshkian-araghchi/.

19 Fabian Hinz, 'Iran's Shattered Missile Strategy', *Survival*, vol. 67, no. 4, August–September 2025, pp. 33–42.

20 See David E. Sanger, 'Some of Iran's Enriched Uranium Survived Attacks, Israeli Official Says', *New York Times*, 10 July 2025, https://www.nytimes.com/2025/07/10/us/politics/iran-attacks-damage.html.